THEY WERE LEGENDS BEFORE THEY WERE HISTORY

Jack Fritscher is the founding San Francisco editor-in-chief of *Drummer* magazine and curator of the *Drummer* Archives. In essays, interviews, and photos, his masterful writing sheds new Gay Pride light on authentic leatherfolk founders, icons, and superstars too often under-reported by gatekeepers of gay-history timelines.

AIDS poet, **Thom Gunn**; race-sex-and-gender photographer, **Robert Mapplethorpe**; **Society of Janus** founder, **Cynthia Slater**; **Mineshaft** manager, **Wally Wallace**; godfather of gay writing, **Samuel Steward**; young Provincetown playwright, **Tennessee Williams**; filmmaker Wakefield Poole's art-director, **Ed Parente**; **Old Reliable Video** hustler-art photographer, **David Hurles**; leather fashion designer, **Rob of Amsterdam**; and the filmmakers of the 1975 classic *Born to Raise Hell*, **Terry LeGrand** and **Roger Earl**.

With his first gay writing (on James Dean) published in 1962, Fritscher at 83 reaches across 60 years of gay life into his journals and heart to examine our lost midcentury world.

Review Comments about the Author's Work

"Jack Fritscher is an icon and pioneer provocateur from San Francisco's sexual hey-day alongside sex idols Peter Berlin, Annie Sprinkle, David Steinberg, Rumi Missabu, and the Cockettes." —*San Francisco Magazine*

"Jack Fritscher writes wonderful books...careful writing...a world of insight." —Geoff Mains, author, *Urban Aboriginals*, in *The Advocate*

"*Drummer* was a map of leather culture; Fritscher and his book are unabashed and uninhibited tour guides."
—Chuck Renslow, founder, Chicago Leather Archives & Museum and International Mr Leather (IML)

"Fritscher is intelligent, perceptive, sensitive, articulate — and a good writer." —Charles Casillo, *New York Native*

"For six decades, Jack Fritscher has been chronicling the world of gay leather, kink, and blue-collar men. His books have captured a large part of gay sexual liberation, fetish, Golden-Age San Francisco, gay art, and photography. Researching leather and kink history is infinitely easier thanks to his meticulous work. Best of all: Fritscher has lived the history he presents, consistently bringing a world to life for the reader.

—Owen Keehnen, Chicago queer historian, author, *Leatherman: The Legend of Chuck Renslow*

"Any new book about San Francisco by Jack Fritscher is cause for celebration. I've followed his writing since the 1970s when I was coming out into leather and bought my first issue of *Drummer*. So I'm acquainted with his knowledge of the leather community, his muscular prose style, his wit, and his commitment to preserving gay history. Yet, familiar as I am, *Profiles* astonished me with its depth of feeling and its sincere reconstruction of that glorious, heartbreaking Golden Age before AIDS. *Profiles* may make readers who lived in the 1970s nostalgic. Younger readers may wish teleportation to those days and nights of "libidinous joys only!" *Profiles* is much more than nostalgia for our *auld lang syne*. In future, it will serve as an invaluable eyewitness resource for anyone researching gay history of the 20th century.

—Hank Trout, editor, *Drummer* magazine (1980), senior editor, *A&U: America's AIDS Magazine* (2016-2021)

"Fritscher is epicentric to gay literature...he is first and foremost an extraordinary American writer. He deserves a broad-based audience because his powerful and original voice rings in one's head long after the book has been completed." —Nancy Sundstrom, *ForeWord* magazine

"Fritscher is a key player in the masculinity of homosexuality...This is 'must reading' for those who want to know more about their past and those who simply want to relive the days when it was fun to be gay. *Gay San Francisco* is history for GLBT people who want to know the diversity of our gay roots."

—David Van Leer, professor, Lesbian and Gay Studies, University of California, Davis, and author of *The Queening of America*

"I stayed up most of the night reading and re-reading Fritscher's memoir of the late Thom Gunn. It was worth every minute."

—Kevin Killian, San Francisco poet, co-founder of the Poets Theater, Lambda Literary Award winner, *Impossible Princess*

PROFILES IN GAY COURAGE

LEATHERFOLK, ARTS, and IDEAS

A Memoir
Gay Popular Culture

Jack Fritscher, Ph.D.

Archival Edition
Jack Fritscher-Mark Hemry Archives

Palm Drive Publishing™

For author history and for historical research www.JackFritscher.com

Cover and book design by Mark Hemry

Published by Palm Drive Publishing, Sebastopol CA
www.PalmDrivePublishing.com
Email: publisher@PalmDrivePublishing.com

Library of Congress Control Number: 2022933010
Fritscher, Jack 1939-
Profiles in Gay Courage: Leatherfolk, Arts, and Ideas / Jack Fritscher
p.cm

ISBN 978-1-890834-61-6 Print
ISBN 978-1-890834-62-3 eBook

1. Memoir. 2. Homosexuality. 3. Masculinity. 4. Gay and Lesbian Studies. 5. Gay Studies. 6. Popular Culture. 7. Sadomasochism. 8. American Literature--20th Century. 9. Feminism. 10. Homomasculinity.

First Printing 2022
10 9 8 7 6 5 4 3 2
PalmDrivePublishing™.com

Special dedication and thanks
to my stoic editor and husband Mark Hemry
without whose remarkable diligence
for over forty years
this material would have been
impossible to collect, analyze, and present.

Bliss was it in that dawn to be alive,
But to be young was very heaven!
—William Wordsworth. *The Prelude*

Give me now libidinous joys only!
Give me the drench of my passions!
Give me life coarse and rank!
To-day, I go consort with nature's darlings—to-night too;
I am for those who believe in loose delights—I share
the midnight orgies of young men;
I dance with the dancers, and drink with the drinkers...
O you shunn'd persons! I at least do not shun you...
I come forthwith in your midst—I will be your poet...
—Walt Whitman, "Native Moments," *Leaves of Grass*

Contents

Jack Fritscher and Robert Mapplethorpe, New York, 1978.

ROBERT MAPPLETHORPE

November 4, 1946-March 9, 1989

Fetishes, Faces, and Flowers of Evil

1

The pre-AIDS past of the 1970s has become a strange country. We lived life differently those many years ago. The High Time was in full swing. Liberation was in the air, and so were we, performing nightly our high-wire sex acts in a circus without nets. If we fell, we fell with splendor in the grass. That carnival, ended now, has no more memory than the remembrance we give it, and we give remembrance here.

In 1977, the Thursday before Halloween, Robert Mapplethorpe arrived unexpectedly at my job and in my life at 1730 Divisadero Street in San Francisco. I was editor-in-chief of the international leather magazine *Drummer*. Robert was a Downtown photographer struggling to be known above 14th Street and outside New York.

He had been lucky on January 6, 1973, when Tennyson Schad at the Light Gallery, 1018 Madison Avenue at 78th Street, took an Uptown chance with his first little show, a one-off, titled *Polaroids*. The invitation was a self-portrait of the photographer as a young man, his crotch shot in close-up, with his two hands holding a Polaroid camera just above his flaccid penis to make the radical equation that his cock was his camera and his camera was his cock.

* * * *

> Street addresses, like Robert's loft at 24 Bond Street in New York, are important in documenting gay history because they help mark the longitudes and latitudes of who's who in class, custom, and gestalt—like the separation of Uptown, Midtown, and Downtown in Manhattan—in a gay culture whose pop-up gayborhoods, venues, and media are constantly rising, changing, gentrifying, moving on to the new, and forgetting the old. Addresses make possible the interactive fun of using Google *Street View* to check out locations where the past happened. It may be

worth noting that fifteen or so years after Stonewall, "gay history" morphed into the hard-nosed "gay history business" in academia, museums, and publishing with the arrival of AIDS alongside the first sustainable gay book publishers and queer studies startups.

* * * *

2

On February 5, 1977, Robert debuted two landmark solo shows, his first foundational coming-out shows, each lasting ten days, both small, both Downtown in SoHo. In the never-ending schism over his work, Holly Solomon took a chance on his career promoting his *Flowers* and *Portraits* at her Holly Solomon Gallery, 392 West Broadway, while the Kitchen Gallery, 484 Broome Street, simultaneously opened with *Erotic Pictures*, his first leathermen and male nudes—which Holly had refused to hang.

In 1978, the schism over his duality continued even in liberal San Francisco when Edward DeCelle hung Robert's erotic pictures in his 80 Langton Street gallery in the leather district South of Market Street, and Simon Lowinski hung his flowers and portraits in his chic antiseptic gallery north of Market Street at 228 Grant Avenue near Union Square. This schism influenced all his future shows. He did not score his first museum show until the year after we met. *Drummer* wanted good photos. Robert was experimenting with portraits of leathermen and urban-primitive scenes of leathersex. Always recruiting new models with kinky trips, he wanted access to the leather community of potential fans, models, and collectors who subscribed to *Drummer* which at that time had a monthly press run of 42,000 copies.

He arrived at my desk and unzipped his big black leather portfolio of photos perfectly suited to my goal to upgrade one of the first gay magazines founded after the Stonewall riot. He knew that one of the civilizing and virilizing things *Drummer* did was teach gay men new ways to live. I accepted every black-and-white photo and hired him to shoot a color cover for *Drummer* 24.

Our mutual professional desires ignited instantly into mutual personal passion. Imagine what it was like to reach inside Robert and feel his heart pumping against your fist. In movie scripts, couples meet cute in less intense ways. We became bicoastal lovers for nearly three years when our erotic love became like Whitman's Calamus love between friends as he moved from white leathermen to black men, and I met marine botanist and film editor, Mark Hemry, the man who would become my husband for life. We knew what we were doing. We both liked ethical polyamory in our crowded love affairs. We weren't kids. He was thirty-one, and I was thirty-eight.

Robert was a serious artist, disciplined enough to play by night and work by day. His "take" (one of his favorite words) on life pleased me. He was a grownup gifted with the discipline that drives talent. That made him appealing. During the wild post-Stonewall coming-out party of the 1970s, he was the opposite of well-intentioned writers, painters, and photographers who wanted to write, paint, and shoot, but instead spent their time in 24/7 fuckerie scoring a dozen tricks a day in the backrooms of gay bookstores, bars, and baths, or spent their cash on cannabis, cocaine, and Crisco. The sex and drugs that drained some, fueled him.

Robert Mapplethorpe's bawdy life was the source of his art. He asked me to write about him. So I did in journals of notes and quotes. "You live it up to write it down," he said. "I expose myself on film. We both have the Catholic need to sin and confess." Handwritten letters and messages sealed our east-west romance. "Jack, if you're not free for dinner tomorrow night, I'm going to beat you up. Love, Robert" (July 26, 1979). To Robert, S&M did not mean sadism and masochism so much as sex and magic.

Robert by the late-1970s was becoming a reciprocal talent in the New York art scene. He shot Warhol. Warhol shot him. He made Warhol look like a saint. Warhol made him look like a blur. In 1978, I introduced him to Tom of Finland. Robert shot Tom. Tom drew Robert. I took him to meet Thom Gunn. Robert shot Thom. Thom wrote the poem, "Song of the Camera," for Robert. Whenever I pissed in Robert's 24 Bond Street loft, I stood facing him, framed, hanging on the wall over his toilet, looking down, insouciant, from the black-and-white portrait Scavullo had lensed of him. Francesco caught Robert, hands jammed into his leather jeans, Kool cigarette hanging from his mouth, torn T-shirt tight around his speed-lean torso, his road-warrior hair tousled satyr-like. He confessed in our correspondence that his main enjoyment in sex was uncovering the devil in his partner. Lucifer, the Prince of Darkness, was avatar for Robert, the prince of darkrooms.

3

Robert, innocent as any victim, was killed by AIDS on March 9, 1989, at the pinnacle of his international photographic success. With his early S&M work first published underground in *Drummer*, he was an archetype of the homosexual artist who struggles up from the gaystream of outsider art to mainstream acceptance in galleries and museums.

At age sixteen, he made his first trip to Manhattan from Floral Park, Long Island, across the border from Queens, where he was born November 4, 1946, and baptized into the Catholicism that infused his art. He attended Pratt Institute in Brooklyn, joining the Army Reserve Officers' Training Corps (ROTC) and earning a BFA bachelor-of-fine arts degree while crafting jewelry and sniffing around the edges of photography, making mixed-media collages from other people's photographs, until, in 1971, art historian John McKendry, curator of photography at the Metropolitan Museum of Art, gave Robert his first Polaroid camera to take his own photographs. McKendry fancied Robert, as did his wife, Maxime de la Falaise, the British fashion model, *Vogue* columnist, and Warhol actress who navigated Robert's *entrée* into European and American high society into which he flowed like sparkling water seeking its own level.

Soon after in 1972, Robert was exhibiting at a small gallery in a group show when, he told me, his life abruptly changed the moment his first lover of three years, the elegant fashion model David Croland—who starred with him and Patti Smith in Sandy Daley's Warholian underground film *Robert Having His Nipple Pierced* (1971)—introduced him to a man admiring his photos. The man took Robert's hand and said, "I'm looking for someone to spoil."

"You've found him," Robert said.

The man was the charming, aristocratic millionaire Sam Wagstaff, the brother of Mrs. Thomas Jefferson IV, who in 1987 contested Sam's will whose beneficiary was the dying Robert. Sam was a patron of the arts, who in the 1970s, came from self-imposed lay monasticism, with Robert in tow, to create a new fine-art market and intellectual respect for photography—including Robert's photography whose esthetic of eros was endorsed by art experts, and acquitted by law a dozen years later in the culture war when seven of his pictures were put on trial for obscenity in Cincinnati in 1990. Robert became Sam's protégé, lover, and friend. They were born on the same day, November 4, twenty-five years apart. Sam was fifty. Robert was half his age.

4

One splendid sunny March afternoon in 1978, after Robert and I had flown from San Francisco to Manhattan, we taxied directly to the restaurant, One Fifth, at 1 Fifth Avenue, with its deluxe ocean-liner decor, where Robert walked us through the maze of tables into an upholstered green banquette. Several people nodded and waved. Robert's chiseled face, porcelain skin stretched tight over classic Celtic bone structure, broke into his easy grin. "I'm not into celebrities," he once told a *New York Times* reporter.

Nevertheless, celebrities and socialite swans, introduced by de la Falaise and Croland, climbed the stairs to his fifth-floor Bond Street loft to sit in the south light of the front room with its silver umbrellas and exposed heating pipes—like the radiator gripped by the limber Patti Smith crouching naked, almost fetally, on the painted wood floor in his 1976 pictures of her. Whether in studio or on location, everyone from the 235-pound Arnold Schwarzenegger in a four-ounce Speedo to Princess Margaret drinking Beefeater Gin in Mustique wanted to be photographed by the fashionable bad boy with the Hasselblad.

"Arnold was cute," Robert said. "He sat with all his clothes on and we talked. He's nice. He's bright. He's straight. The gay bodybuilders I've been with are so roided out they're like fucks from outer space. I can't relate to all that mass. It overshadows personality."

Robert's relationship with bodybuilder Lisa Lyon was a seditious gender-spinning upgrade of the physique photography he found on 42nd Street in gay magazines like *Physique Pictorial*, *The Young Physique*, and *Tomorrow's Man*. Lisa was the first of the new wave of female bodybuilders and Robert promoted her because she was, like him in his gender-fluid self-portraits, changing stereotypes into archetypes on the androgynous cutting edge. Lisa at our supper directly across the street from the Castro Theater at the clone café Without Reservation, 460 Castro, seemed yet one more psychic twin to Robert. She was his good-looking, poised, and charming collaborator.

The culturally predictable pin-up pictures of her in *Playboy* gain an edge because Robert's transgressive photos of her subvert the "Playmate" cliché. In a related way in the Mapplethorpe universe, Robert's pictures often explain one another like pieces in a meta-puzzle of his design. The Mapplethorpe photo of a calla lily hanging in an elegant condo dining room gains *frisson* from the Mapplethorpe fisting photo hanging in the bedroom.

I inhaled the atmosphere at the posh One Fifth. Robert lounged comfortably close, waiting for Sam. "Did you ever go to Max's Kansas City?" Robert asked. "Did you ever *have* to go to Max's Kansas City? I went to Max's every night for a year. I had to. The people I needed to meet were there. I met them. They introduced me to their friends."

Robert delighted in acting the cool edgy artist with clients, celebrities, and editors of magazines. *Vogue* rang us awake one morning. Was it Grace Mirabella, frequent publisher of Helmut Newton and Richard Avedon, begging Robert to shoot Faye or Fonda or Gere or Travolta or somebody hot they needed fast? I could hear only his side of the conversation, our bodies tucked spooned together, my front to his back, a fine fit, lying slugabed in his twisted sheets on his mattress on the floor.

"Ah, a *principessa!*" Robert said. *Vogue* wanted some princess, maybe some rising hot soon-to-be royal like Gloria von Thurn und Taxis headlined in the tabloids as "Princess TNT," or anyone part of the stylish Eurotrash invading the New York club scene. The climbing Robert liked climbing the climbers. He had a soft spot for princesses and a hard-on for nasty sex.

While waiting to meet Sam at One Fifth, I realized what confidence Robert had pushing the activism of his queer art against the mainstream prejudice against homosexuality, and into prominence by identifying himself as a society photographer while assaulting mainstream conventions with phallic nudes and hydraulic leathermen. Yesterday, the kidnapped torture victim John Paul Getty III. Today, Elliott Siegal, the toughest S&M hustler I'd ever hired for the cover of *Drummer*. Tomorrow, Eva Amurri, the three-year-old daughter of Susan Sarandon.

In a decade of fashion designers like Saint Laurent and Halston and Vivienne Westwood democratizing their brands by sucking up the DNA of young street-smart punk styles, he sired the perfect frames of his layered signature look on the streetwise DNA of leathermen, fetish clothing, and chain-link jewelry—all *de rigueur* at bars, baths, and sex clubs like the Mineshaft.

Cinematically, in the genesis of gay popular culture, Robert was indelibly inspired by Kenneth Anger whose stunning rapid-fire frames in his 1963 montage film, *Scorpio Rising*, previewed to the teenage Robert the very leather bikers, S&M action, piss fetishes, film stars, occult rituals, Satanic costumes, machine guns, death's-head skulls, and blasphemous Christian and Nazi images whose shock power—to the tune of black rock-and-roll on Anger's soundtrack—he would soon source and morph into the static "queer cinema" of the single frames in his own narrative canon—where he very often framed several photos together *à la* Warhol's *Nine Jackies* as if they were successive frames in a film strip from a private movie: *Self-Portrait* in 1972; *Candy Darling* in 1973; *Charles and Jim, Kissing* in 1974; *Holly Solomon (Three Portraits)* in 1976; and *Jim & Tom, Sausalito* in 1977.

5

With his *nostalgie de la boue*, his love of slumming which was pivotal to his art, Robert cross-pollinated the flowering divine decadence of Manhattan society with the sticky gay seed of the leatherman esthetic that captivated him in Times Square porn shops where 42nd Street became his teenage Road to Damascus.

In the conveniently archival adult bookstores, the boy from Queens was converted from a photographer into an artist who was a photographer when he divined the difference. A delicate distinction often lost on gays with cameras who wanted to be Mapplethorpe but were not artists. He changed the way he thought about developing his own esthetic when he discovered, in addition to Anger, the radical photography of homomasculine artists like Bob Mizer of AMG Studio, Chuck Renslow of Kris Studio, Don Whitman of Western Photography Guild, and Bruce of Los Angeles. At sixteen, he was a junior midnight cowboy coming out into an art tutorial he could only get on the pop-culture strip of the gloriously decadent 42nd Street.

Walking on the wild side of Warhol's black-and-white movie portraits of faces shot close-up in *Screen Tests*, and cruising with the acumen of a street photographer, he assessed random faces and bodies he imagined he might upgrade from down-low Polaroid screen tests to formal studio shoots. He took up smoking. White men smoked Marlboros. He smoked Kools because black men preferred Kools.

On his own, he began collecting original photographs. To buy pictures for his cut-and-paste collages of other photographers' work, he hustled. Like Caravaggio, he turned a trick or two.

Imagine if you could buy the one and only original Mapplethorpe offering himself on sale around Times Square for twenty bucks sulking cocky inside the Haymarket hustler bar, or nursing his "French Drip Coffee, 10¢," eyeing the Johns over a "Tongue Sandwich with Lettuce and Relish and Potato Chips, 65¢," at the Horn and Hardart Automat at 1557 Broadway.

He studiously spent snowy afternoons and hot humid evenings tramping 42nd Street searching and researching deeper into dozens of dirty book stores. He fingered his chewed nails through thousands of wooden filing bins of a million gay photographs in mint condition selling at ten cents each. Nothing grabs a viewer like sex. Sex seduces. He told me he preferred "intelligent sex." He wanted his elegant pictures to excite viewers' brains and bodies the exact way that porno succeeds because its interactive power causes brain and body responses that pleasure the viewer.

6

Across the crowded room, Sam Wagstaff entered, making his modest way through tables of celebrities, blue-haired ladies, and out-of-towners. His handsome granite face was eager for Robert who introduced us before they touched. They were too cool to more than air kiss in public. When Sam held out his hand, Robert pulled back in surprise at the diamond ring Sam slipped into his palm. "Welcome back," Sam said. Robert, swear to God, bit the diamond with his teeth. I nearly died. To Robert, who fancied himself an imp of the perverse, nothing was sacred.

Sam laughed, and after lunch whisked us into the building's one elevator, up past his 8th-floor apartment devoted to his photo archive, up to the 27th floor where he lived in his all-white penthouse atop One Fifth. His zillionaire digs were Spartan, but what was there had all the comforts of old money, good taste, and safe home. Historical photographs of all kinds lay shuffled about like playing cards stacked in casual treasure piles on the white tile floor. Robert's interest in photography had kindled Sam's. Inspired by Alfred Stieglitz's push to include photography as a fine art, they had bought up—and cornered the market on—the best of nineteenth- and early twentieth-century photography, including male nudes and physique photography shot in the covert homoerotic style of the times.

The past in that present met the future. Sam and Robert built up a keen-eyed blue-chip collection of early photography that we three carefully handed back and forth, including sepia-toned photographs of Native Americans shot by the white Edward S. Curtis whose own millionaire patron was J. P. Morgan. Robert studied his way through thousands of photographs, exactly the way he had self-educated himself in the commercial porn archives on 42nd Street. He absorbed the history of content, style, and ethnography and folded it into his images of race and gender and sadomasochism, several of which saw first publication in my 1978 *Son of Drummer* feature article "The Robert Mapplethorpe Gallery (Censored)." In 2016, that *Drummer* issue, laid open to that feature article, was displayed as an art object itself in a glass case at the Los Angeles County Museum of Art linking its Mapplethorpe exhibit to the simultaneous Mapplethorpe exhibit at the Getty.

That *Drummer* article, which I opened with the shaved skull of *Cedric, N.Y.C.*, was intended as trial-balloon publicity for his *X Portfolio*. Robert was obsessed with skulls: *Skull and Crossbones*, 1983; *Ken Moody and Robert Sherman*, 1984; human *Skull*, 1988; and *Skull Walking Cane*, 1988. The four-page feature introduced to the national media culture of leatherfolk his transgressive pictures of bondage; black rubber body suits; a nude male self-mutilating cutter with torso scarified by razor blades; a leather master standing with a leather slave seated in chains in a designer apartment (*Brian Ridley and Lyle Heeter*); men sucking piss-dripping jockstraps (*Jim and Tom, Sausalito*); men with fists up their butts; and a celebrity leatherman, Nick Bienes (*Nick*), with a Satanic tattoo on his forehead.

When I met Nick in 1972, he lived in a tiny apartment decorated like a subway car with rubber mats on the floor, and several black-and-white video monitors inserted like small subway windows into the walls papered metallic gray with tinfoil. Under his pseudonym "Judith Gould," Nick wrote a sensational bestseller that became the Joan Collins' TV mini-series, *Sins*. Robert photographed him specifically for a *Drummer* cover that never came to pass.

"You could do the same," Robert said. "Write a mini-series. Make some money."

Robert was as well acquainted with the English and American smart set as he was with after-hours sex clubs like the Mineshaft where he was the official photographer, shooting pictures like his 1979 portrait of leatherman David O'Brien, *Mr. Mineshaft*. As self-dramatized in *Robert Having His Nipple Pierced*, he liked consensual, ritual, sexual action that philistines mistake as violence. He gloried in human flesh and courted statuesque male and female dancers and bodybuilders who were athletes of the kind who were artists sculpting themselves.

His taste ran from perversatile leathermen to finger-licking freaks to majestic blacks. His time as a junior cadet marching in his ROTC uniform during the controversial Vietnam War, that dragged on until 1975, alerted him to the cultural fetishes around the American flag and American guns. The Sixties hippie he was, who could be simultaneously traditional and subversive, photographed both flag and guns, as well as warships like the aircraft carrier *Coral Sea*, to exploit the extra bonus of their patriotic sales appeal. During the mid-decade when Bicentennial fever was sweeping the country merchandising Americana collectibles, he shot his tattered *American Flag* in 1977, followed by a second flag in 1987. In both, he digested the red, white, and blue in black and white.

7

In the sweet polyamory of 1980, wanting my San Francisco lover Jim Enger, a most handsome championship bodybuilder and one of the most sought-after men of the 1970s, to be preserved forever in all his transitory muscle glory by the permanence of my New York lover's camera, I set up a shoot on March 25, in a Twin Peaks condo perched high above Castro Street, that we three ultimately found satisfying even though it was upended by Robert's pique at Enger's not-unreasonable refusal to sign a release without photo approval.

Standing between my two lovers, I saw what happens to a good deed when egos collide. The handsome blond champion bodybuilder with his many first-place physique trophies thought he was the star of the shoot. The dark photographer working with the power tool of his camera thought that he was the star. Even so, we three, ever so cool, shot the shoot and went like athletes who compete on the field and bond in the pub, out to another supper with Lisa Lyon.

Afterwards, she and Robert and Jim and I took a cab together to the opening of his show at the Lawson DeCelle Gallery where gay society photographer Rink captured all of us together in the same frame chatting with the anthropological photographer, Greg Day.

The civil rights activist Day had been Enger's roommate in college before Day migrated to New York and documented his own 1970s "take" on leathermen, Warhol superstars, and the gutter art of "genderqueer" performance artist Steven Varble.

Months later, in his Bond street darkroom, Robert cut off Jim's head and re-framed one of the gorgeous V-shaped nude rear-torso photos into a headless full-color greeting card sold in gift shops in Provincetown.

In early 1978, Robert suggested we do a book together. He copied me with fifty photographs of some of his most edgy work so I might write the introduction to our book, *Rimshots*, pairing his erotic pictures and my erotic writing. As happened at that pressurized time of competing representations by galleries, and of the censorship wars caused by Anita Bryant, our venture fell through because of New York reasons, and some of those deep dark photos have yet see the light of day as have his once forbidden fisting photos. The proposal manuscript for *Rimshots* is housed at the Getty Museum Research Institute which in 2011 the Mapplethorpe Foundation made the official archive of his work.

In 1983, Robert had curator Edward DeCelle hand-deliver to me a package whose personal value far exceeds offers asking me about buying rumored "private images" Robert might have given me for safekeeping. In 1978, DeCelle had displayed several of the same Mapplethorpe photos I had printed simultaneously in *Son of Drummer* in his *Censored* exhibit—which Robert and I helped him hang—at his Lawson DeCelle Gallery, 80 Langton Street, San Francisco.

At that time, DeCelle introduced Robert to San Francisco high-society blue bloods like Gordon and Ann Getty; Judge William Newsom, the Getty lawyer and environmentalist who was related by marriage to Nancy Pelosi, and was the father of future mayor and governor Gavin Newsom; and the regal Katherine Cebrian. At the same time, I introduced him to underground socialites in the alt-world leather salon around *Drummer.* In DeCelle's delivery, Robert gave me, in gratitude for the Enger shoot, two stunning silver-gelatin prints of Jim—one with face. Robert is likely laughing at my sentiment against selling his work; but some things, Roberto, have no price.

In 1986, just as his AIDS was diagnosed, eight of Robert's pictures managed to dominate and vivify Rimbaud's text in a luxe quarto version of *A Season in Hell.* He pictured himself on the cover as the pagan Pan, the horned devil out for a Mapplethorpe dance around the bacchanalian Maypole.

One of his most expressionistic role-playing frames is his contorted *Self-Portrait with Whip* (1978). In this campy comic photograph about pulling art out of your ass, his butt cheeks framed in leather chaps dramatize S&M penetration and scatology with the bullwhip handle inserted petulantly up his skinny bum—its long tail, evacuating turd-like down its full braided length, and trailing out the bottom of frame. This polite shit picture showing a snarling rugged look on his otherwise sensitive face is remarkable autobiography because in it the artist who never wrote a monograph about his process reveals his challenging attitude and agency in front of and behind the camera by showing the cable-release bulb in the fuck-you fingers of his left hand.

8

"This is," I told him our first night together in 1977, "your first reincarnation in three thousand years."

"How so?"

"Intuition. I get re-incarnational readings off some people."

"I'm one?"

"The most intense."

The world and Robert Mapplethorpe were on no uncertain terms with each other. In his New York incarnation, or in past goat-footed Dionysian lives, Robert demanded, managed, and delivered what he wanted from life. He lived on an ascending arc of creativity, ambition, and success. He died with seven books in print; a large bibliography of critics and social historians appraising him, not the least of whom was Susan Sontag who wrote the introduction to his portrait book, *Certain People*; a top-tier list of more than one hundred international gallery exhibitions, the triumphant epitome of which was the successful showing at the Whitney Museum of American Art from July 28 to October 23, 1988, which Robert gallantly attended in a wheelchair and an oxygen mask.

Like Jesus taken to the mountaintop by Satan who promised all the kingdoms of the world and their glories, the dying Catholic Robert Mapplethorpe if taken to the top of the Empire State Building could have ascended to heaven looking down on the city he conquered. He was a definitive New Yorker. In 2016, poet and theorist Kenneth Goldsmith in his comprehensive book *Capital: New York, Capital of the 20th Century* presented Robert as "the Ultimate New Yorker of the 20th Century" in his chapter written by Patti Smith, Patricia Morrisroe, and me.

Robert took from life all he wanted of its quality, if not of its longevity. He lived fast romancing the 1970s pop-culture paradigm of Byron, Shelley, and Keats who died young like James Dean, Janis Joplin, and Jim Morrison, whom he most resembled in look and style. Rimbaud died of cancer at thirty-seven. Robert died at forty-two, the same age as the androgynous Elvis who had also turned to black culture for inspiration.

Among all the apocalyptic photos giving absolutely necessary personal faces to the genocide of AIDS, one of the most appalling photographs is Jonathan Becker's photo of an emaciated Robert Mapplethorpe attending his Whitney opening. AIDS is a time-lapse speed trip of the aging process. Robert looks a million years old in the stark realism of Becker's candid news photo illustrating Dominick Dunne's essay, "Robert Mapplethorpe's Proud Finale," in *Vanity Fair*, February 1989.

The year before, Robert the formalist—assisted by his dedicated brother Edward Maxey Mapplethorpe, himself a noted photographer—had shot the perfect moment of his mortality in his *Self-Portrait with Skull Cane* wherein Edward, assisted by Brian English, makes Robert's ghostly head float disembodied, with the death mask of his face fading in soft focus in the upper right on a field of black, while in the lower left field his right hand in crisp focus holds the cane topped with a skull. The penitential choice of the skull makes death his subject the way the choice of one of his lilies in his hand could have made resurrection his point. Soon after the stark salute of this "morituri" photo, Robert, who wore the Roman torture device of a cross on a chain around his neck, returned to Catholicism.

Predicting his short life, I wrote about Robert in my 1978 short story that was republished in the 1984 anthology, *Corporal in Charge of Taking Care of Captain O'Malley,* that Robert, "forever reincarnating, will, when his next death-passage is appropriate, take his life with the same hands with which he has created and crafted it. He will neatly, stylishly even, finish it." Dunne and Becker confirmed Robert's stylishness right down to that insouciant death's-head skull cane that was his final prop in his final self-portrait.

9

Robert's early work, sexually explicit leather images, many of them shot in his hidden life in San Francisco, shocked the New York art world in the 1970s. His was an assault with a deadly camera. What succeeds better than calling society's bluff? He double-dared squeamish clients: "If you don't like this photo, maybe you're not as *avant-garde* as you think."

His reputation spread beyond Manhattan chatter of a new talent in SoHo. The bad boy had tuxedo elegance and leather attitude. His ironic smile charmed the cold cash from the checkbooks of clients, patrons, and gallery mavens. At $2,000 a shoot, the right people sat in Robert's studio. The right runs of platinum prints and lithographs, dispensed in wallet-whetting limited editions, found their way into the right galleries, the right magazines, the right addresses.

Robert was a new shooting star, a lone rider, a nova-bright guy in the fast lane, careening with me, one October night, up 6th Avenue, both of us happily stoned on pot, but less loaded than the wild Travis Bickle taxi driver who, driving quite recklessly, scared us both so much we crouched cuddled on the floor of the backseat.

He sometimes acted out what he wanted me to see. He wanted intimate biography. Although he rarely read books, he admired the publication of books and courted writers who could be his eyewitnesses. He liked that this tenured university professor had already written three books on subjects he could relate to: a dissertation on Tennessee Williams, a leather novel, and a university-press book on the occult featuring the High Priest founder of the Church of Satan Anton LaVey whom, like Tennessee Williams, he should have photographed. "You do write well," he wrote me on April 20, 1978, "I think we should go fast on the book [*Rimshots*]."

He confessed, late one night, walking elbow to elbow from our signature haunt, the Mineshaft, that, as a starving student at Pratt, he had depended on the survivalist Patti to live. Patti became Robert's first patron the day she went to work to earn money to support him. She was a hyphenate poet-singer-artist who in tandem with Robert set out to score the soundtrack of their fifteen minutes of fame. The photogenic waifs stylized their androgynous Jack-and-Jill look while each entertained other lovers. Building on pop culture, they conjured their new identities as artists in the flophouse drug den of the Chelsea Hotel. Robert said that Andy Warhol's 1966 film, *Chelsea Girls*, inspired him to move to New York in 1969.

During the free-wheeling open-access of the swinging 1960s and 1970s, more than one handsome young man walked into gay venues like Warhol's Factory and was hired immediately on the cheap. Teenage juvenile delinquent Joe Dallesandro met Andy in 1967 and became a Superstar. The teenage artist Jed Johnson, delivering a message in 1967, was hired as a janitor, and became Warhol's lover. At the same time, Robert scored first blood and respect when he became a staff photographer for Warhol's *Interview* magazine.

Wherever doors were open, in walked Robert. By 1971, Robert was *tête-à-tête* with the Catholic Bob Colacello, the platonic-ideal of an editor at *Interview*. By 1972, when David Croland introduced him to Sam Wagstaff, Robert may have needed Sam emotionally in the world of polyamory to cope with Patti's romance with cowboy-playwright Sam Shepard. There were two Sam's in their relationship. Years later she told *FarOutMag* in 2020 what the gay Robert, who was not a jealous man, may have sensed about the straight Shepard in 1971: "…We [Sam and I] had an equal but masculine/feminine relationship…it was like having a man in my life."

With Shepard, Patti co-wrote and co-starred in their play *Cowboy Mouth*, a one-act about their affair in which a rockstar woman kidnaps a man she holds at gunpoint in a motel where he claims she ruined his life while begging her to tell him stories about Rimbaud and Verlaine. It opened and closed like a subway door at the American Place Theatre in Midtown Manhattan in April 1971. After opening night, Shepard reportedly fled New York while Patti, staying forever friends with him, headed back Downtown. After Hilly Kristal opened CBGB at 315 Bowery Street in 1973, she became one of the first female punk rockers in a CBGB roster that included singer-composer-poet Camille O'Grady and her band Leather Secrets.

Just before Patti retired from public view and left New York for Detroit in 1979 to marry rocker Fred (Sonic) Smith, Camille and her punk boys performed at the Mineshaft, as documented in French director Jacques Scandelari's 1978 film, *New York Inferno*, scripted by my playmate and friend, *Village Voice* film critic Elliott Stein. O'Grady, who in 1978 paired up in San Francisco with Robert Opel who had wowed a billion people when he streaked the live 1974 Academy Awards telecast, said she had also dated Robert in 1970s New York. In my video interview of Camille, she said she always referred to her rival Smith as "Ms. Myth." Patti's music and Robert's gender-bending simpatico cover portrait of her channeling "Frank Sinatra 'cool'" for the Patti Smith Group album *Horses* was a trophy to their bond. With Sam's money, Robert had earlier funded an indie record label, Mer, to self-publish and release Patti Smith's first single.

"Patti," Robert told me, "is a genius. She deserves to be a legend." He who was no sexist Pygmalion said it proudly when he screened for me *Still Moving*, the new thirteen-minute black-and-white film he had directed and shot of Patti who was her own parthenogenetic person—and no man's Galatea.

10

Robert was a legend in his own time. Mapplethorpe! His name—which he demanded his photographer brother not use professionally—acquired mystique, and entered popular culture as a meme. It's twice been an answer on the game show *Jeopardy*, a punchline in the film comedy *The Bird Cage* (1996), and a "security password" in Season 1, Episode 7 of the Canadian sci-fi series *Dark Matter* (2015). Under Sam's guidance and through the Robert Miller Gallery, 524 W. 26th Street, limited prints of branded Mapplethorpe photographs zoomed up in price, a sure sign of success in America where money is the way of keeping score. His New Orleans mentor, the painter and photographer George Dureau, told me on videotape shortly after Robert's death: "Robert ran himself like a department store."

Robert's opening at Robert Miller in 1978, in which his pictures hung alongside Patti's drawings, was marketed to capture a diverse demographic of suits, pearls, black leather, and New Wave punk. In 1981, a Mapplethorpe sold for $2,000; in 1984, $5,000; in 1987, $15,000; in 2017, his portrait of Milton Moore, *Man in a Polyester Suit*, one of the most recognizable photos in the world, sold for nearly $500,000. When Sam died of AIDS in 1986, he willed Robert, whom he truly loved, $5,000,000. Because Warhol died a short two years before Robert, there has been a postmortem competition in the press between the two rival estates as to which is worth more. Artists all die, but their estates go on forever because that's where the money is.

By 1987, Robert's name and face were so commercial a commodity the handsome devil posed with fashion photographer Norman Parkinson in a campy full-page ad for Rose's Lime Juice shot for the May issue of *Vanity Fair* by Annie Leibovitz whom Robert had in turn lensed earlier wearing a leather jacket in 1983. What a send-up for a man whose favorite cocktail was poppers and MDA.

Beginning with *Drummer* in 1978, his photographs slowly began to grace the covers of other alternative magazines like *New York Rocker* and *East Village Eye*. By January 1988, at the height of the AIDS crisis, *American Photographer* featured a Mapplethorpe cover photo and lead story "Mapplethorpe: The Art of His Wicked, Wicked Ways." The June 1988 *Harper's* published some of his photos of blacks in Shelby Steele's lead essay, "I'm Black, You're White, Who's Innocent: Race and Power in an Era of Shame."

By 1989, he had worked, not clawed, his meritorious way up to the pop-culture pinnacle of the cover of *Time* magazine with his portrait of AIDS hero U.S. Surgeon General C. Everett Koop, shot just thirty-seven valiant days before Robert died. Moralizing critics might autocorrect and remember it was not ambition that killed him. He was killed by a virus.

11

Late one morning, he sat me down in his Bond Street loft. An amusing redundancy of sex and religion was in the seasonal air for leathermen raised as altar boys with a taste for erotic blasphemy. It was Catholic Holy Week from Palm Sunday to Easter, March 24, 1978. Each day of this ritual Passion Week was a scene in the unfolding S&M drama of a male-male kiss leading to Roman soldiers capturing, stripping, mocking, binding, whipping, crucifying, and stabbing the bearded athletic Christ who was mummified in total bondage and closeted in a tomb from which he escaped. Like a night at the Church of the Mineshaft. Truth be told, Robert and I didn't create out of our Catholicism as much as we created out of our PTSD from Catholicism. The sun slanted through the four south-facing windows and hurt my eyes. We had kept each other going for days. It may have been Wednesday before Good Friday.

"You okay?" He unscrewed the legs of his tripod.

"Yeah." There was a fire escape outside the windows.

"Come on, Jack, you're lying."

"How embarrassed do you want me?" We were perversatile together, but while he set up his gear, I shied away.

"Why should you be embarrassed?"

"I don't know why."

But I knew why. Robert's eye was true. The third eye of his camera proved it. I understood why primitive cultures feared that the camera stole their souls, but maybe he was trying to save my soul, or at least examine it out of curiosity. He always wanted everyone to go farther than far out. He wrote to me on May 21, 1978, "I want to see the devil in us all." We both played at being cynics abroad in the world, but back up, buddy. As a journalist, I may have written a book on popular witchcraft, but I was no Faust like he was. Maybe he wasn't playing. Even though I frequently traveled for extended cultural sex-tourist stays in New York beginning in 1957 when he was eleven, maybe I was only California attitude. Maybe he was existential reality.

Helping found the American Popular Culture Association in 1968, I had academic purpose, and loved immersing myself in the gay underground of New York in the 1960s when he was in school. While neither of us was present in Greenwich Village the night of the Stonewall riot in June 1969, I did march in May 1970 alongside the newly founded New York Gay Liberation Front protesting the U.S. bombing of Cambodia which I shot on Super-8 film that can be seen under the opening titles of Todd Verow's 2021 film, *Goodbye Seventies.* Robert never covered live events, not even candid shots at the Mineshaft. He was a formal studio photographer who did not like to shoot from the hip.

So, I sat in his studio, the visiting West Coast writer, submitting to the East Coast photographer's camera eye that made me anxious about appearance and reality. His sight and insight cut through bull. In conversations, we traded quips for fun, but now he was dead serious. He was a man at work, assessing me, his hands arranging me, re-arranging me, deconstructing me frame by Duchamp frame, his Irish green eyes darting between me and his viewfinder. I remembered the first night we made love he licked his tongue across my eyeball. That homosurreality was a probing first. No one had ever so literally fucked my vision. Sitting for him in his sunny studio, I feared his eye, *malocchio,* his evil eye, his wonderful eye that through the omniscient third eye of his lens might burn through my appearance to my reality and tell me something I needed to know.

I had seen others whom he had photographed. Each person seemed different from the visage he captured in a single frame. I did not want to be victim of a single shot. Not JFK shot in a Zapruder 8-mm frame. I wanted to be Mapplethorped, transformed, if not into an exotic persona, then at least into the guise he fancied for gay writers the way he staged and shot Allen Ginsberg in the lotus position; Truman Capote barefoot in a chair; William Burroughs standing with a rifle; and Fran Lebowitz holding a cigarette. So my fear of his camera was primitive. He was a sorcerer. I surrendered to a magic process that X-rays a person in a single frame as a negative and then as a positive. I wanted to give the devil his due. I wanted him to have his way with my face.

Appearing nightly in the performance art that was his bed was not enough. Pillow talk was not enough. We were both tactical. I wanted what he wanted: to experience him working so I could write what it felt like to be objectified inside his process. Yet, for all my personal trust in him, I feared he might find the private face I thought I hid from the world. Photographs say what is true despite the sitter's wishes.

Lebowitz, who is an influencer, said she made a big mistake in 1979 when she, who admits she's hard to please, petulantly threw a dozen of the photos Robert had given her into the trash because, she said, he was "a rich man's toy," and she preferred his competitor, photographer Peter Hujar. Robert's work always provoked reactions. Edward DeCelle told me Robert's San Francisco portraits of my friend, Cynthia Slater, the leatherwoman co-founder of the BDSM Society of Janus, were "mercilessly harsh."

In fact, Robert shot me effortlessly and quickly. He sealed the rolls of film and handed them to his assistant working in the darkroom in his loft. Because he had little interest in the hands-on process of printing beyond some editing and tweaking, he hired various assistants like his brother Edward, and Tom Baril who became his master printer.

Years later, when Sam bought him a luxury apartment at 35 West 23rd Street, Robert kept his 24 Bond Street man-cave into which he had moved in 1972 and kept unchanged, like his "Rosebud," until the day he died. He loved the storied art and jazz music provenance of the building once owned and rented to artists by the painter Virginia Admiral who was Robert DeNiro's mother. His funky Bond Street loft—not his designer and cocktail-party showplace on West 23rd where the BBC interviewed him—was always his safe home where his brother helped him shoot his final-exit selfie, a kind of Alas-Poor-Yorick *Self-Portrait with Skull Cane* (1988).

"The contact proofs will be ready tomorrow." He hugged me.

I made us instant coffee in the jumble of his tiny kitchen. Under his framed silver screenprint of Warhol's *Jacqueline Kennedy* in the pillbox hat she wore in Dallas, an ashtray broke from smolder to blaze on the table littered with Con Edison electricity receipts and please-please-please letters from galleries. Robert brushed the small fire from his discarded Kool to the floor and stomped the flames with his black pointy-toed snakeskin cowboy boots.

12

Minor disasters stalked us: that insane Saturday-night kamikaze ride in the taxi up 6th Avenue; a car crashing into a corner diner spilling lunch-counter donuts all around us; a run-in with organized Italian businessmen; a young gay man shot in the shin, before our eyes, by a mugger in the lobby of 2 Charlton Street; a naked man falling headfirst out of a piss-filled bathtub to the concrete floor of the Mineshaft. It was dangerous, dirty, and divinely decadent New York in the 1970s still vivid on screen in Martin Scorsese's *Taxi Driver* and William Friedkin's two films, *The French Connection* and *Cruising*, a gay detective story of leathersex S&M murders.

Robert laughed at my concern over the fire in the ashtray. "You're paranoid," he said.

"Signs and omens are everywhere."

"Homosexuality can cause paranoia."

"Homosexuals have reason to be paranoid."

I thought of our friend and mutual model, Larry Hunt, whom I had photographed outdoors in bondage for *Drummer* during the 1977 Satyrs Motorcycle Club bike run at Badger Flat in the California foothills. Robert had photographed Larry the same year indoors in New York sitting on his Mission couch, feet and legs laced up tight to the knees in leather logging boots. That was Robert's first and only photo exhibited in Robert Opel's pioneering Fey-Way Gallery at 1287 Howard Street in San Francisco's leather district SOMA on March 23, 1979, four months before Opel was shot to death in his gallery.

At the opening, Opel, mixing media with an S&M "Happening," exhibited everyone's favorite masochist, the sexy and fun Larry Hunt himself, live and in person in a cage near Robert's photo, titled *Larry Hunt: Boots and Bench* (1977). Because Robert had decided on a whim, and too late for printing, his name was not listed on Fey-Way's First Anniversary invitation, and is omitted from listings of his more proper exhibits. When Larry Hunt disappeared from a Los Angeles leather bar during the winter of 1981-1982, all that was found of him years later were his lower jaw and teeth in Griffith Park. There were rumors of a Mapplethorpe Curse.

I remember Robert lowered his eyes at my mention of paranoia. His mouth grew tighter. Robert resented resistance. Robert loved compliance. Shit happens, same as magic. Wordlessly.

We walked a silent fifteen minutes to Jack McNenny's flower shop, Gifts of Nature, at 251 6th Avenue and Houston. It was not the first or only afternoon he and I hung out there. Robert was as famous for his subliminally sexy flower photographs as he was for his threatening *pars pro toto* phallic fetish pictures such as *Mr. 10½* and *Man in Polyester Suit* in which the thick uncut black penis of his unrequited lover, Milton Moore—whom he presented headless in this 1980 photo at the same time he decapitated Jim Enger—droops succulently like a pollen-wet reproductive organ of a flower from the unzipped fly. Were Robert's worshipful pictures of black men racist or racial? His derring-do in an age of civil rights encouraged people to think about larger questions around race, ethnicity, and sexuality.

The sweet Jack McNenny, the Irish-American floral designer with the drop-dead breath of an outhouse, always saved Robert his filthiest jockstraps and his best blooms for Robert's Baudelairean *Fleurs du mal.* The name of Jack's shop where he lived upstairs was a scatalogical pun. For a moment, the altar boy in me recoiled.

Jack was swamped with local orders for his handmade Easter bouquets. He was a character, and the neighborhood, except for the Mafia, loved him—but that's another story of life compressed into docudrama. Four years earlier he had walked into Doc Siva's corner pharmacy and announced to the proprietor of thirty-eight years that his store ought to become a flower shop. While Siva watched, stunned, McNenny removed the suppository display from the corner window and replaced it with a philodendron Doc had behind his counter. The plastic bust of the provocative Clairol Lady ("Does she or doesn't she? Hair Color So Natural Only Her Hairdresser Knows For Sure") gave way to an over-watered Swedish ivy. He got the shop on one condition. He promised to maintain the 1930s wooden cabinets, the frosted glass panels, and the marble floor.

As I had on other occasions when as a writer I wanted to experience what it felt like to have a hands-on creative job in New York, I picked up a florist knife to help trim stem ends from tulips and baby's breath. All his bouquets were bespoke art; he could not bear commercial arrangements. Robert sat among the pots of Easter lilies, smoking on a high wooden stool near Jack's brightly lit floral cooler. He was reading my vibe, suddenly, intuitively, knowing from my eyes I did not want to go to bed with him. Not that night. Maybe not anymore. Definitely not just then. He wanted to know why. I didn't know why. I think it was because the devil had touched my soul with his magic camera.

13

Robert was miffed but congenial that afternoon when I stepped back in that moment just as the gay orgy of the 1970s, launched at Stonewall, was rocketing to its awe-inspiring zenith. Not since Rome. Not since Weimar. I wanted some neutral time together to sort things out. He wanted time to further his seduction. He suggested supper at Duff's, 115 Christopher Street, where we lingered long and late over pasta and coffee. He plied beautifully subtle ways to untangle my mood. For some reason, he wanted me, not in any way forever, just for that night of the afternoon he had shot me.

"There's been a madness on us all for some time," I said. Like a good and proper gay man quoting books and movies, I was channeling Sarah Woodruff standing windswept on a dangerous sea wall in John Fowles' *The French Lieutenant's Woman.* Like her, I was faced with three different endings to my postmodern story. I knew Robert kept a copy of Fowle's *The Magus* on his bookshelf, and hoped he could relate.

"You're afraid to go as far into nasty sex as I want to take you."

The hanging green-glass lampshades in Duff's lit pools of light over separate tables.

"You want to be dirty." He spun his web.

"Let's pay the check."

At the door, the cold spring night chilled straight through our leather jackets. Robert headed out onto the crowded midnight sidewalk. A hundred guys cruised slowly up and down the block loitering outside Ty's Bar, 114 Christopher, and the Boots & Saddle bar, 76 Christopher. Feeling our musical comedy was turning into a disaster movie, I kept pace past the bagel shop we liked—that had been the Mafia-owned Stonewall Inn, 51-53 Christopher—all the way to Sheridan Square. The drama was coming right on cue. Across the street from the bright red signs of the landmark Village Cigars shop, we stood on the dark curbing a long time, not talking, stoned on grass, two still points in the rushing headlights and clamor of cabs and cars honking and streaming past us down 7th Avenue.

Finally, Robert said, "It's stupid."

"Everything is."

"It's stupid." He wasn't even holding one of his usual Kools to punctuate his gesture. "I'm not in love with you."

"I never thought you were."

"But when two intelligent people make love, if they don't do it when they can, it's stupid."

"That's it?"

"That's that."

This sexual short circuit was about the fuck of intellect?

He hailed a taxi. No hands on each other's knees now. Where was that curious lesbian photographer, Nita? Whatever became of Nita? Earlier that week, she had shot us together when she discovered us sitting in painter Lou Weingarten's new Stompers Gallery and Boot Shop, 259 West 4th Street, where Lou exhibited Tom of Finland, Dom "Etienne" Orejudos of Chicago, and Don "Domino" Merrick of New York. She was shooting a book on gay couples, and she liked the way our arms and legs wrapped around each other. We gave her the poses she wanted which were so like the dozen selfie poses Robert shot of us lounging affectionately together sharing a joint on his Mission couch.

She was right. Our bodies were a perfect fit. Our heads were another matter.

I ordered the cab to go to the Mineshaft.

"You need fresh meat," the devil said.

In the Meatpacking District, the cab pulled over at 835 Washington, and into a street-life painting by William Hogarth. Leathermen uniformed in black-leather assless chaps, codpieces, and jackets stood in the shadows smoking outside the club's metal door on the loading dock shared with a hundred burly meatpackers in bloody white butcher aprons, yelling, unloading trucks, shouldering huge sides of raw beef striated with fat into the florescent abattoirs, hanging long halves of cow bodies on overhead conveyor lines of meat hooks, ready for processing. Just like the sex action next door.

I pushed a twenty-dollar bill for cab fare between Robert's clenched fist and his leather-chapped thigh. I turned full face to his, and the rhythm spilled out: "What you said you're not, I think I partly am." I meant "in love." I climbed out, closed the door, and walked off without looking back. Inside the Mineshaft, a man could control the organ grinders.

14

Two mornings later, lying in bed with Robert in his loft, I felt his arm wrap around my neck. We were both repentant.

"What I said the other night," he whispered, "I didn't mean."

I kissed his long artist's fingers. I said nothing. I didn't need to.

"I wanted to get really crazy. I want to go so far with you. Get so nasty."

"This is my farewell tour to New York. I'm joining a monastery. This is it for sex."

"Yeah. Sure." He pulled from his leather jeans pocket one of those little plastic MDA bags he was always dipping his finger into and shoving up noses.

"No. I mean it, Robert. I'm tired of fistfuckers and dirty people. I'm tired of everybody always being sick with hepatitis and amebiasis and clap and crabs and you name it. You can glamorize sex all you want with your pictures. I can glamorize it with my writing. When did gay sex become a constant search for new ways to be disgusting."

"You're dirty, Jack. You have a face that could have been drawn by Rex. You have dirty eyes."

"What I may want to do is not what I ought to do," I said. "What about my eyes?"

"You've got dark circles."

"I won't after two weeks of rest. I'm not kidding. I'm heading back to California. I'm doing my own private version of being born again."

"Dark circles are what I look for. Interesting people have dark circles."

"Robert Mapplethorpe's famous raccoon effect."

"Stay through the week. It's still spring break. Andy's throwing an Oscar party at Studio 54." The Academy Awards that year were April 3. "I have to go."

"Don't tempt me."

"Mario Amaya will be there."

I hesitated. I liked Mario. He was an art critic and a longtime friend. I had felt sorry for him when he had been shot, wounded, along with Warhol, when separatist feminist Valerie Solanas, the schizophrenic founder of SCUM (Society to Cut Up Men), had opened fire on Warhol for, she screamed, taking too much control of her life. Maybe Valerie, who died a year before Robert, felt about Andy the way I feared Robert's pushing us beyond my common sense.

"Hard sex," I said, "leads to hard times." None of us knew then that gay liberation would soon play out its next act in an intensive care unit.

15

That lovely morning, I could have gone his way or mine. Were our night ships linked in convoy for so long never to connect again? If so, then I knew that what-was must remain always so dear to my heart and my head. We rarely dared say "love." We had no need. Life is a series of Gatsby's beautiful gestures: a look, a lick across the eye, a touch, a word, sex verging on love—each and all again.

Leaving on a jet plane, I fled the island of Manhattan for the peninsula of San Francisco. "I want, I need, I love, yes, love, with incredible respect, this man, Robert Mapplethorpe," I wrote at twenty-five thousand feet in my journal, "even though we may never really be together again."

When Robert sent me a package with a print of his photo of me, or perhaps not-me, or, more, what I was then, I hesitated. I wanted to see what my visionary bicoastal lover had found in me with his scrying lens. I had to see if I looked dirty, not from the inside out, but from the outside in. I had to know if I had a gay face: the haunted, hunted, distorted, stereotypical kind of the balding crewcut leatherman with a big brush moustache.

I had to find if my face had become like the Otto Dix faces in the opening scene of *Cabaret*, or like the *Fellini Satyricon* faces emerging in the bars and the baths and the Mineshaft: a dead giveaway of whatever *vampyr* night hunger it was that made us terminally different from other men. Had Robert exposed my soul to save it? Was this beautiful picture I treasure another "harsh" photograph like Cynthia Slater's? Was this a Dorian Gray portrait warning about behavior modification? Was he saving my life?

Like Patti, I pulled back gently from the overload of the thrilling 1970s that were the heyday and last hurrah of my youth. At that time, forty-two years ago—the exact length of Robert's short life, I was turning forty. *Non, je ne regrette rien.* He and I continued on ribald in person and raunchy in phone sex, modulating gradually into counseling and consoling each other in our late-night conversations and in the letters he wrote when he was lonely.

16

I saved the phone bills and his letters that ached with the isolation of the gifted artist for whom life was never intense enough. In his left-handed slant, he wrote on April 20, 1978 (which he misdated as 1977): "I think you're right about me needing a psychiatrist. I'm a male nymphomaniac.... Just can't get sex out of my head. I'm never satisfied. It will drive me mad.

But otherwise, life doesn't seem worth it. I'm probably going to have to find one person somehow that can keep me in. Otherwise my energy will just pick up and leave."

On May 21, 1978, he wrote: "It's midnight...I almost forgot to tell you. I let some creep stick his hand up my ass. I've been fisted—even came—but I think I prefer being the giver. I don't seem to have any great desire for it to happen again. In fact, I can't help but to give preferential treatment to the feeding process. I want to see the devil in us all. That's my real turn on. The MDA is coming on stronger. I have to take a dump, but I'll save it. I'm sure somebody out there is hungry. It's time to get myself together, pack my skin in leather. The package is always important. Goodnight for now. I feel the pull to the West Side. The night is getting older. Love, Robert."

September 12, 1979: "The 'punk' leather boy [Marcus Leatherdale] from San Francisco is getting more and more on my nerves. I hate naïve people. He just left wearing his motorcycle jacket. I feel as though he shouldn't be allowed to wear it as he just doesn't have a sophisticated sense of sex. I hate happy, naïve people. I guess I believe in total dictatorship with someone who thinks exactly like I do in charge. How's that for ego? ...I took pictures of Nick [Bienes] *in color* last week for a second possible *Drummer* cover.... I met that publisher from *Drummer* a couple of times in the bar. Nothing much else to report. Blood is in the air. Love, Robert."

As he progressed into his *Mandingo* period of shooting black men, he confessed: "I'm still somewhat into [N-word plural]. I even have a button that spells it out that I wear to the bars. It seems to attract the dirty jiggers. Sex Sex Sex Sex—that's all I think of. Let me out of this place. It's driving me crazy."

On April 10, 1978, on Hotel Boulderado letterhead, Robert, bored in Colorado, wrote: "Dear Jack—I just arrived here from New York. The London *Times* sent me to Boulder to take a picture of Allen Ginsberg. It sounds good, but I would prefer to be under the sheets in New York or even better in San Francisco. It makes me crazy when I travel, especially this sort of trip which is for less than 24 hours.... Thanks to you and your friends I've been spoiled. I haven't really been satisfied since I left San Francisco. I miss you, Jack. I regret we never got into anything more while you were in New York the last time...It's 10 P.M. I'm in bed already. I checked out the 3 bars near the hotel and nothing was happening on a Monday night in Boulder—at least I saw nothing. Besides, life has exhausted me.

"Ginsberg was a Jewish drag. He made me sit through his lecture on William Blake which was OK except that it reminded me of when I was in school as I had to make a great effort not to close my eyes and fall asleep. Then he complained about the *Times* spending the money to send a photographer out here as he's had so many pictures taken already."

Ginsberg, whom I had shot on Super-8 film on May 9, 1970, at the protest march on Washington after the shootings at Kent State, did not seem to catch on that this was not just another motor-driven camera hack; this was to be a portrait by Robert Mapplethorpe.

"Then he complained about having no time to make an effort. He finally decided to sit in the Lotus position barefoot. I quickly set up my lights which I had to drag out here and took 2 rolls (24) of film. I had wanted to do more than that as I came all the way and I do get nervous about the results. Somehow I brought up the subject of S&M and he did say (still in the Lotus position) that he was getting into it. No blood, however. Anyhow, by the time I was through, he was apologizing and invited me to meet him later at some Rock 'n' Roll club. I said I would, but I won't. His day is up. The time for chanting is over. As far as I'm concerned, it never existed.

"I'm going to turn out the lights and try to muster up enough energy to 'Jack' off," he fantasized. " I'm going to think about having my fist up you while you.... Love, Robert."

17

Let the art critics recount the international art world's loss at the death of Robert Mapplethorpe so beloved by his own dear family. Let them explicate the wonders of his fourteen different printing processes, of his still-life studies of floral genitalia, of marble sculptures, of male and female nudes and fetishes and celebrity portraits, of all his shocking American gun photos, and of his cool sexualism. Let them wax jealous over his rich patron who knew art when he saw it and who saw the genius in Robert's art.

Let them muse over his distinctive esthetic edge in sinister and beautifully violent, perhaps subtextually racial, pictures of a watermelon stabbed with a butcher knife: a black man's hard shaft paired close-up and parallel with the barrel of a handgun held in his fist (*Cock and Gun*, 1982): and Robert himself, wearing a high-society white bow tie and a film-noir leather jacket, standing aspirationally as a Satanic terrorist in front of a pentagram holding in his gloved hands an automatic rifle.

In this 1983 *Self-Portrait,* Robert was quoting the iconic 1975 SLA "Tania" poster of the kidnapped San Francisco socialite and heiress Patty Hearst—who shot to fame in pop culture renamed "Tania" by Cinque, the handsome black leader of the Symbionese Liberation Army that had abducted and brainwashed her. In the "Tania" poster on the April 29, 1974, cover of *Newsweek,* Hearst was pictured solo wearing a revolutionary beret, brandishing an automatic rifle, and standing in Stockholm Syndrome solidarity with her kidnappers in front of the SLA's terrorist symbol of the Seven Headed Cobra. Patty Hearst was a muse to Robert five years before she became a muse to filmmaker John Waters.

Let Paloma Picasso, and Willem de Kooning, the Louise's Nevelson and Bourgeois, and Philip Glass, and the punk princess Gloria von Thurn und Taxis, and the royal San Francisco socialite Katherine Cebrian whom he photographed as a quote of "Whistler's Mother" and adored because she was so rich and privileged she pronounced: "I don't even butter my bread; I consider that cooking"—let them all be grateful Robert Mapplethorpe ever existed at all.

So many dead from AIDS, let us sit on the ground and tell sad tales of the death of kings and queens. Let me say I wonder and waver about the moody chiaroscuro portrait Robert shot of me. It's a leap for a person to look at their portrait as art. Let me distance myself from whatever truth he sucked from my face that is so different from the truth I think of my face. Perhaps he broke the mask I had polished for forty years. Perhaps Robert, the salvific artist, forced me to look into my soul and change my ways. I wonder, did Richard Gere and Grace Jones and Yoko Ono feel somehow changed? Robert's tongue never licked their eyeball. Robert's lean body never made love to them. But his camera did. With his camera, he maybe saved my life. With my writing, I couldn't save his.

I confess now that in my May 10, 1978, letter I lied to him: "Caro Roberto, ...the portrait you took of me arrived. You're good.... I see the way you slanted me. I should be so kind to you in the slant of my written vision of you. Two pieces are completed in which you figure: the article, short, in *Drummer,* and another piece, a barely fictionalized short story, in *Corporal in Charge*.... Take care, my good friend, I love you with all my head."

Let the art world assess the artist and his art. Leave the private man—what does not belong to other friends and lovers—to me. We were too hot not to cool down, but how bright we shined in the Titanic 1970s before the iceberg of AIDS. As writer and photographer, as men, as fuckbuddies, as friends, something special passed between us. Revelation.

Lust. Joy. Darkness and light. Good and evil. Understanding. Maybe even love.

18

We were what he said: intelligent people making excellent sex. That's the value of ships passing in the night: reassurance that in the dark sea-swells, with Robert gone, his art living on, other talented lights, rising and falling, will certainly loom closer out of the distance, learn from his brilliance, and, in their own brief passage, prove once again that none of us, as I learned from him—playing Nick Carraway to his Jay Gatsby—borne back against the current, is forever alone.

Centuries from now, people will look at Mapplethorpe's photographs, but what will they know of Robert, the kind sweet man who has no more memory than the remembrance we give him? As a monument to him, the Mapplethorpe archive at the Getty Museum Research Institute valued at millions contains his eye, head, heart, and gender in 120,000 negatives, 500 Polaroids, and 200 artworks of drawing, collage, sculpture, and jewelry. Robert through his Mapplethorpe Foundation bequeathed millions to AIDS research including grants to the two hospitals that treated him for AIDS: one million to Beth Israel Medical Center in New York and $300,000 to New England Deaconess Hospital in Boston where he died.

As he lay, oh, so very ill seven months before he died, he showed a visiting journalist a typed manuscript he kept close to his bed. Holding it out, he said, "This story is about me." It was my 1978 short story, "Caro Ricardo," which should have been titled "Caro Roberto." But in the political turmoil of 1978, only six months before Harvey Milk was shot by an ex-cop, and with Christian soldiers marching onward with Anita Bryant and the Moral Majority, I felt that because of the story's intimate eyewitness "take" on Robert, I needed to change his name to protect his private person who was not then at all as famous as he became in the 1980s when he courted any and all publicity—including the dramatically perfect moment of his brave performance art of "dying in public" at the Whitney exhibit to show the world, as had Rock Hudson in 1985, a personal face of AIDS.

From first to last with Robert, the danger from fundamentalist flame-throwers never stopped as the culture war revved up to burn women and gays at the stake. One hundred days after Robert died in 1989, tobacco-funded Republican Senator Jesse Helms, pitchfork in hand, dared denounce him on the floor of the U.S. Senate. In 1990, the outlandish city of Cincinnati dared to put seven of his photographs on trial for obscenity. I felt I had the right, the duty, the mandate even, assigned by him in 1977, to write that *à clef* metafiction "Caro Ricardo" while protecting him, because he had told me in pillow talk one rainy night on Bond Street, "I want to be a story told in beds at night around the world." That private line, that caused us to giggle, became the iconic tag line under his self-portrait on the poster for Fenton Bailey and Randy Barbato's 2016 HBO documentary, *Mapplethorpe: Look at the Pictures.*

Robert Mapplethorpe was a creature of the night. Take a walk down Christopher Street after midnight. Peer in the windows of shops where we browsed for antiques. Robert was an offhand collector. He wrote impulsive, enormous checks for small bronze sculptures of the goat-footed devil. I think he will haunt those Village streets until his next incarnation. I think I am happy to be left with the memory of him and with the evil-smirking cover of *Drummer, Biker for Hire,* which is perhaps the most authentic color portrait work he ever shot. He so liked my friend, Elliott Siegal, the biker model I introduced him to, that he immediately shot him and his partner Dominick in multiple frames of religious martyrdom for his *X Portfolio.*

19

Robert came, saw, and conquered, but did he get what he wanted?

In the 1980s, Robert went to Heaven.

British film director Derek Jarman, who was his UK competition, remembered that one night at a party at Heaven—the psychedelic London disco under Charing Cross railway station—he was going down one crowded stairway as Robert was climbing up another, and Robert shouted out, "I have everything I want, Derek. Have you got everything you want?"

In his radically American book *Representative Men*, Ralph Waldo Emerson following Plutarch and Thomas Carlyle wrote about society's need for Great Men whose talents have a decisive historical effect. Robert had the primacy of personality and the heroic genius necessary to change culture. The altar boy from Floral Park dared rise up to reveal how vulnerable and strong and valuable we homosexuals can be as seers and sayers explaining truths of the human condition to a blind and deaf society. In all my writing about him in books, magazines, and newspapers, I carry him in my heart where the memory of his mind, heart, sex, and seed sustains me. Is this the reminiscence you wanted from me, Roberto? *Caro* Roberto!

Cynthia Slater photographed by Jim Wigler for *Faces of AIDS*, 1984. Wigler's 101 Portraits, *Faces of AIDS*, premiered in San Francisco in 1986 at Grace Cathedral and the Moscone Center before touring nationally with the Names Project Quilt including the 1987 National March on Washington for Lesbian and Gay Rights. Under auspices of the International Red Cross, the exhibit traveled to venues from Stockholm to the House of Commons in London to the National Cathedral in Washington, D.C.

CYNTHIA SLATER

1945-1989

Kink Queen of Folsom Street
Mistress and Myth: A Memoir

In 1974, Cynthia Slater, after a challenging solo startup, partnered with Larry Olsen to found the Society of Janus. In 2017, the San Francisco Leather History Alley set her metal boot print in cement like a star on Hollywood's Walk of Fame. She was a writer, an activist educator, a pansexual "good ol' gal," almost my sister-in-law, and the first woman profiled in *Drummer*. In 1979, she spoke vividly when interviewed for my feature, "S&M The Last Taboo: The Society of Janus," which was the first national press coverage of Cynthia and her Society.

History is *Rashomon*: a story told with multiple points of view. Everyone enjoys private memories of Mistress Cynthia who was a legend before she was history. She ran fast in her life cut short at forty-four years: August 7, 1945-October 26, 1989. My recall, personal rather than canonical, remembers her as a sex pioneer so earthy she'd laugh a chain-smoker's laugh if labeled saint or visionary. What fun watching her provoke the 1970s San Francisco scene to satisfy her libido by recruiting local leatherfolk and European sex tourists like Michel Foucault. Her politics came after the sex. She was not a gender separatist. Sex was her business. She broke straight and gay male privilege around kink.

Because her paying heterosexual johns were mostly vampire bottoms, she pulled off a r/evolutionary diverse-gender Hat Trick. To grow a pool of mutualist partners, she ran Janus as a mixer to bring out the unaddressed bisexuality of gay men for whom S&M, especially fisting by a lusty woman with small hands, was one more erotic experiment bonding our perversatile community.

Sexpert Susie Bright, founding author of *On Our Backs*, told me: "Cynthia was founding Janus in my aunt Molly's gay bar, the Bacchanal, in the East Bay, where the *Women in Print* idea started. Her erotic avatars her entire sex life were gay men. Although a million dykes were in love with her, she knew her lane. I always hoped she'd find the perfect 'Kinsey 4' man to love her unconditionally."

The two-fisted Cynthia introduced the woke reality of female body, mind, and energy into 1970s leather culture where men's image of leather women was Ann-Margret in *Kitten with a Whip* and Dyanne Thorne in *Ilsa: She-Wolf of the SS.* Cynthia was a kittenish Ilsa, and a highly wired trapeze artist in the 1970s sex circus. Her portrait should have been drawn by the gloriously decadent carnival-sideshow artist Rex.

Cynthia's lover, photographer Honey Lee Cottrell, who became lovers with Susie Bright, documented Cynthia in thousands of female-gaze pictures, including Cynthia galloping nude, riding bareback, on a Marin client's horse. *Drummer* photographer Gene Weber, my traveling companion, also shot 35mm transparencies of Cynthia with her preferred Top/lover John Pfleiderer for Gene's invitation-only multimedia kink screenings in his art deco apartment atop Buena Vista Avenue West with Cynthia laid back on his couch channeling Madame Recamier. Among the horsemen in her stable, the most famous was a very out Earl Baxter, M.D., whose column, "Ask the Doctor," Cynthia featured in her Janus newsletter, *Growing Pains.*

Cynthia idolized the tall and commanding Baxter who was her physician and a master fueling feel-good revels in the Catacombs fisting club founded by Cynthia's lover, Steve McEachern, and his lover Michael Shapley, with whom she lived part time. In Baxter's medical office on the first floor of his white stucco mansion across from the San Francisco Marina Yacht Club, he cured teens of pregnancy, and leatherfolk of clap. He loved Ketamine, fisting, and stallions on weekend S&M runs to the Redwoods.

Like all us lucky Folsom Street players in that first post-Stonewall decade, Cynthia was right-place right-time. Like her friend, Larry Townsend, author of *The Leatherman's Handbook*, she helped organize emerging leather identity. She had the humor of Chaucer's bawdy Wife of Bath. Her friend HypnoKink Priestess Kaye Buckley told me: "A gay man called Cynthia a 'sexual witch.' She called herself 'a gay man with a cunt.'" She was the Kink Queen of Folsom Street.

Back when we were all friends together, my publisher and intimate from 1968, the fabulously fallen Roman Catholic leather priest Jim Kane (who was as thin and white as a Communion wafer), and I were part of the variegated gender circle sitting on the floor of Cynthia's tiny apartment for one of her first meetings. The question was: "What's absolutely necessary for you in any S&M scene?" Cynthia shouted: "Pain!"

Cynthia was a force of nature whose twisted-sister female energy helped make *Drummer* the 20th-century's BDSM magazine of record. In issue

27, she wrote: "*Drummer*, because of its kinky authenticity, is becoming a solid favorite among kinky straights and kinky gays." In *Drummer*, I wrote my feature documentation of her body, words, and aura from my intimacy with her as longtime human friends behind the sex scene.

* * * *

> BDSM culture exploded in a speed trip of ten gestational months. August 1974: Cynthia and Larry founded Janus with the first issue of *Growing Pains*. May 1975: Steve founded the Catacombs. June 1975: *Drummer* published its first issue. July 4, 1975: Richard Goldstein wrote his poison-pen essay attacking S&M in the *Village Voice* fueling the feminist sex wars trashing sadomasochism.

* * * *

Cynthia's Janus Salon, Steve's Catacombs Salon, and the *Drummer* Salon latched onto the nationwide vogue of bisexuality popularized by Studio 54 and the most polyamorous film of the decade, *Cabaret*. More straight women than Liza had a gay leatherman walker on her arm: Jackie Onassis had Jerry Torre escorting her to the Anvil; Patti Smith had Robert Mapplethorpe; leather singer/poet Camille O'Grady who played CBGBs with Lou Reed had Oscar Streaker Robert Opel; and Cynthia had the arm of many a man she sleeved on her arm.

Her male friends besides Kane, who was her mentor, landlord, and Father Confessor, included modern-primitive performance artist Fakir Musafar; *Urban Aboriginals* author Geoff Mains; whipmeister Peter Fiske, founder of The Fifteen Association; and Mr. IML Guy Baldwin—her roommate for three months—who assisted her Janus startup in 1975 and gave the speech introducing Cynthia into the CLAW Leather Hall of Fame in 2014.

Native New Yorker Peter Fiske, a veteran of the 1960s Stonewall bar, but fated to be out of town for its 1969 riot, remembered: "Cynthia made sure gay men were welcome in Janus and gay men made sure she was welcome at the bars and clubs."

In *Drummer* 27, I portrayed Cynthia as a sex missionary who labeled herself a humanist: "Cynthia Slater, an earth-woman in her hot 30s, wearing stiletto-heeled boots and spurs, demonstrates her human bridle. Slater shoves the bit into her Bottom's mouth, straddles her, and yanks the reins....Catholic leather priest Jim Kane smiles benediction at her wisdom. If he is the priest, she is the priestess."

San Francisco's emerging leather salons networked in bars like Ron Johnson's No Name, Hank Diethelm's Brig, and David Delay's Ambush which was Cynthia's favorite. Those fuck groups creating kink power exchanges were a leather Bloomsbury of art and sex.

In 1978, I introduced my lover Robert Mapplethorpe to Cynthia because I thought the star leather photographer should shoot the star leather woman. Standing in the Catacombs, leathered up in front of Robert's Hasselblad, She Who Must Be Obeyed stood boldly bare-breasted, with an insouciant Eve cigarette, as if posing for a dominatrix ad in the *Berkeley Barb* where in 1973 she had placed her first classified announcing Janus.

Leave it to La Slater to create a diva moment. She threw her aggressive "Biker Chick Look" at Robert to pair with Robert's *Drummer* cover that she knew so well of Elliot Siegal flaunting his defiant "Hells Angel Biker Look." That afternoon, Mapplethorpe made Slater iconic in 16x20 gelatin silver prints now in museums like the Getty. For a true two-faced Janus leather moment, some exhibit should hang the binary portraits of Elliot and Cynthia side by side.

Art critic Edward DeCelle, whose San Francisco gallery championed Robert's pictures, told me, "The Slater photographs are mercilessly harsh." For Robert and Cynthia, that was the radical point. The authentic collision of beauty and terror is why moralists fear women like Cynthia speaking her mind and men like Mapplethorpe shooting photographs that assault conventions.

In 2009, while assisting Gordon Baldwin in his curating the very not-nude *Mapplethorpe: Portraits* exhibit for the Palm Springs Art Museum, I made certain, for female leather representation, that Cynthia be displayed alongside other legends Robert lensed: Patti Smith, Yoko Ono, Grace Jones, Keith Haring, Tom of Finland, Thom Gunn, Peter Berlin, and Arnold Schwarzenegger.

In 1978, Cynthia was having an affairette with my brother whom she liked because he was a straight Vietnam-era USMC recruiter. Inside their inside-straight, I, who would never have heterosexual coition, often participated, simultaneously, catering to her inner slave girl with seductive talk and toys. Thinking like a gay man, she liked threeways, and orgies, because one single partner rarely brought it all. Cynthia was a swinger and sexual immigrant seeking sanctuary like most of us in 1970s San Francisco.

She had a party hostess's passion for welcoming displaced persons, sex refugees, and new meat in town. Few knew that after she quit my brother in 1979, she went down to City Hall, with her lover Steve McEachern as best man, to marry handsome Australian immigrant, Frank Sammut, a cleaner at the Catacombs, to get his Green Card so he'd not be deported. Frank gave me their hippie-chic wedding pictures with drag queen bridesmaids.

When her groom gave her the choice of a plane trip to meet parents and friends in Sydney or to receive a cash equivalent, Cynthia nixed going Down Under. Two years later, on August 28, 1981, Steve died of a heart attack in a sling at the Catacombs which quickly closed. He passed nine months before the first headlines about "gay cancer" ended the 1970s Golden Age of Sex on May 11, 1982.

With her anxious sobriety, HIV diagnosis, and telephone hotline work around sex information and AIDS, Cynthia sent out a commanding invitation to her own college Graduation Party, December 22, 1984, 32 Walter Street, San Francisco, insisting: "Please bring food and drink to share. No alcohol or drugs, please!" Photographer Jim Wigler shot her in 1987 for his exhibit *Faces of AIDS*.

On October 22, 2004, the Society of Janus celebrated its thirtieth anniversary with "A Special Leather Tribute" dinner, hosted by Angela di Tenebre and Iain Turner, honoring kink pioneers at 942 Mission Street. The program, with a Honey Cottrell photo of Cynthia on the cover, listed a dozen Leather Pioneers as "special guests" invited to speak about Cynthia and the fetish roots of leather: "Guy Baldwin, Dossie Easton, Amber Rae, Jack Fritscher, Fakir Musafar, Cleo Dubois, Sybil Holiday, Mistress Lana, Robert Morgan Lawrence, Mark I. Chester, Josh Shaw, Karen Furr, Carol Truscott, and Chris Schwertfeger, with Carol Queen as emcee."

At the head table, Guy Baldwin and I sat reminiscing about our auld lang syne. Guy, her lifelong friend, was the first gay man seated on her first board of directors. He was particularly moving when he stood to propose his toast. History ends in tears. The crowded room was full of love.

In that moment of nostalgia, I recalled the eulogy that transman Patrick Califia, an early coordinator for Janus, read at Cynthia's memorial, as well as the poignant obituary that Carol Truscott wrote for *Sandmutopia Guardian*, issue 8.

When she died at 44 in 1989, Cynthia was renting rooms in the 42 Pearl Street building owned by Jim Kane (1927-2004) who lived next door at 11 Pink Alley with its once busy dungeon pictured in *Drummer* 17.

Sorting Cynthia's estate, Susie Bright said, "She really knew her shit, and she saved so many leather souls; you know what I mean?"

Her friend David May, author of *A Nice Boy from a Good Family*, told me she even wrote her own obituary. She also wrote short stories like her first-person feminist S&M tale "Discovery" in *Drummer* 125.

At our last goodbye at the corner of Pink and Pearl streets, she gave me manuscripts of her unpublished short fiction which, in her evolution to kink humanism, contains the beating heart of a free woman who helped gay culture re-brand S&M as "Sensuality and Mutuality."

Our Intrepid Editor dares to put it all on paper, so if you've always wondered how San Francisco's SM scene got "that way," the answers are here, in her tightly-compressed article, **SAN FRANCISCO: A REVERENT, NON-LINEAR, NECESSARILY INCOMPLETE HISTORY OF ITS SM SCENE**, Page 6.

If you want hot, we got hot! **SANDMUTOPIA PUBIC LIBRARY's** T. Mirabela reviews the Beauty books. You'll be rushing out to buy all three of them. Page 20.

And you'll find our regular features: **Report**, with news from SM clubs around the country, page 22; **Soundoff**, what our readers write to us, page 4; **News From the Front**, the good news and the bad news from the rest of the world, page 5. Ready to think about joining an SM club? They're listed in our **Club Listings**, along with various professionals who are SM-aware, on pages 18 and 19. And don't forget our **Classified Ads**, beginning on page 24. If you don't see the possible partner you've been looking for, you can place your own ad!

At right: Cynthia Slater, 1989

Cynthia Slater, nude on horseback ©1983 Honey Lee Cottrell. Used with permission. Cynthia Slater wedding to Frank Sammut. Photos courtesy of Frank Sammut.

SOCIETY OF JANUS

BDSM Boys and Girls Together

Author's Note: While continuing for years with my longtime intimate, the Irish-Catholic priest James H. Kane, Ph.D. (1927-2004) and with Cynthia Slater (1945-1989) who co-founded the Society of Janus with Larry Olsen, I conceived this 1979 feature interview-essay, which as editor-in-chief of *Drummer*, I bylined as "Eric Van Meter" — as demanded by publisher John Embry who said, "It looks like you're writing the entire magazine."

Because of my personal relationship with Cynthia Slater, I wanted to introduce versatile women like her and Pat Califia into *Drummer*. So this article published in *Drummer* 27, February 1979, is the first leatherstream mention of women advancing into male venues of S&M, and is also the first mention in *Drummer* of the person then known as the woman Pat Califia — later the beloved transman author Patrick Califia who spoke against the anti-Janus mentality typified by "Women Against Violence in Pornography and Media," and against the "San Francisco Gay Freedom Committee" who denied Janus float privileges in the 1978 Pride Parade until, under pressure, it begrudgingly relented.

My erstwhile writing partner since 1969, Jim Kane had been born fifty-one years earlier in the Roaring 1920s, and asked me to code him as "Frank Cross." In this reprint, I restored his name to the text. Was it characteristic that the leather patriarch who quit the Diocese of Colorado Springs soon also quit his "parish of Janus" when he realized he was unable to enforce his priestly authority on straight men coming into the Society? He had become distressed with the power struggle among genders as straight males dismissed his diktats and continued pushing their sexist dominance over women and gays. Even so, he remained a friend to Cynthia and a colorful fixture in leather culture.

* * * *

SOCIETY OF JANUS

BDSM Boys and Girls Together
Published in *Drummer* 27, February 1979

Frank Cross [Reverend Jim Kane], a 51-year-old former priest and proficient S&M Top, demonstrates his homemade trapeze, a wondrously wicked device for securing a Bottom to tit clamps. The clamps attach to ropes. The ropes go along a pulley, and on the other side of the pulley are knots in the rope for hanging lead fishing weights. "If he's a heavy Bottom," Kane says, "you can increase the weights to increase the pull on his tits."

HIGH PRIEST

Kane, who wears leathers and sunglasses like they were papal vestments, pulls out a large leather hide. An admitted fetishist, Kane adores black leather. He speaks of its "bouquet" and handles it with the awe and respect one associates with fine wine.

Kane moves to the subject of flagellation, speaking in rhythmic, ritualistic tones. "You're possessing the Bottom's mind, his body, his sensitivity," he says. "You're whipping out every sense of reality except pain. Pain...your brain...pain. Pain. You get his full attention."

"I love this man!" a woman shouts out.

Kane smiles, just slightly. He respects adoration from the Bottoms.

SHOW AND TELL: CYNTHIA SLATER

It's Show-and-Tell at a Society of Janus meeting, and the motley San Francisco crowd, sardined into a small room above a Market Street bar, gobbles up Kane's bits of S&M lore like manna from heaven. Kane was, after all, once a priest; and once a priest, always a priest. Now, the Society of Janus is his parish.

Society of Janus founded August 1974
Catacombs opens May 1975
Drummer first issue June 1975

Cynthia Slater, an earth-woman in her hot thirties, wearing stiletto-heeled boots and spurs, takes the floor moments later, demonstrating particulars on her human bridle. Slater shoves the bit into her Bottom's mouth, straddles her, and picks up the braided reins that extend back from the headpiece. Slater yanks on it expertly. "Some people," she cautions, "have sensitive gag reflexes."

The litany moves along to thumbcuffs, more whips and cats, ideas on shaving a partner's genitals prior to splashing hot candle wax. (Never use beeswax. It burns for real, not ritual!) When handcuffs get locked, and the key is lost, we're told, don't panic. Call the San Francisco Fire Department. "In this town," Slater says, "they don't even bat an eye."

In all, 16 "toys" that Mattel never heard of are discussed. What one person doesn't know about the most sensual refinement of a device, another provides.

"Grease up the end of the flange for whipping," Slater says. "It makes a greater sting without any mark."

Kane smiles his benediction at her wisdom. If he is the priest, she is the priestess.

Janus members know the best saddle-and-tack shops in the Bay Area, the friendliest leather gear outlet, the finest surgical supply store. You might say what the Juilliard School is to music education, Janus is to S&M.

EDUCATION BREEDS SAFE PLAY

All information, by Janus policy, aims at safety tips and precautions. Toys aren't capriciously brought in and creamed over, but instead discussed reasonably and practically. The erotic element is primary. "We try to tell people to never play over their heads or beyond their skills," Kane explains. "You can achieve an S&M high without crucifying people."

The meeting charges on with good-humored, and even playful camaraderie. These folks are all friends.

"Sensuality," Kane says, with no note of preachment in his voice, "is the name of the game."

"And mutuality," Slater adds. The lady knows pleasure in private, and guest-lectures on human sexuality at college symposiums.

A surge of applause endorses the sentiments.

Nobody's here to score. Not officially, anyway. The assortment of men and women, gay and straight and bi, Tops and Bottoms and Negotiables, comes not to orgy or to swap, but to share information. Janus was formed, according to the group's literature, "to exchange insights and to learn more about S&M in an accepting social atmosphere."

GROUP PURPOSE

Janus, almost unique in the United States, is rivaled only by the older Til Eulenspiegel group in New York. Til Eulenspiegel also features rap [rapport] and consciousness-raising sessions. Aside from the Show-and-Tell described above, Janus schedules programs like "Bondage Workshop," "Ask the Doctor," "The Gentle Art of Flagellation," and "Playroom Tours." Interested in an S&M speaker's bureau? Call Janus for a good time. A monthly bulletin with consumer reports, occasional S&M book and film reviews, as well as social events like a Halloween party are included in the membership package.

Janus has roughly (no pun intended) 50 members, and has recently branched into a women's C/M group named *Cardia*, and a Lesbian offshoot, *Samois*. Janus maintains a plurality of gay men. (Home-base is, after all, SFO.) A membership survey determined that 20% in the group are clearly-defined Tops, 55 to 60% are exclusively Bottoms, and the rest are Negotiables.

TAKE MY WIFE. PLEASE.

I ask Slater what motivates a person to join Janus. "First a chance to share information and learn more," she answers. "Second, a chance to meet partners. And third, a chance to be in a supportive, validating environment. Like when you first find out you're gay, you're afraid you're the only one in the whole world."

Slater, who founded Janus [with Larry Olsen], frequently lectures on the group's behalf. She identifies herself as a bisexual-Negotiable basically into sensual bondage. She sprinkles her talk with pop-psych vocab. "Validating" comes up a lot. The "OK-ness" of being a Top or a Bottom. Slater stops well this side of est. What she says is intelligent, eye-opening, and well-reasoned.

Slater moved to San Francisco in the 1970s, and began actualizing her S&M fantasies. She and her male lover had problems making "trips" and Tops "click" in the scenes because of their lack of information. You can't go to the library and check out a book on *How to Safely Tie Up Your Partner*," she says.

The groups they discovered by reading *Berkeley Barb* ads were mostly swing-swap-n-clap clubs. Commercial. Heterosexist. Very much "I'll kiss-off my wife for yours." The women were traded around like fuckable commodities on the New York Stock Exchange.

At the same time, Slater grew tired of her non-S&M friends whose "heavy vicarious curiosity" became a judgmental mindfuck. "They never really shared themselves other than saying, 'I'm not into that.' At the same time they'd be squirming on the edge of their seat and clenching their wet thighs. I felt ripped off. Even psycho-sexually molested."

Slater never minces, despite the psycho-babble sentiments.

Finally, she and her lover decided that in order to meet other S&M people, without the bullshit of the existing clubs, they'd have to start their own organization. It was August 1975. Their first move was a newsletter, advertised in the *Barb*, listing the monthly meetings at Cynthia's house. In those early days — before gay men started joining — a lot of heterosexual men persisted in "dogging the women," Slater says. "That was the only reason they came."

NO PRESSURE-PUNKING

Today, there's a firm Janus rule regarding pressure. If someone asks for a date, gets turned down twice, he or she must drop it.

"Anyone looking for a hot conquest," Kane said, "or for a bunch of men stalking and menacing each other, won't find it here."

CROSS [KANE] PURPOSES?

The focus of Janus has been changed in the past three years. Whereas information and support were the steady diet before, now there's a kind of communication between Tops and Bottoms as well. "We try to get both sides be more tolerant of each other," Kane says. "So many times a Bottom lets the Top take over completely, thinking he's done everything the Bottom needs to do just by presenting himself. Big deal! He expects the Top to be his animated dildo." Kane strokes his heavy leather. "On the other hand," he says, "Bottoms complain that Tops lack patience. They keep saying the Tops need to go to school."

"The real coup," Kane says, is getting away from inflicting your fantasy on someone else. Both need to recognize the need for mutual turn-on, mutual susceptibility. Sharing. I found I have a built-in circuit-breaker. Unless my Bottom is enjoying, I don't want to play."

JANUARY: TWO FACES

The name *Janus* comes from the two-faced Roman god of doorways, symbolizing beginnings and endings. To quote Janus literature: "Some of us believe that the intertwined drives toward domination and submission are common to all humankind…[and when] expressed creatively S&M can develop an exquisite and beautiful trust."

Trust is the operative word.

Slater corroborates: "The more I have gotten in touch with my S&M fantasies," she says, "the stronger a human being I've become. Even a bit of a humanist."

Fantasies. Myths. Guilt. What S&M person ever had a smooth coming-out? Cynthia is articulate and moving on this subject. Perhaps she's used the speech in her lectures. No matter. With Slater, practice makes perfect.

"Anyone who's a member of a sexual minority in this country," she says, "no matter how much work they've done on their head or how much external support they get, always carries a remnant of the crap that society has laid on them. You never get 100% clear of it. I have my moments when someone looks at me funny, and it pushes those buttons for me. But I deal with it now because I have something that balances it out. I can walk into a Janus meeting and be surrounded by great people who validate me."

SOME CRAP NEVER DIES: GAY PARADE SAYS "NO"

The crap she recalls lives right now, alive and sick, within the uptight, vanilla-gay, kissy-face gay community. Feminist circles, like queenly circles, go down in a nosedive of fear, resentment of, and a downright attitude toward S&M.

A tremendous amount of flak rained down on the Society of Janus when they applied to the SFO Gay Freedom Committee for float privileges. Janus was finally begrudged a space. When they paraded that day on Market Street (with a placard saying "A Woman's Right to Choice Is Absolute!"), the howl could've been heard in San Jose. Middle-class gay pressure groups ultimately caused the parade committee to say: "We're sorry we let you in."

S&M COMING OUT: PAT CALIFIA

Women probably have the toughest time coming out as an S&M person. Even in "soft" or "vanilla" sex, society's heavy thou-shall-not hand tells them to be less exploratory and adventuresome than men.

"If you want to come out with gay men," Slater says, "you'll find a lot of men equate being a Bottom with the traditional woman's role in the home. They show the same insensitivity that exists in daily life, so that playing with them can't be mutually satisfying. It's awfully scary to be a *maitresse* to any American male considering the lack of permission women are given to be assertive and initiatory."

"Coming out to gay women," Slater continues, "you can expect to be trashed. I've been verbally attacked and abused by my so-called sisters in ways that utterly appalled me."

Pat [now Patrick] Califia, 24, one of the coordinators of Janus, says the anti-S&M mentality is typified by Women Against Violence in Pornography and Media. The WAVPM is a righteous group that made news by getting the giant billboard for the Rolling Stones' album *Black and Blue* (depicting a bruised and bound woman) removed from the Sunset Strip.

"Spanking, bondage, torture, and murder are lumped together in their minds," Califia says. "They want to ban pictorial sex altogether." She sees the group as reactionary and playing directly into the hands of neo-right anti-gay and anti-porn groups. Instead of attacking S&M people and the erotic art industry, she feels WAVPM should focus its tight little vaginal wrath on ineffective rape laws and capricious police enforcement.

Califia, who took her name from the Amazon figure that appears on the California State Seal, is also incensed by WAVPM because of its bigotry toward gay men. "If there's any group in our society that's supportive of sensual sexuality, it's gay men. It also infuriates me to see one minority dump on another; it's like watching lobsters fight in a bucket."

Califia seems to have her head "right on."

"The majority of lesbians think sex is nasty unless it's someone you want to spend your life with," Califia says. "I like to play in public. I'm exhibitionistic. But there's no way I could march into a dyke bar and drag out a hot woman in handcuffs. Those lesbians would be up in arms."

Califia has two lovers (one Top and one Bottom), a budding career as a writer of women's erotica, and an insatiable desire to transfer some of the "privilege and power of male S&M" into her own life. She has the distinction of being the first woman to violate the once all-male sanctum of the Black and Blue, a once popular San Francisco leather bar. The bouncer refused her admittance, but she brazenly marched past, dragging two women with her.

THE VILLAGE VOICE

Pain. Torture. Should one believe the famous Richard Goldstein piece on "Flirting with Terminal Sex" in the *Village Voice* some years ago? Goldstein suggested that the S&M aficionado ultimately loses control, finding his passion spiraling into realms of the senses he never dreamed of entering — like death. It's that old "slippery slope" fallacy so beloved by conservative moralists: marijuana leads to heroin, etc.

The Goldstein piece used words like *Satanic*. It equated S&M with Nazism.

Kane, who hated that piece, insists S&M is not a progressive thing. "You don't go from dressing up in uniforms, to bondage, to pain, to torture, to blood. No. As I've observed it, people have their own functioning level, and as long as they're comfortable they usually remain at that level."

"Most of the men at the Black and Blue were amused and titillated," Califia says. "When I handcuffed both the women, threw them up against the wall and did a number on them, the only one who got blown away was some guy in a jockstrap and dog collar who kept saying, 'Is nothing sacred?'"

Jim Kane sometimes offers tours of his totally maxed playroom and water sports den near the corner of Pink and Pearl just off Market Street. Kane is also concerned with dispelling myths. He says, "Phil Andros [aka Sam Steward, legendary erotic writer for *Drummer* and other publications] is always quoting to me a major psychiatric researcher who says that a person's main interest in S&M lasts seven years and then burns out." Kane is confident and reassuring. "I've been into S&M for fifteen years, and I'm probably better, more accomplished and patient than ever. One of the nice things about S&M is that it's not ageist, like so much of the homosexual culture. Leather and S&M can add a whole additional decade to a man's active sex life if he understands it and uses it properly."

Goldstein also isolated fistfucking as the pinnacle excess of S&M, an "apocryphal gesture." Kane argues that, though FF and S&M occasionally intersect, most fisting doesn't carry an S&M element. "It's purely sensual; it doesn't have that exchange of domination and submission. It's more of a direct trust exchange."

SENSUALITY AND MUTUALITY

Overcoming the kind of incorrect and malicious information in the Goldstein piece is one of the objectives of the Society of Janus. The introductory Janus pamphlet defines S&M as "an exchange of power between two or more mutually consenting persons." Nothing more.

S&M does not necessarily involve leather or rubber, the literature says, or pain, or even sex. It is "by definition consensual…(and) therefore antithetical to rape, violence, and murder." Take that, you WAVPM ladies!

THE IDEA! OF A UNIVERSITY?

Is Janus working?

Cynthia Slater replies: "I see us making progress. We've gotten some very good press from non-S&M magazines. I see changes in the professional world. When I started knocking on doors at institutions like San Francisco Sex Information and the University of California, I said, 'You're the frontrunner in the human sexuality field. You're taking the most humanistic view of sexuality ever. What are you doing about S&M?' They all said, 'Nothing. We don't know anything or anyone who's qualified. Will you help us?' So now S&M is part of their program."

Slater smiles through opalescent skin and lights up an Eve cigarette.

"Across the country, there are some people in the counseling and helping professions who don't follow the old approach of 'curing perversion' when they encounter an S&M-identified person. Perhaps more important are the changes in S&M people. It's just my instinct that Janus has something to do with it,"

Cynthia Slater finishes with a grin: "But I think people feel better about themselves because Janus is here."

"Yeah," says Kane. "You can see it from the way they walk when they're out in leather."

For more information on the Society of Janus, write to: Box 6794, San Francisco CA 94101. [Address not valid after 1984]

Ike Barnes, Ohio State football half-back (1959 Rose Bowl), and the Reverend Jim Kane, Catholic priest, Golden Gate Park, San Francisco, June 20, 1972. Photo by Jack Fritscher.

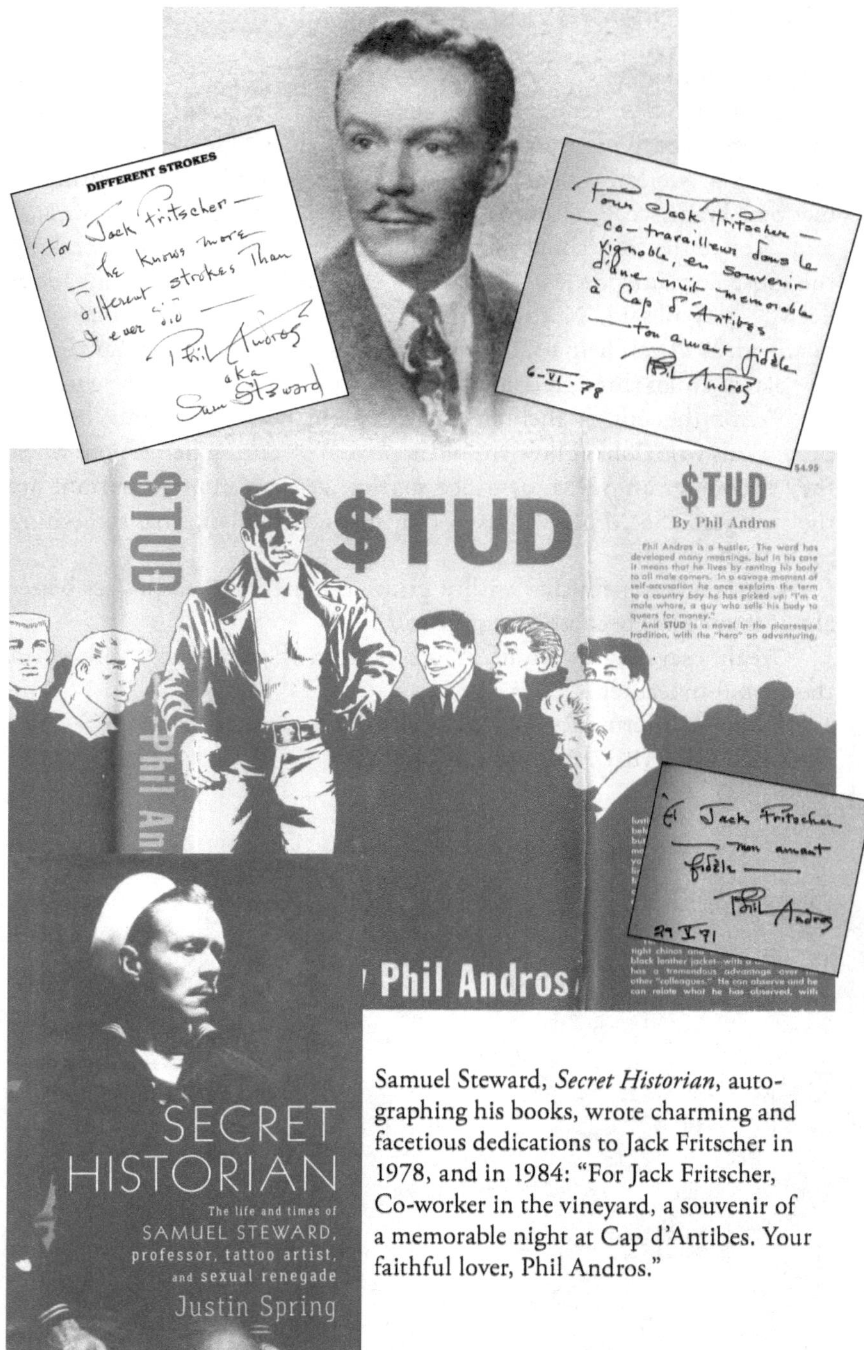

Samuel Steward, *Secret Historian*, autographing his books, wrote charming and facetious dedications to Jack Fritscher in 1978, and in 1984: "For Jack Fritscher, Co-worker in the vineyard, a souvenir of a memorable night at Cap d'Antibes. Your faithful lover, Phil Andros."

SAMUEL STEWARD

1909-1993

The Talented Mr. Steward

San Francisco's Connection to the Gay Bestseller Shocking the Nation

Secret Historian: The Life and Times of Samuel Steward, Professor, Tattoo Artist, and Sexual Renegade,
by Justin Spring, 478 pages

In transparency, rather than review the brilliant *Secret Historian*, I can best, as a San Francisco SOMA historian, give heads-up endorsement of my friend Justin Spring's important and authentic biography of my longtime friend Samuel Steward. Born in 1909, Steward defied the stress of the anti-gay century when owning one gay photograph meant jail. He defiantly documented gay culture in his books, sex diaries (1924-1973), tattoo journals, and activist input to his beloved mentor Dr. Alfred Kinsey at the Institute for Sex (1949-1956).

Spring chronicles Sam's anxiety-driven life that was an existential pile-on of family dysfunction, literary ambition, alcohol, celebrities, speed, hustlers, censorship, inter-racial S&M, rage against ageing, and a soul shared with an unborn twin in his left testicle. As Gertrude Stein warned her "dear Sammy," his every gorgeous vice sliced away at his self-esteem until he died December 31, 1993.

New York author Spring was researching his book *Paul Cadmus: The Male Nude* when in 2001 he discovered the "cold case" of Steward stored in a San Francisco attic. Since 1969, I have been eyewitness to Steward's story, and can testify to the pitch-perfect authenticity of Spring's character study which downloads Sam's analog diaries and letters without overpowering his outrageously risque voice.

At Stonewall, gay character changed. Reading *Secret Historian*, you see why it had to. And, why, if it hadn't, you'd still be in the closet.

Sam Steward, famous for his pen name as the artful dodger "Phil Andros," was a *bon-vivant* chum whose life, like Christopher Isherwood's, was a cabaret. Sunbathing in France in 1938 with Gertrude Stein and Alice B. Toklas, fleeing Nazis by ship, he was an ambitious boy from Ohio who knew how to sing for his supper at the tables of Stein-Toklas, Thornton Wilder, Oscar Wilde's lover Bosie, George Platt Lynes, Tennessee Williams, Kenneth Anger, the Hells Angels, and, even, my lover Robert Mapplethorpe and me when Steward joined what he playfully dubbed our "*Drummer* Salon" which included San Francisco poets Ronald Johnson and Thom Gunn.

Author Steward, always pursuing publishers to print his "Phil Andros" stories, loved *Drummer*, San Francisco's longest-running gay magazine which resurrected his career. When I put him in touch with the founding Los Angeles editor-in-chief Jeanne Barney, she revived two of his previously published stories: "Babysitter," *Drummer* 5, March 1976, and "Many Happy Returns," *Drummer* 8, August 1976. As the founding San Francisco editor-in-chief, I printed his new cop-fetish story, "In a Pig's Ass," in *Drummer* 21, March 1978, and his Catholic short story "Priest: This Is My Body" in my *Drummer* spin-off zine *Man2Man Quarterly* 2, December 1980.

From my editorial desk for February 9, 1978, *Drummer* art director Al (A. Jay) Shapiro and I arranged an iconic dinner party "mixer" at the home of leather-priest Jim Kane and chef Ike Barnes who later managed Sam's eldercare. Our five guests, whom we introduced to each other for the first time, were individually famous *Drummer* contributors: Sam Steward; Tom of Finland and his lover Veli on Tom's first visit to America; Oscar streaker Robert Opel, founder of SOMA's first gay gallery Fey-Way; and my lover Robert Mapplethorpe with whom Steward shared a taste for kinky Polaroids and black men. I watched Steward, a graduate of Stein's "Charmed Circle," glow in the convergence of the kind of shining company he had adored since youth.

In 1972 on audiotape Sam told me when he was seventeen in 1926, he knocked on the hotel door of silent-screen star Rudolph Valentino, walked in, and blew him while sneaking snips of the actor's pubic hair with a manicure scissors. When Valentino died later that year, Sam enshrined the film icon's short-and-curly Italian DNA in a gold reliquary he kept forever. He showed it to me like a sacred relic. Some may doubt his teen movie-fan story, but that was the moment when he started creating documentation of his sex partners, writing sex stories, and collecting a fetish hoard of police patches. His gay trophies piled up in his Berkeley cottage, and then in the San Francisco attic of his executor, expert librarian Michael Williams.

Steward, immensely generous to friends, romanced straight women; adored lesbians; fetishized black, Latino, and straight men; and spouted Old School queer theories knocking the "fake masculinity" of the new generation of post-Stonewall leathermen. He chased Gide and Genet, ran from James Purdy, balled Rock Hudson, tattooed James Dean, and adapted his novel *$tud* as the screenplay, *Four More Than Money*, for San Francisco filmmaker J. Brian. His sex-tourist diaries of San Francisco (1953-1954) give eyewitness to local bars, baths, and "sailor sex" so wild at the Embarcadero YMCA he was banned from Y's everywhere.

As a popular university professor and zealous masochist (1930s-1980s), he worshiped students and rough-trade Navy seafood. To get his hands on young recruits, he learned tattooing and, while still teaching university classes, opened "Phil Sparrow's Tattoo Joynt" (1956-1963) in a sleazy Chicago arcade with coin-operated sailors whom he paid thousands of dollars at three bucks a pop. Wrongly accused of child murders, he fled west to Oakland, opening his "Anchor Tattoo Shop" (1964-1970) where the Hells Angels adopted him.

Inking 150,000 men, Steward pioneered today's tattooing style, mentoring young San Franciscan Ed Hardy and Chicago leatherman Cliff Raven who, like Steward, was intimate inside Chuck Renslow's Chicago Family. Spring reveals that Steward documented how Renslow, the great unrequited love of his life, and the artist Etienne organized their business ventures of 1950s homomasculine leather culture around their Kris Studio physique models, their *Triumph* and *Mars* magazines, their Gold Coast bar, and their 1960s physique contests that evolved into their annual International Mister Leather contest (IML).

Steward and I met in 1969 when he was sixty, and I was thirty. With Kinsey dead since 1956, we both feared he might die without a post-Stonewall update. Circumstances made this university professor who was there for him the first gay scholar to interview him. Our 1972 session was recorded in his Berkeley cottage on Ninth Street just before the *Advocate*, the *Bay Area Reporter*, *Drummer*, and gay book publishers existed, and a dozen years before younger writers such as Joseph Bean, John Preston, and Gayle Rubin paid him court.

Their keen literary crushes on him in the 1980s bucked up his self-esteem the way he had felt validated by my government arts grant to record him in 1972 for the *Journal of Popular Culture*. After our interview, he put a fly in our fun that was really rather charming. And understandable. He stipulated I never use his recorded narrative while he was alive, "because

I have to live off my story." He meant dinner parties, autobiographical essays, and university lectures.

On my digitized audiotape, Sam's voice rings as clear as in Spring's perfect narrative. He spoke frankly about his literary life, affairs, beatings, arrests, and divine lunches in Paris, Rome, and San Francisco. He smoked his cigarettes, tilted his glass, and told his oral history of sex, intrigue, revenge, and literary gossip in phrases so authentically measured word for word that I realized he had long ago rehearsed and decided precisely how his story should be told.

I believed every vivid word Sam said, and loaned my thirty-year-old transcripts to Justin Spring who, empowered by Michael Williams' salvific attic archive, fit eighty-four years of Steward's drama into his astute and charming book that finds—and here's its human value—a universal gay story in Sam's specific life.

Steward would have loved Spring. Resurrected once again, through Justin, Sam sings for his supper. *Secret Historian* succeeds as an amazing cautionary tale and awesome depiction of how gay men built up the gay courage to construct personal survival tactics against all odds in the homophobic last century before and after Stonewall. Justin Spring's entertaining page-turner with its strong narrative plot and fierce characterizations deserves to be made into an art-film biopic of the kind international gay film festivals applaud. Til then, Sam's story is perfect bedside reading.

* * * *

April 10, 1994

Friends of Sam Steward are invited to meet one another on Sunday, April 10, 1994, from 3:00 to 5:00 PM at Sam's favorite restaurant, Le Bateau Ivre [named after Rimbaud's teenage poem, "Le Bateau Ivre"/"The Drunken Boat"], at 2629 Telegraph Avenue, Berkeley, California, to share memories and the joy we have had in knowing Sam. Refreshments will be provided. There is no need to RSVP, but for information, call Michael Williams at [phone number]. Also you might let me know if you need a ride or could provide one.

"The Girls All Go for the Man with a Phil Sparrow Tattoo."

Sam Steward wrote novels as "Phil Andros" and tattooed as "Phil Sparrow." He drew his own window posters often showing curvaceous Lorelei temptresses meant to lure straight sailors in through the front door of his parlor and into his private backroom where tattoos were "free."

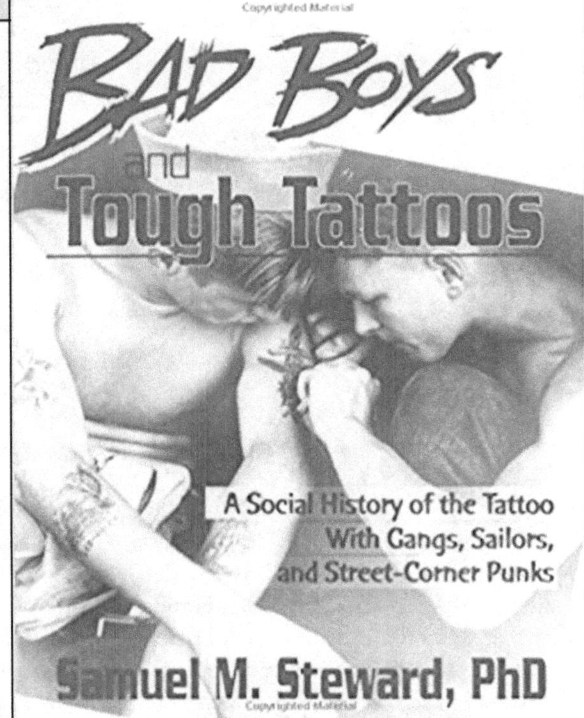

New Year's Eve, 1982. Mineshaft manager Wally Wallace with Mineshaft artist Rex exhibit Rex's 1983 Mineshaft calendar. Publicity photo attributed to George Dudley for Wally Wallace. Courtesy Wally Wallace.

Mineshaft member Camille O'Grady (left), muse/poet/artist/singer, Fey-Way Gallery, 1287 Howard Street, San Francisco, April 17, 1979. Photo by Jack Fritscher. Mineshaft member Jack Fritscher (right) wrote the first national feature on the Mineshaft in June 1977 for *Drummer* 19, December 1977, and the second in *Drummer* 20, January 1978. Photo by Mark Hemry.

THE MINESHAFT

October 8, 1976-November 7, 1985
Legendary Twentieth-Century Sex Club

If You Don't Know Jack Shit About The Mineshaft, Pull Up A Chair

"The first rule of Fight Club is: you don't talk about Fight Club." But the legendary Mineshaft wasn't Fight Club. Macho men who survived Mineshaft nights bragged every morning after about the night before. Wally Wallace managed that Roman orgy pit that ran 9 years and 9 days from October 8, 1976 to November 7, 1984, at 835 Washington Street in the Meatpacking District in Greenwich Village. Located, without irony, next door to an all-night loading dock with burly butchers in white coats shouldering bloody cow carcasses from trucks into florescent abattoirs after midnight, the Mineshaft was one of the great performance spaces in New York. Freddie Mercury came for the sex and bought the T-shirt designed by Rex. It was at the Mineshaft that music producer Jacques Morali zeroed in on the four fetish archetypes that became the pop stereotypes of the Village People. Glenn Hughes, the leatherman biker in the Village People, was a sex-player at the Mineshaft as well as part of the leather salon around *Drummer* in San Francisco.

"MACHO, MACHO MAN"

The Mineshaft changed the character of sex and ritual in the 1970s when homomasculine men came out to try everything to make up for time lost in the closet, and to create erotic interaction, no matter how existentially extreme, to achieve fully human male pleasure. Wally encouraged negotiation and consent. "I made our music tapes ranging from country-western to standards and Ella and jazz. No 'Let's Dance.' My policy was the music was never so loud you couldn't hear the person next to you." He helped men turn sex fantasies into floor-show performances in his theatrical set designed to keep hundreds of stoned players moving up, down, and through scaffolds of stairs, slings, and bondage rigs while circling the drain of the sacred watersports bath tub. "A regular Saturday night," Wally said, "would be 500 to 600 guys. Special events, a 1000." Like the Stonewall Inn, the Mineshaft was owned by the Mafia who told Wally to do his thing as long as he sold lots of beer. On March 28, 1990, I shot a two-hour video interview of this iconic New Yorker who lived 1938-1999.

100 NIGHTS x 20 MEN A NIGHT

Wally said, "I always felt the Mineshaft was everybody's bedroom. New Yorkers often live in single rooms or small apartments with nosey doormen. Guys went to the baths for fun they had no room for at home. It was safer than taking strangers home. We had some pickpocket problems we controlled rather well. We weren't like the club called the Toilet that hired its own pickpockets to work its crowd. When we caught pickpockets, we'd throw them out on the street without their clothes."

Through the years, I played at the Mineshaft more than 100 nights with armies of men uniformed in jockstraps and combat boots. We tucked brown bottles of popper into the necks of our gray wool socks while searching for any scene and any kink with any freak from anywhere around the globe. "The Mineshaft," Wally said, "attracted very hot men who got into S&M action that turned everybody on: fisting, bondage, whipping, worship, tit play, water sports, humiliation, dirty stuff. But it wasn't just handsome hot men. All kinds of faces and bodies made for great scenes. It's not always muscle and looks. It's a sensuality some people have."

IMPROVISATIONAL EDGE PLAY

Mineshaft sex was not about wham-bam as much as it was about sustained edge play in a gladiator arena where leathermen could turn the magical thinking of masturbation into reality. Every night Wally's stage set encouraged improvisational actors to arrive from closets around the world to produce their performance art with a new cast of thousands. Fetish scenes escalated from one intensity to the next, from the mud to the stars, while players changed identity within a scene, so that a man could enter any intimate scene upstairs, or leave any orgy scene downstairs, or go up on the roof where a shirtless blacksmith tended a fire to heat branding irons. The erotic dynamic was pitched so far beyond the boundaries of civilization that a man had to have self-discipline not to get swept away in action or voyeurism too extreme for himself, but not for the other guy.

SEX TOURISTS & THE MACHO DRESS CODE

"Air fares were low," Wally said. "We had lots of Europeans. I had a doorman keep tabs for ten-days over two weekends. It was something like 33 states and over 40 countries. The only countries missing were behind the Iron Curtain. I had fun with the Germans and the Dutch. New York is supposed to be this cold city, but we did everything not to be that way."

The Mineshaft's "Dress Code" came about by popular demand. "It was basically leather and Levi's," Wally said. "At an open meeting, the one rule people wanted was no cologne or deodorant. Everybody wanted sweat. Then some people wanted to go totally leather. I pointed out that the business could not exist if it was just leather because a lot of young guys couldn't afford leather. We agreed on jock straps, raunch wear, fetish gear, but no suits, ties, dress shirts, or sweaters. Because of fire codes, people always had to have their shoes on. Rudolf Nureyev played at the Mineshaft many times, but was refused admission once by a doorman for wearing a fur coat. So he took off his coat and was in full leather, but the doorman wouldn't let him in because he still had the fur coat—and this arrogant employee refused to check the coat! Nureyev vowed never to come back, and he never did—and neither did the doorman."

Wally made a point about leather fraternity: "The Mineshaft employees were a working fraternity. On Saturday night, I'd have one doorman and maybe fifteen guys on duty. We had three bars, with three or four guys in coat check. We had one assistant manager to make the money pulls from the various bars. We didn't have cash registers and couldn't keep money in the house due to the Mafia owner's policy. So our three floor men were constantly collecting money from our three bars." Wally hosted hundreds of community fund-raisers at the Mineshaft, including the Metropolitan Community Church benefit for the survivors of the fire at the Everard Baths, 28 West 28th Street, where nine patrons died May 25, 1977. "Whatever money I made for the benefits went directly to the causes we supported. The owners, the Genovese crime family, were not generous, but I sure was."

CAMERAS, VIDEOS, & THE MOVIE, *CRUISING*

Wally said the most basic sex was cocksucking and rimming with most fierceness going to bondage, fisting, and hazing "torture" not unlike Navy SEAL SERE training. He rarely allowed photography except for the Mr. Mineshaft Contest portraits shot by Robert Mapplethorpe who used the Mineshaft as a casting couch for models and ideas. In the early 1980s,

Wally allowed the Skulls of Akron biker club to shoot several S&M videos, like *Fisting Ballet*, which can be viewed online as a documentary of the Mineshaft space with its hoists, slings, crosses, and whipping posts.

Wally told me that, contrary to urban legend, the "interior leather bar" scenes in William Friedkin's film *Cruising*, so hated by the politically correct, were "not shot at the Mineshaft although to this day a lot of people think they were. I didn't want the exploitation. The bar scenes were shot at an after-hours place now called the Cell Block which was in the basement of the Little Triangle Building at 14th Street and Ninth Avenue. They decorated the interior to look like the Mineshaft." Friedkin's casting director did, however, hire Mineshaft leathermen as atmosphere extras so a viewer can freeze-frame old friends streaming on Netflix who are authentic Mineshaft faces now all gone with the wind.

AIDS & THE MAFIA

The Mineshaft, which did not cause AIDS, is a textbook example of how some first-class party people cruised on full speed toward the iceberg of HIV that no one knew lay dead ahead. When AIDS and the Mafia killed the Mineshaft, it was the end of an era. While it lasted, the Titanic 1970s was a perfect moment in time when we men liberated "our bodies ourselves" at the same time that women like Susie Bright empowered their sexual identities in 1970 with their movement and book *Our Bodies Ourselves*. It remains a veteran's badge of honor for a man, alive or dead, to have been one of the men who dared play at the Mineshaft.

It's important to gay male history to note that the first guys to die were not necessarily into the Mineshaft, S&M, or fisting despite the calumnies spread by puritanical haters. Needles were more dangerous than sex. A person was more likely to contract AIDS shooting up inside Studio 54 than fucking inside the Mineshaft. Wally said, "I was rather naïve about drugs unless somebody was falling over. The FFA [Fist Fuckers of America] was a very heavy drug scene—as I finally realized when their orgies at the Mineshaft went on for days. It took me awhile to realize some of my staff were addicts."

Always rolling with the punches, Wally kept the Mineshaft safe from being either a firetrap or the Black Hole of Calcutta. He opened exits and hosed down the concrete interior with bleach and distributed condoms and safe-sex pamphlets. As a community service, he permitted the Gay Men's Health Crisis to shoot a video inside the Mineshaft. When AIDS caused beer sales to drop off sharply, the Mafia accused Wally of embezzling the profits. He quickly schooled the straight hoods that there was a fucking plague killing the patrons.

When the Mineshaft was raided and closed in 1984, the excuse was AIDS, but the reason was taxes. Wally explained how a former NYPD cop, known as the "main man" behind the Mineshaft, was arrested on charges that the Mineshaft ownership had no liquor license and had failed to pay sales tax and income tax. It was the same reason the NYPD in 1969 had raided the Stonewall bar controlled by mobster, Matty the Horse Ianniello.

GOODBYE TO ALL THAT

The Mineshaft existed in the wonderful window between penicillin and HIV. If any talent was required at the Mineshaft, it was "perversatility." Thinking of what gay saint Yukio Mishima wrote in 1968 about ecstatic gay male pleasure and pain in *Sun and Steel*, I feel the Mineshaft was a graduate school of sex education, physical discipline, and existential identity. As we survivors raise our heads above the fallen field of our beloved AIDS dead, we eyewitnesses recall that at the Mineshaft, in the Dionysian fuckerie of all we were doing, we were simply evolving away from a fundamentalist society towards being fully human.

Publicity photo attributed to George Dudley for Wally Wallace, 1978. Courtesy Wally Wallace.

Wally Wallace, video interview, 206 Texas Street, San Francisco, March 28, 1990. Photo by Jack Fritscher.

WALLY WALLACE

1938-1999

The Mineshaft

October 8, 1976-November 7, 1985

Wally Wallace Tells All
Performance Art, Gay Space, Mapplethorpe, AIDS Disruption, and the Provocative Film *Cruising*

Wally Wallace founded and managed the Mafia-owned Mineshaft at 835 Washington Street in the Meatpacking District in New York City where the club ran nine years and nine days: October 8, 1976, to November 7, 1985. While his eyewitness memories were still fresh, I interviewed him for nearly three hours on March 28, 1990, when he sat for my video camera in the attic at 206 Texas Street where he stayed on his visit to San Francisco. When the interview ended, he opened a small suitcase and gave me eighty priceless photos snapped inside the Mineshaft. Our relationship was fourteen years old. We had first met around the opening of the Mineshaft, and he remembered me as the first national journalist to write about it. Having promised to publish his story, I wrote the very detailed "Mineshaft" chapter in the leather history book *Gay San Francisco: Eyewitness Drummer.* What follows is my transcription of Wally's exact spoken words lightly edited for flow and clarity.

START VIDEOTAPE #1
TIMECODE: 01.00

Jack Fritscher: Please tell me about yourself as background for how you managed the Mineshaft.

Wally Wallace: As long as I can remember, I was on stage in plays. As a kid I had a lot of fantasies and was left on my own a lot. I was born May 12, 1938 [died September 7, 1999], during the Depression and grew up during the war years. We lived in the suburbs of New York. My dad worked for the government. My weekends were spent in the city at my grandmother's house, a big sprawling West Side apartment which I sort of roamed in. I played games by myself: hide and seek, games like that. I was sort of an introvert with a lot of fantasies. Later I got involved with theater.

Jack Fritscher: So you enjoyed a "fantasy theater" boyhood.

Wally Wallace: Sort of like cowboys and Indians. I always enjoyed the men in the movies more than the women. Before the Mineshaft, I worked at a bar called the Ramp. I also worked for JC Penney developing their early mail-order catalog, sort of production manager. At the same time, I did a lot of theater in New York.

Jack Fritscher: Yes. Weren't you part of La MaMa [Experimental Theatre Club]?

Wally Wallace: Oh, yeah. Mainly in small parts. I did a lot of lighting too. Stage manager. That sort of thing. We opened La MaMa in three different locations because the police kept shutting us down or the rent would go up and we'd have to move somewhere else. Of course, now, La MaMa is long lasting and has done very well. At the same time, I was involved in day-to-day operations, public relations, etc. I was making travelogue films at one point, directing, writing scripts. After I got out of the army in 1963, I moved into New York [into an apartment] that an army buddy of mine was vacating. Got my first job. Of course, in those days one could afford to live in New York with a rent-controlled apartment.

In about March of 1976, Terry McNulty, a friend of mine, a club brother, founder of a small [gay leather biker] club called "Excelsior M. C. [Excelsior Motorcycle Club]"—still around—was managing a bar on 18th Street near the highway called the Ramp. He wanted to go into the clothing business, leather goods. So I said I would try managing the bar. I knew a lot of people, used to give a lot of parties. I thought I would just be a bartender, but soon it became too busy for that. The place really took off. It was a couple blocks from the Spike and the Eagle. It was the upper floor, and it had kind of a game room. We cleaned up the rest of the deserted building and expanded the bar. It became the most popular backroom bar in the city, and also kind of a "leather bar" that summer. The people [the Mafia] that I worked for weren't too nice. That's the best way of putting it. As it made more money, instead of bringing in the people that I wanted, they brought in their own bartenders. Then they lost their license. So I left.

Then somebody called about this disco place in the neighborhood called the Mineshaft. It was called that before I took it over. It had been through several semi-legal incarnations: one was a leather bar called the Den; another was the Zodiac.

So, in 1976, this disco place called the Mineshaft was running concurrently with the Ramp, but it wasn't doing very well. Michael Fesco's Flamingo was the place to go for disco fans.

Jack Fritscher: How is Michael Fesco? We had an intense four-day affairette in San Francisco during Jonestown weekend in 1978, the week before Harvey Milk was shot.

> [Michael Fesco (1934-2019) was a drop-dead-hot-and-handsome Broadway dancer and cultural influencer of New York nightlife whose pioneer disco enterprises from his Ice Palace on Fire Island (1969-1974) to his Flamingo disco (1974-1981) to his "Sunday Tea at Studio 54" (1981-1984) to his Sea Tea gay party cruises (1997-to his death) around Manhattan gave seminal soul to gay popular culture and made the always hale and hearty impresario a beloved figure.]

Wally Wallace: He's still around. He runs a tea dance on Sundays at a place called 20/20 (opened 1988) at 20 W. 20th Street. A nice space.

So I left the Ramp. There are things about the Ramp that are very special to me personally. It was my first endeavor in taking a space and utilizing it in my way. The Ramp was a safe space in the sense that we had the [Christopher Street] piers going at the time and we had the trucks. The actual piers and docks were not safe places for guys trying to have a good time and sex. There were murders and things like that. So by bringing sex indoors, I made it safe. This was the success of the Ramp.

I was then offered a position running a club at the Mineshaft. I had been there a couple of times but didn't really like it. It didn't seem to be successful and there were a lot of underage kids there. I said, "The only way I can do this is completely close it down, take a few weeks, spend about $500, and turn it into a leather bar." I sent out a mailing. Here's a copy of it. This was in the fall of 1976 when it opened. When I first looked at it, my intention was to change the name because it had this bad reputation, but when I went to see it, first of all you entered through some stairs and you went to a second floor and the operation at that time was all on the second floor where there was a bar and a pool table. I remember a false ceiling with white florescent lights and when it was lit up, it looked like a butcher shop [like the butcher shops on the same loading dock as the entrance to the Mineshaft].

To the right there was a hallway, then another big room which was the dance floor. In the middle of the floor was a box which they used as a small stage for go-go boys to dance on top of. I said, "I have other uses for this room. It should be a backroom because that's what people want these days." The owners agreed. I said, "I want to move this box," and I discovered the box was on top of a door. A metal trapdoor. I said, "What's this for?" They said, "It goes downstairs to an old freezer." So I opened up the door, went down a flight of stairs, and then realized that we were on the street-level floor where there was a big meat freezer with drains. I remembered seeing a place. It was in San Francisco, a place called the Barracks on Folsom Street. I had only been to San Francisco once at this point. I saw somebody was in the bathtub at the Barracks, which I thought was very hot.

Jack Fritscher: The Barracks was the hottest place in San Francisco next to the Slot.

> [The Folsom Street Barracks South of Market was a post-1906-quake corner building whose street entry was at 72 Hallam—with a second entrance into the bath itself through the Barracks' Red Star Saloon in the front corner of the same building at 1145 Folsom Street. It was a four-story former skidrow single-occupancy hotel for working men that changed to a bath when it opened May 15, 1972. It quickly became an S&M orgy scene and dream destination for locals and for sex tourists who could spend entire vacations enjoying private rooms, lockers, sauna, continental breakfasts and lunch in the bar, and thousands of international men in towels and leather treading the carpeted halls, showers, and orgy rooms. Its poster suggested: "Stay a night, or a weekend, or as long as you want!" I reserved the same room, 326, first door to the left at the top of the stairs, every third weekend and every New Year's Eve beginning in May 1972 when the Barracks set the bar for what a kinky gay play space should be. Wally Wallace distilled that inspiring essence for his Mineshaft. On July 11, 1981, an arsonist destroyed the Barracks that had been closed for remodeling in the worst fire San Francisco had seen since the 1906 earthquake.]

Wally Wallace: It had a bathtub, where somebody was in the bathtub, fully clothed, getting soaked with piss, surrounded by a big crowd pushing in to piss on him, which I thought was even more hot.

Jack Fritscher: So you put a bathtub on the ground-level floor of the Mineshaft.

Wally Wallace: That bathtub became famous. I didn't realize how many people were into bathtubs.

Jack Fritscher: Into piss…

Wally Wallace: Ha! The point is, I kept the name of the Mineshaft, because I had found an actual shaft under this metal door which went to the lower level.

It was also safe. Over the first year, the Mineshaft went through a lot of problems with police and building codes, etc. But one thing about the space was it was totally safe because the lower level, which always seemed subterranean, was actually on street level. By the time it closed, the Mineshaft had five exits, three with double doors, to the street. In that sense, it was perfectly safe. In time, we had to put in a water sprinkler system. We had to do so much for building codes, etc., probably harassed to the point that… But we were probably the safest place in the Village. About six months after we started, there was a terrible fire at the Everard Baths. Several people were killed. [On May 25, 1977, nine men died.] When the Metropolitan Community Church went to find out which places were safe in terms of discos, etc. to host an Everard benefit they were putting on, our papers happened to be on the desk of a local fire marshal, having just gone through an inspection. So the benefit that was done for the fire victims was put on at the Mineshaft. There was just a fire last week where 83 people were killed at a social club in the Bronx. That would never have happened in the Mineshaft.

Jack Fritscher: So you were practicing "safe sex" from the get-go.

Wally Wallace: Our building was safe, but the sex definitely wasn't. AIDS was still in the unforeseeable future.

Jack Fritscher: What was the dominant sexual activity at the Mineshaft? It seemed, "Anything goes."

Wally Wallace: The most basic thing was cocksucking, then fucking, then fisting, then other things. Oh, rimming. And a lot of tit play. S&M. You know, you start at the top and go to the bottom.

Jack Fritscher: That's gay sex to a T.

Wally Wallace: Before AIDS, there were a good four or five years when people were pretty wild and abandoned. They did almost anything they wanted.

Jack Fritscher: That was the Seventies. How did you change the image from the disco?

Wally Wallace: We were closed for a couple of weeks. So I went to a mailing list. It was a private club from the beginning. A men's club plus a couple of women. The night of the opening, the word had got out through my newsletter; but then also just word of mouth. People were looking for something different. The Eagle and the Spike, which were the leather bars at the time and still are today, had become rather inundated with other people who were just out slumming and not into the leather scene. So people were looking for a new place to go. I promised a dress code, although at the time I didn't know what it would be. It was to be a membership club.

Well, the first night we opened! We were on the second floor. I was standing at the entrance greeting friends, etc. Then I noticed an attractive female standing halfway up the stairs. I said to her, "I'm sorry, but you can't come in here. This is a men's club, a gay men's club. It might be embarrassing for a woman."

Jack Fritscher: I know this story. I love this story. It's canonical. She herself told me.

Wally Wallace: She said, "Well, I go to the Spike and the Eagle." She was dressed in leather and a very attractive girl. I said, "I'm sorry, but we determined that this was to be a private club for leathermen." I was worried about getting into trouble with women's rights groups. We had had some trouble at the Ramp with women trying to get into the backroom, but that was a public bar. But when she left, all these hot men standing on the stairs also left with her. So I said to myself, "I've got to find out who this woman is."

So I made inquiries to find out who she was, and that's how I met Camille O'Grady.

> [Camille O'Grady (c. 1950-2020), my longtime friend, a brilliant mind, a great beauty, flawless skin, raven-haired, Irish-American from New Jersey, Pratt student, punk poet/artist/singer who identified as a "gay man in a woman's body," toured with Lou

Reed, dated Robert Mapplethorpe, performed at CBGB before Patti Smith, and was nearly murdered when her lover Academy Awards Streaker Robert Opel was shot standing next to her (with a shotgun held at her throat) in their Fey-Way Gallery in San Francisco in 1979. Having been ill for years, she died of unannounced causes in the Coming Home Hospice in the Castro at 115 Diamond Street on St. Patrick's Day, March 17, 2020, two weeks into the first Covid lockdown.]

Camille became our sort of token female member of the Mineshaft; but she could only go to the bar area, and she couldn't bring any of her women friends, which she didn't. She pretty well stuck to those rules. I know that sometimes when I wasn't there, she would end up in the backroom; but I wasn't supposed to know. I'm sure she got involved in some pretty hot scenes. Lots of other people — men as well as women — who bragged they made it into the Mineshaft were lying.

There was another bar running nearby called the Anvil [owned by my friends and playmates leathermen Frank Olson and Don Morrison]. The Anvil had staged sex shows. Guys would get on the stage and be fisted, and there were stories of various female celebrities who would go there. [Jerry Torres, the star of the Maysles documentary, *Grey Gardens*, once took Jackie Kennedy Onassis to the Anvil.] And the guys on the stage: one was named Toby Ross [not gay film director Toby Ross], and he could take anything and he did. So there was a place for other people to go. The Anvil was a little bit of everything. In time, it became more of a drag bar. In the beginning it was a leather bar. They had backrooms too, but we never paid anybody to do anything or to perform.

I always felt the Mineshaft was like a gay man's bedroom. In a city like New York, you had a lot of people living in very small accommodations at that time. Single rooms, very small apartments with doormen. Guys went to the baths to have their sexual fun. They also knew it was safe in the sense that whoever they carried on with was not going to rip them off or whatever. We did have a number of pickpocket problems, which I think we controlled rather well. We were concerned about it. A lot of clubs didn't even care. There was a place called the Toilet which used to hire their own pickpockets to work the house. This is true. That place went out of business in our second year.

Jack Fritscher: When did you know you were a solid hit? How long did it take?

Wally Wallace: Wasn't long. We opened in October and by December. Hmm. It didn't take that long. I'm sorry I'm very bad on chronology. But the Mineshaft was always more than just me. I was very fortunate to have some very good guys working for me. Like any place there are those who work with you, those who work for you, and then there are those from the day you hire them are working against you or want to change things to their own. There was one particular incident I remember in the early days. The Ramp as I mentioned also had a backroom. There was a very big celebrity who used to go to the Ramp.

Jack Fritscher: For the record, who was it?

Wally Wallace: Rudolf Nureyev used to come to the Ramp and play there. And he loved to create scenes. He was an exhibitionist, a performer, but in a different way than on the ballet stage. When he went off to make the movie *Valentino* [directed by Larry Kramer's friend Ken Russell; released 1977], he stopped at the Ramp. It was a very dead night, maybe Tuesday or Wednesday, and he had this chauffeured limo stop at the Ramp so he could make his farewells. And I think it was something like $1 to go upstairs at the Ramp. There was an extra charge if you wanted to go upstairs to play around.

At the Mineshaft we had something like a $3 door charge. It was never very much. So one day Nuryev came to the Mineshaft when I wasn't there, and we had a French-Canadian fellow working for us who felt it was his job to enforce the dress code to the nth degree. Because Nuryev had on a long fur coat, he was refused admission. So he took off his coat and was in full leather, but the doorman wouldn't let him in because he still had the fur coat with him and this arrogant son of a gun who worked for me wouldn't even check the coat! Nureyev vowed never to come back, and he never did. I never had a chance to talk to him personally. We gave him his privacy when he was there. Obviously, the French-Canadian kid didn't stay there very long. He had an attitude.

The dress code at the beginning was basically leather or Levi's. In those days leather was *sub rosa*. You didn't talk about S&M which, of course, was connected to leather. But after a while, we decided to have a meeting of the members. The only reason for making it a membership club was to keep open later than the official closing time for public bars, which was 4 AM every night except for 3 AM on Saturday night. Beyond that, you had to be a private club. At that time, nobody who had a private club bothered about getting a liquor license in New York City. There were hundreds of social clubs, some still to this day. I mentioned the Bronx fire.

Anyway, we had a membership meeting to decide on a dress code. It was packed. I presided and we appointed a secretary. Interesting things were brought up, but the number one thing that irritated people, and the specific thing that they wanted in this dress code, was no perfume, cologne, scent, etc. Of course, everybody wanted people to smell like sweat. People appreciated the "natural" scent. Then some people wanted the dress code to be totally leather. I pointed out that the business could not exist if it was just leather. One thing was a lot of the young guys couldn't afford leather, and we definitely wanted guys to be naked if that was their thing. Because of the New York fire code, people always had to have their shoes on.

We would allow jockstraps, raunch wear, torn T-shirts, that sort of thing—anything that would make a guy look or feel sexy. We would not allow dress shirts and ties, suits, dress pants, sweaters. That was a big thing. People should not wear sweaters in leather bars, even though there is a hot military sweater. In the early days, in time, as the uniform clubs evolved, there were things like military tights and sweaters we could allow. "No turtlenecks," I think I said. How can you get the guy's tits when he's got a turtleneck on?

A lot of things like this came out of this meeting. The thing I did allow was sneakers. If they were too white, of course, we had to do something about that. We dirtied them up. Technically sneakers were never against the dress code, but people thought they were [likely because Chuck Arnett's Tool Box bar (1961-1971) in San Francisco had a sign made famous in *Life* magazine in 1964, saying "No Sneakers Allowed"]. Even then, some members would sometimes say something about the color of sneakers, red or yellow, maybe, but I had nothing against the basic sneaker.

Jack Fritscher: When did the Mineshaft take on its character of being more than just a backroom, into being, well, "Grand Opera"?

Wally Wallace: I don't know exactly what you mean by "Grand Opera"?

Jack Fritscher: I mean a sort of way larger-than-life Living Theater with no fourth wall like Julian Beck in *The Brig* or Artaud's Theater of Cruelty where your members could act out so many spectacular high-performance scenes in so many different stage sets with a cast of thousands.

Wally Wallace: The secret was the space itself. In time, we expanded the space to accommodate the sex and the crowds. I mentioned that we had found under that go-go box an actual shaft that had a wood-frame stairway where you could go downstairs, and there was a tub down there. The exact dimensions of the building I don't really know offhand, but it wasn't as large as it seemed to be. It was about a half-block long, but New York City blocks are like alley blocks elsewhere. They're really not that long. And it was relatively narrow. In time, we took over the entire street floor, which had included the Den.

The Den was at one time a straight bar in that building which for some reason went out of business—tax problems or something. When we moved in, well, let me say first of all, the Mineshaft is in the middle of the Meatpacking District, and, at that time, with all the meatpacking firms, there were a lot of straight truckers who wouldn't be caught dead going into the Mineshaft. But there were three places in the neighborhood where straight guys would go in and watch strippers, go-go dancers, naked women, that sort of thing, and drink beer or whatever. The Den had become one of these places, kind of a club. When there was a crackdown on that sort of club, the space became vacant, and then we took that over. The other part of the building—the northern part—was some sort of a carpenter shop. Eventually, we got that too. So we had the whole building. The owners of the Mineshaft did not own the building, but rented it from someone. I think from lawyers. The Mineshaft became very notorious when—I can't remember the year. When was *Cruising* made?

Jack Fritscher: It was shot in summer 1979 and released in 1980.

Wally Wallace: Because that was a crucial time. A lot of things changed then, which we should probably talk about. Anyway, what happened was the lawyers or agents for the owners of the building represented an estate, and it turned out that the beneficiaries of the estate were underage kids getting a trust fund. So when the movie *Cruising* came out, the owners of the building offered to sell it to the Mineshaft owners. *Cruising* was not filmed at the Mineshaft, but it did give us notoriety.

Jack Fritscher: Let's sort this out. The Mineshaft had gained a certain notoriety well before *Cruising*.

Wally Wallace: Right. Certainly, in the gay scene, it had become the place to go. New York and San Francisco at that time were the hubs of the gay tourist industry for a lot of reasons. They were known as gay cities. Big gay populations. Air fares were low. Europeans' money went a long way. We had lots of tourists from all over Europe.

One time I had a doorman who for one week kept tabs on where everybody was from who came through our doors. We called it "Seven Days in May," but it was really ten days over two weekends. I think it was something like thirty-three states of the Union and over forty countries in that period. About the only countries not represented were from behind the Iron Curtain. It was just amazing. I knew a little bit of German from my army days—"G.I. Deutsch"—so I had fun with the Germans. New York is supposed to be this horrible cold city, but we did everything possible not to be that way. I am basically a friendly person. I have trouble with attitude. As long as you're not hurting someone, do it if it gives you pleasure. So we had guys from all over the world. The Dutch especially were wonderful.

Jack Fritscher: When did you notice that the Mineshaft was getting to be a lot kinkier than you first thought?

Wally Wallace: When did I first think that? Because in the beginning I thought it would be just a basic fuck and suck in the backroom. Well, it was fairly early on that we put up slings. I don't know exactly. I'm sorry that I didn't keep a diary, but then if I had...Wow! But we had a good group. The FFA [Fist Fuckers of America] was older than the Mineshaft. You have to realize that for any business, anywhere in the world except maybe in Las Vegas, there are so many dead times during the week. When the Mineshaft opened, there were maybe thirteen leather bike clubs in the city. There was besides the FFA, the T.A.I.L. Chapter [Total Ass Involvement League], and the Interchange [biker club]. A lot of these bike clubs were relatively new. So we tried to attract these clubs in there, for events or whatever to fill the slow nights [like inviting GMSMA—Gay Men's S&M Association—to run seminars advertised as "The School for Lower Education"].

Jack Fritscher: Promotions.

Wally Wallace: It's part of the business.

TIMECODE: 51:56

Wally Wallace: I think the slings changed the game. I always had a problem with being fisted, although I tried it, as I've tried a lot of things. I was naïve about a lot of things. I missed the drug culture along the way. I was certainly naïve about a lot of the drugs in the gay scene. Unless somebody was so stoned that they were falling over, I was not aware of them being on something. The FFA was a very heavy drug scene—as I finally realized when their orgies went on for days. It took me awhile to realize that some of my staff were addicts. I wasn't looking the other way, but I wasn't seeing things as they were.

Jack Fritscher: Do you think it was your wild staff who encouraged wild sex to happen?

Wally Wallace: Oh yes, some of the guys came in with bright ideas for personal fetishes. I had learned at the Ramp, and also as a customer for many years in bars, that the "professional bartender" was not necessarily the person you want behind your bar. First of all, we had a limited drink menu. We didn't make Zombies or all those cocktail concoctions at the Mineshaft. No name brands. The basic drink of the Mineshaft was beer. We sold a lot of beer. Beer and soda were the basic drinks. Bud and Bud Lite. No Perrier. We got a lot of requests for it, but we had no Perrier. We had house brands. Our drinks were not expensive. Our door entry was maybe $10 towards the end on a Saturday night, otherwise $8. This was for non-members. Members were about half that. We gave out freebies to other bars.

People talk about the sex at the Mineshaft, but sex was not what it was all about. First of all, I had a policy that the music was never so loud that you couldn't hear the person next to you.

Jack Fritscher: Who created your music tapes? I remember your reel-to-reel tape deck perched behind the bar.

Wally Wallace: I did. I made them. So did Jerry Rice…

Jack Fritscher: *Mon amour*—for a minute—and houseguest back in 1971. He borrowed my copy of Bill Carney's leather novel, *The Real Thing*.

Wally Wallace: …and Michael Fesco and a guy named Ashland. I asked all kinds of people to make new tapes to fit our scene [including Thom Morrison in San Francisco]. We played anything in the world, from western to classics. A lot of classics, actually. Electronic variations on classic themes. Ella Fitzgerald, jazz. Tomita, new wave.

Jack Fritscher: I remember hearing Kitaro, and Kraftwerk's *Trans-Europe Express*, and Tim Buckley. His "Sweet Surrender" was more seductive than poppers for fisting.

Wally Wallace: We tried to avoid basic disco, references to females, references to "let's dance," things like that. But our music became kind of famous because we didn't follow the mainstream. We had a somewhat older clientele. When the New York drinking age went up from 18 to 21, the Mineshaft was one of the places least affected by that loss because our guys had generally grown to a point in life where they were old enough to know what they wanted. They knew what kink was. They were single guys. They weren't out to blind date, nor to emulate the straight world in terms of sexuality, lovers, dogs, and family.

But getting back to the main room at the Mineshaft. It was a very creative space. We had sawdust on the floor. It was a basic western motif. No black walls in the main room. In time, we did have video; but when video got big, we wouldn't play it all the time. Movies a few nights a week. Porn in the early hours when it was slow, not during the rush, because I figured people weren't there to watch sex. They were there to do it. I would discuss things with my staff. The one that I was closest to, he was there almost the entire time—our official run, incidentally, from opening to closing, was nine years and nine days. The guy's name was David Fishman, known as "Butch." Butch did the matinees. He had another job in the straight life. Worked Saturday and Sunday during the days. On weekends, we were open 2 PM to 10 AM. None of the guys worked more than eight-hour shifts. Other places make their bartenders work twelve-to-fourteen-hour shifts, but I didn't believe in it. That's no good.

Jack Fritscher: Let's talk about size...crowd size.

Wally Wallace: The biggest crowd we ever had was on the night of the circus, an annual benefit by Ringling Bros. and Barnum & Bailey Circus at Madison Square Garden [where the elephants linked trunk to tail come from Long Island into the city parading out of the Queens Midtown Tunnel to the Garden], and we had a party afterwards. That night we did have a lot of women there, but not downstairs.

Jack Fritscher: How many?

Wally Wallace: I don't know. It wasn't a normal night. A regular Saturday night would be 500 to 600 guys. On the circus night, there must have been over 1,000. We had a roof—I didn't mention that. Eventually we opened up the roof, and that was a very popular space up there. Guys could get away from it all up there.

Jack Fritscher: I remember. It was kind of romantic up there with the moon over Manhattan.

Wally Wallace: Yeah, it had a wall around it. We were right next to a factory of some kind where there was nobody on weekends. The roof was kind of a hot place. We put benches up there. In the summer, we would sometimes cook hamburgers up there. One anniversary, we had a blacksmith from Ohio, Larry Schwartzenberger, who had a forge for handcuffs and things like that. He came up and set up a forge and anvil and we had a branding.

Jack Fritscher: A lot of noise from the forging and yelling?

Wally Wallace: We always had to worry about that. Some of the S&M stuff, slings, and so on. Sure, there was some screaming. We had to use gags sometimes. There wasn't a lot of S&M going on; everybody wasn't into that. But we did have bondage equipment developed over a period of time. I would get ideas from going to Inferno [an annual S&M outdoor leather bike run] in Chicago, A-frames and crosses, that sort of thing. We had them available for guys.

Jack Fritscher: What was the most outrageous S&M scene you saw in the Mineshaft?

Wally Wallace: I don't know if you would call it outrageous, but we had a back bar. You couldn't depend on the customers—once they disappeared into the backroom—to come out again to the front bar. Of course, the owners of the business were mainly interested in selling beer. So on weekends we added this little back bar to sell beer. Then we eventually added a bar downstairs, which was also very popular on weekends.

Anyway, I had become very good friends with Leather Rick.

> [Leather Rick shot and starred in outrageously extreme S&M videos at the Mineshaft featuring guys from the biker club called "Skulls of Akron." In their feature, *Fisting Ballet*, the action is typical rough and real Mineshaft play. The videos also incidentally document some of the interior set, the gay space, of the Mineshaft rooms.]

I had met Rick at the first Inferno weekend I attended, and we remained good friends. It was on a New Year's Eve, I think, he nailed somebody's cock down on the back bar. The guy was sitting up there on the bar waiting to be nailed. Somebody asked if the nails were sterile. I happened to be there. "Of course, they are," I said. I had no idea if they were or not. This was before AIDS. I didn't know a lot about S&M. I knew about leather. I've never been a big reader of gay porno, although I like *Drummer*. You were the first person to write about the Mineshaft.

Jack Fritscher: Thanks for remembering. I wrote about you twice. [*Drummer* 19, Christmas 1977; *Drummer* 20. January 1978]

Wally Wallace: The only porno films I really liked were the Joe Gage films, *Kansas City Trucking Company*, etc., because there was a story built into them, showing environment and context along with actual sex. I did read *Mr. Benson* by John Preston, a lot of which revolved around the Mineshaft, but I don't read a lot of fiction.

TIMECODE: 1:14:45

Jack Fritscher: Did you know John Preston?

Wally Wallace: Yes. I had a run-in with him once. The very first year there was a New York "leather contest." It was hosted by Interchange. John Preston was sent by the owner of *Drummer* to photograph the event. This was the second year of the contest which was held in the Paradise Garage. My job was as Special Events committee, involving security and photographers. Because there were already two other people covering the event for *Drummer*, we had to tell John Preston not to take pictures and he got very upset. He wanted to get in free and we said, "This is a benefit. There are no comps." He argued about it, but eventually paid. He definitely had an arrogant streak that just rubbed me wrong.

Jack Fritscher: Preston was problematic inside *Drummer* as well [during and after I was editor-in-chief]. After he was fired by *The Advocate*, he came hat in hand to us to work freelance, but he didn't stay long.

Wally Wallace: Rules get set up and sometimes get followed to extremes. For instance, at Inferno in Chicago, there are very strict rules about photography because there are people there who don't want to be exposed, do not want anybody taking their pictures. In the Mineshaft for the first four years, we would not allow photos. I remember one time we let a guy, George Dudley, come in and shoot some pictures, including our flag and flagpole.

[George Dudley (1949-1993, AIDS) was a photographer and artist who founded and owned the nostalgic American Postcard Company and also served as the first director of New York City's Leslie-Lohman Museum of Gay and Lesbian Art.]

In those days, because of all the Bicentennial celebrations, most leather bars, including the Mineshaft, had an American flag. Not the case today. Our flag was cloth with Christmas lights behind it. Later I bought a hand-crocheted flag from a friend. We would use that flag when we did our Mineshaft Man contest.

TIMECODE: 1:20:58

Jack Fritscher: Robert Mapplethorpe shot pictures of that.

Wally Wallace: Yes, I have one of his shots right here.

Jack Fritscher: That's David O'Brien, Mr. Mineshaft. I have a copy Robert gave me.

Wally Wallace: Bob only shot one of our Mineshaft Man contests, and David O'Brien was the winner that year; so it was about 1979-1980. Somebody thought Bob could take pictures of the event. But that wasn't his thing. But he took some posed pictures of David. I don't remember if he ever shot anything else there.

By the way, the Mineshaft Man contest was not to pick "Mr. Leather," or "Mr. Muscle," or even "Mr. Mineshaft," but to pick a guy who epitomized what the Mineshaft was all about: "The Mineshaft Man." The judges were people who usually went there, or who were in gay businesses. One guy who did look "like a recruiting poster" was Mark Pongie [approximate spelling]. He was partially deaf, and read lips: a sweet, nice guy. I was really proud to see him win.

Rex did three posters: for the first contest, of a miner with arms raised hoisting a big Mineshaft sign; for the second one, of the guy with the pick and hard hat; but the third one never turned out the way it was supposed to. It was of a guy with a jackhammer in the street. Something was lacking. Rex himself was wonderful. Not easy to get to know, but he's a wonderful human being.

Some of the male pornographers, you know, are like Michelangelo. There's our Tom of Finland and A. Jay [*Drummer* art director Al Shapiro]. A. Jay's posters from the Caldron [This is the correct spelling.] were wonderful. I hope someone saved them. I got to know Jim [Gilman] and

Al [Shapiro] at the Boot Camp [a pissoir-bar on Bryant Street in San Francisco]. When Jim and Al were putting together the Caldron [with Hal Slate who managed the Castro Theater in San Francisco], they came to New York City for a long weekend to observe things in the Mineshaft.

What did they observe? Did they observe the backroom activities, etc.? No, they looked at our coat-check system and adopted that. They were interested in exploring how the Mineshaft systems worked. And I think it paid off for them like it did for us. We didn't lose checked clothing because we had a good system that guys trusted and we lost very few coats. The ones we did lose, we paid for. The Mineshaft was pretty safe that way. That's important in an operation.

Jack Fritscher: At the time you mention, 1979-1980, Robert Mapplethorpe was just beginning to become a sort of a celebrity in his own right.

Wally Wallace: Yes, right, but I knew him as a person. I liked Bob. We weren't close friends, but we'd talk and compare notes. I remember one time [hesitates], well, he liked black men. He had heard of a place in Times Square called Blues, which was a black gay bar. One of the few places that was openly promoted as a black gay bar. And Bob was afraid to go there. I don't why, but he was. So I went up there with him one time. He was like a kid so eager to go, but so afraid to go alone that you might have thought it was in the depths of Harlem. The night we were there, there weren't many hot men, but only a couple of drag queens with their white boyfriends. It was not what he imagined. I know he went back there a few times. I know he went to Keller's a lot. That has now become a black bar. It was one of the original New York leather bars. It's still there; one of the longest-running gay bars. Never talked much to Bob about his work. You didn't talk about work at the Mineshaft. You talk about what's going on in town, neighborly talk.

Jack Fritscher: Let's talk about some other celebrities who came to the Mineshaft. I heard Mick Jagger was once turned away.

Wally Wallace: Yes, Mick Jagger was turned away because he was with a girl [Jerry Hall, the Texas model who became his wife for a Warholian fifteen minutes]. He probably would have been let in if he was alone. I know that because I was there that night. I was there a lot, but not always, and I can't vouch for some things that are reported to have happened. I may have been home sleeping. I certainly was not there all the way from Friday night to Monday morning.

Jack Fritscher: What was it like to scrub the place up after a long weekend?

Wally Wallace: It was pretty bad. We would have a problem in the tub room if the guys used too much bleach because the vapors would come upstairs. I think the Mineshaft was a lot cleaner than people perceived it to be. We kept it pretty clean. It was an old concrete building. We eventually had to nail up plywood over the plaster wallboard because people having rough sex and shoving up against the plaster board would put holes in it and the inspectors were always having to tell us to replace it. One of the biggest problems we had was the *scatzies* [scatophiliacs] what with their drugs and everything. We tried to discourage that kind of dirty sex, but people would do *scatzie*. We always had floor men on duty to clean up.

The Mineshaft employees had a certain camaraderie. On Saturday night, I would have as many as fifteen guys on duty. We had three bars, with three or four in the coat check, and doormen. We had one doorman and one assistant manager to make the money pulls from the various in-house bars. We didn't have cash registers and couldn't keep money in the house due to the [Mafia] owner's policy. So we were constantly collecting money from the various bars. Then we had three floor men. Then, when the can-recycling thing came in, that was a whole new operation.

TIMECODE: 1:40:59

Jack Fritscher: Tell me about the time the Skulls of Akron biker club came to make a video in 1981 or so. Was that the first video shot in the Mineshaft?

Wally Wallace: No, the first video happened like this. One of the guys who worked at the Mineshaft had a friend who made movies. He came from France and wanted to shoot a porn film at the Mineshaft. Supposedly, this would only be seen in Europe and not in America. We got a little money, but it was a strange film. It was a French version of what they thought the Mineshaft was. They tied one guy up and put Christmas lights around him so he looked like a Christmas tree. I remember Camille O'Grady was in it.

Jack Fritscher: I know the movie. It was *New York City Inferno* [1978, directed by Jacques Scandelari].

Wally Wallace: When you're recording music for a movie, you have to pay attention to the sound balance. The music on the video had a horrible echo and did nothing for Camille's career. She thought it would. She did sing at the Mineshaft a couple of times for benefits. We did a lot of benefits. We would also hold casino nights during the week, no sex.

> [The first Mineshaft flyer for Christmas 1976 advertised: "Upcoming special events include the opening of our new tunnel playroom, a 'Criscomas Party,' and a repeat performance by Camille O'Grady." Wally also invited Camille to sing her piss song "Toilet Kiss" at the Mineshaft 1978 anniversary party.]

But getting back to the French movie, the plot was that a Frenchman came to the U.S. to find his lover who has been made a slave. And his way to find his lover was to take the seven days of letters he had received and follow them from place to place, which was totally ridiculous, of course. But there were a lot of hot things in the movie. One of the hottest was when he arrived in the States, he meets a taxi driver who takes him to the meat market where he is seen having sex in the freezer with all these sides of beef hanging around.

And then he's seen in the Mineshaft, but it didn't look like the Mineshaft. They only used a little piece.

> [Scandelari featured Camille and her band on a raw wood stage which was a landing half-way up the interior wood stairs in the middle of the Mineshaft that Wally had found under the go-go boys' box.]

The only time the Mineshaft looked like the Mineshaft in a video was one made later by the Gay Men's Health Crisis. It was in three segments. The first segment was a couple getting together for a date while they talk a lot about having safe sex, put on rubbers, etc. The last segment was about something out on Fire Island. The middle segment was filmed at the Mineshaft and was about S&M, but there was no narrative to explain what parts of S&M were safe and which parts weren't.

Jack Fritscher: What is the most outlandish gear you ever saw worn in the Mineshaft?

Wally Wallace: Gear?

Jack Fritscher: Well, costumes, leather, rubber, the hottest thing?

Wally Wallace: The Mineshaft didn't make that big a thing out of Halloween. We were on the north end of the Village, twelve to fourteen blocks away from the center around Christopher Street where everybody went on Halloween. But we did some things. I think the hottest costume gear was, maybe, [sounds like] Bo Shear, one of the regulars—he was Dracula cuming in his coffin. He had a big dick and an air pump, and some fluid would come out every once in a while. As far as day-to-day gear, I can't think of anything other than leather. We had masks sometime, usually made out of metal rather than leather.

Jack Fritscher: Tell me more about how you managed the action to keep the party under control.

Wally Wallace: So, to get into the Mineshaft you had to walk up some stairs and at the top of the stairs was the doorman. Now he had to determine whether the guy coming up the stairs—if he was too drunk or too stoned he couldn't get in. The same ones would show up again and again.

We did have a few problems with pickpockets. These guys were professionals and would sometimes work in teams. They would get into the Mineshaft, and one of the guys on the team would get naked. Now we would do everything possible to get guys to check their wallets. We had signs. We made announcements. We did everything possible because we never lost that sort of stuff when it was safe in our coat check. Through all the years we had never had anybody lose anything in terms of money he'd checked. We lost a few jackets by transferral. Like I said, these guys would work in teams in the tub room, which got pretty crowded. The naked one would pass the wallet to his cohort. It's hard to accuse a naked man of hiding a wallet. When we caught these guys what we did was throw them out on the street without their clothes. I know of at least three occasions where somebody was thrown out totally nude, sometimes in winter. This kind of thing made me mad. We sometimes wondered what happened to them.

Jack Fritscher: Just like an Old West saloon, throw them out through the swinging doors. What is the sexiest thing you ever saw there?

Wally Wallace: Saw? OK, but I won't tell you about anything I participated in. Well, there were some men there—whatever they were engaged in was sexy. We had some very hot men come in to play. Hot. It's not always body. It's a sensuality that some people have. We had some events—one was called the "School for Lower Education." One was called the "Black Mask" where everybody wore black masks. These events were once a year, special. We had some demonstrations mentoring S&M. We let the GMSMA do a demonstration for a part of the door, that sort of thing. They would put on some wonderful things. A lot of the bondage stuff.

Another thing that went off very well the first few times we did it—and then it died because you couldn't get contestants—was a body painting contest. We would supply the paint and one guy would paint another.

> [In the cross pollination of *Drummer* and the Mineshaft, *Drummer* featured Val Martin, star of *Born to Raise Hell*, with his body painted by Chicago tattoo artist Cliff Raven on the cover of issue 8, published September 1976, one month before the Mineshaft opened.]

I remember Camille was involved in one painting contest. She was a talented artist. Greg Maskwa was one of the artists doing the body painting. He did some nice things [kinky drawings of leathermen and women]. One of the most interesting things was a lot like the "Emperor's New Clothes." This one guy was painting this other naked guy forever with this solution. It was invisible. I didn't know what it was. It didn't look like anything, but it was a sort of clear plastic that peeled off. The guy was totally encased in it. Cock, balls, everything. It was like a third skin. You think of leather being a second skin. This was an invisible skin. I've never seen that again.

Jack Fritscher: Is there anything special you'd like to say about the Mineshaft? What do you think the Mineshaft esthetic did to help create the 1970s as we know them, that high golden age? Maybe you could say something about the movie *Cruising*.

END VIDEOTAPE #1
START VIDEOTAPE #2
TIMECODE: 01.00

Wally Wallace: Well, you know the book was based on gay murders [in the 1960s], but it had nothing to do with our leather scene. [The book *Cruising* was a fact-based novel written by *New York Times* reporter Gerald Walker in 1970, six years before the Mineshaft existed.] I don't know how the director [William Friedkin, director of *The Boys in the Band* and *The Exorcist*] found out about the Mineshaft. I heard he got in at some point or other before filming, maybe six months before. He recruited a lot of guys in our leather scene to be in the film. Most were not actors. He held auditions for quite some time and got a lot of legitimate leather people involved in it. I was approached by one of his crew who wanted to come into the Mineshaft to shoot stills for their storyboard. So I let him come in just to hear his pitch, but he said the ceilings were not high enough for the lights and cameras necessary to shoot a movie. So I met him—before I met Friedkin, but finally I would not agree to them coming in. I could not see any point, any advantage for us. We had that rule about photographs. We only let friends like Mapplethorpe shoot pictures.

We didn't do commercial things. The Mineshaft never advertised, except for inserts in benefit programs. Whatever money I made hosting a benefit went back to the benefit. The mob owners were not generous, but I sure was. We didn't advertise because we were supposed to be a private club and the members were supposed to introduce us to new members. Of course, word of mouth was our best source. We got the people we wanted that way.

So I refused Friedkin, and then a couple of my staff got involved in the movie. Others on the staff didn't want anything to do with it. Their main objection to the film was the portrayal of gays as murderers. There was a boycott protesting the movie led primarily by a guy named Joe Smenyak [who that same summer of 1979 helped organize the first National March on Washington for Lesbian and Gay Rights, and later appeared in the 1983 production of Doric Wilson's *Street Theater* which had premiered in 1982 at Theater Rhinoceros in San Francisco]. So it was never filmed at the Mineshaft, although to this day a lot of people think it was.

The bar scenes were shot at a place now known as the Cell Block, but at that time, it was another after-hours place—before that space became the Hellfire Club—in the basement of the Little Triangle Building at 14th Street and Ninth Avenue. I can't remember the name at that time. It is a unique space. It is underneath the street, not under the building. Historically, there was a canal from the river up to that building. The Little Triangle Building at the time of the Civil War was a Union Army barracks. After the war it became a hotel. I think Herman Melville lived there when he was writing *Typee*. Later I ended up in a loft space on the top floor, but that is another story.

Anyway, let me backtrack to when they still wanted to film *Cruising* at the Mineshaft. They kept trying to get permission to shoot still shots [for their set designer], but I refused. And later, when we had our first raid on the Mineshaft, it had to do with liquor violations and a few other things. Actually, and here's the point. It turned out that the raid had been staged [arranged] by some guys in the movie company, because their security force were ex-New York City policemen. One was Sonny Grosso, who is now a big author and producer of some of the big TV crime series. [Grosso played the part of Detective Blasio in *Cruising*.] These were ex-cops who had been involved with the famous "French Connection" crime case, who had since left the force and were now doing movie work. [Friedkin had directed the cop drama *The French Connection* in 1971 after he had directed *The Boys in the Band* in 1970.] So these guys arranged a police raid on the Mineshaft on the basis of liquor violations [when all they wanted was photos of the interior.] This all came out later in a grand jury investigation. Everybody working at the Mineshaft was taken downtown in a paddy wagon, including me. I wasn't even there when the raid took place; but when I went there to find out what was going on, I was put in cuffs, totally illegally and taken down to the station house.

While we were downtown, a crew from the movie company went into the Mineshaft and photographed everything.

I was arrested illegally, but all charges were eventually dropped after going to court.

I think Friedkin, or maybe his set designer, had this obsession to re-create both the interior and exterior. After I refused, in order to create the exterior, he hired the meat company which is right next door to the Mineshaft where he filmed all his entrances and exits to the bar in the bar scenes in the film. In the movie, people go downstairs after entering, whereas in the Mineshaft, of course, you had to go upstairs. Otherwise it looks exactly the same. We didn't have a sign that said "Mineshaft." We just had little arrows that said "Private Club," and that was what he re-produced.

Jack Fritscher: It's interesting that sometime later when you first began to have a movie night at the Mineshaft, the first 16mm film you projected on the screen in the main bar was *Cruising*.

Wally Wallace: It was interesting to see the faces of so many Mineshaft regulars on screen.

TIMECODE: 11:52

Jack Fritscher: What do you think has been the Mineshaft's contribution overall to the way we are, the way we were?

Wally Wallace: I think we allowed—we gave guys—a sense of freedom, to sort of sow their oats.

Jack Fritscher: Sow their oats and spill their seed.

Wally Wallace: Right. Sex is many things, never a cut-and-dried subject. The form of sexual activity that we had at the Mineshaft is, in one sense, like people going to the gym to work out. It is an exercise, recreation. But it also spiritual, like going to church. Of course, it was hedonistic. You can't deny that. But it was a form of recreation for a lot of people.

Without going into names, we had people who were famous in their professions. We had the cream of the crop. We had a lot of clergymen, including Catholic clergy, theatrical people, stage managers, directors. A lot of gay marriages happened out of the Mineshaft. I know several couples are still together who met at the Mineshaft. Partnerships, collaborations. The front bar was a great place for talking. People at other bars would stand there all night in those bars posing or cruising. At the Mineshaft, people could relax.

The Mineshaft was a neighborhood bar, but it included all of Manhattan. After all, Manhattan is a relatively small island and most of the people live south of 80th Street. So nobody was that far from the Mineshaft in terms of where people actually lived. It was a form of recreation. You needed a place to go after working at a high-pressure job all week and we provided the place to relax. We had dress codes, but they were for a reason. We dealt with a particular clientele, but we didn't see it only as a business.

Other people have tried to imitate the Mineshaft with only money in mind, and haven't succeeded. You have to have other concerns. We, including my staff, gave a lot back to the community. One thing I am personally proud of is that we happened at a time when a lot of things were being created in the gay community, like the Gay Men's Chorus, gay bankers, gay businessmen. We were there at the start of AIDS. We raised a lot of money along with other gay bars like the Badlands for serious and fun things like "Butts for Tuxes" for guys in the Gay Men's Chorus to wear their first tux to their concert in Carnegie Hall. Gay theater.

The Mineshaft opened seven years after the Stonewall riot. Stonewall was political, but it took a good ten years afterwards to create cultural organizations. Some of the discos were happening at that time.

> [The original Studio 54 opened five months after the Mineshaft opened, and ran from 1977-1980 when it was shut down because owners Steve Rubell and Ian Schrager, defended by Donald Trump's then attorney Roy Cohn, were convicted of tax evasion.

Schrager was fully and unconditionally pardoned by President Obama in 2017. In 1981, Robert Mapplethorpe shot a revealing portrait of the gay Roy Cohn making his evil face a mask floating disembodied in a field of black. In the 1950s, Cohn had conspired with the severely anti-gay demagogue Senator Joseph McCarthy and had prosecuted Jules and Ethel Rosenberg who were executed in the electric chair at Sing Sing. In 1986, Cohn was disbarred for forcing a dying client to sign his fortune over to him—five weeks before Cohn died of AIDS.]

The gay churches too. My aunt and uncle, a childless couple, went to a church in Washington Heights, and they couldn't understand why their minister would go from Washington Heights down to the Village to "work with those homosexuals." Little did they know that only two weeks before, I had hosted the Everard fire benefit with that very minister.

TIMECODE: 21:43

Jack Fritscher: You're so generous to share your story. You must be exhausted—unless you want to name some names, for the record.

Wally Wallace: Well, I know Rock Hudson was there once. He came with [unintelligible] Wilson [not Henry Willson, the agent who discovered him]. Al Pacino definitely was there—but not as a gay man—for his role. I think he was duped into that role. I heard he didn't really want to do it. As far as I know, he's heterosexual. That was a weird movie, *Cruising*. It was being filmed at the Hellfire. There were protestors day and night. Cops guarding the set. And the company [he alleged] was passing out dope to the gay extras. Pete [unintelligible] was in the film for a couple of days before peer pressure got to him. He can vouch that everybody was stoned. The guy that danced with Al Pacino, Bruce [Levine], was a friend of mine. You would think all that publicity would get them a great movie, but it didn't work out. Not just because of the gay protest, but because it wasn't a very good movie.

Jack Fritscher: That protest was probably the highest public profile the Mineshaft had.

Wally Wallace: Well, sure, except when we were closed.

Jack Fritscher: Tell me about how you were closed.

Wally Wallace: Well, it was so unofficial. The cops came down during the day. We had been closed the night before. They sent in inspectors. This is really important. This was a task force. This [NYPD] task force was advised that there was a gay, kind of self-policing group, working internally within the city government and state too, I guess, to self-police sexual activity in places where sex was taking place.

One of the people on this board was a woman who may be gay, Ginny Apuzzo, but what does she know about our lifestyle?

> [Wally meant the "leather lifestyle." In truth, in her long career of service, Virginia "Ginny" Apuzzo, a former Catholic nun, was executive director of the National LGBTQ Task Force and served as executive deputy of the New York State Consumer Protection Board and as the vice chair of the New York State AIDS Advisory Council, and was the most senior openly gay person in the Clinton administration. On March 24, 2020, under gay archivist JD Doyle's Facebook photo of her, she wrote in response to a comment I posted about her and the Mineshaft: "It's curious…nearly half a life of advocacy and recalled for closing the Mineshaft." Sometimes history writes us. I reassured her that neither Wally nor I meant to be reductive: "In your valued career, you did a good thing for the community and public health in helping close the Mineshaft. Thank you."]

A couple people from the Mineshaft met with this board, and we did everything they asked, like condoms and passing out literature.

They sent in employees from the Consumer Affairs Office. They did not send in police to make reports. In the reports—and there were something like twelve different reports—not one mentions any sort of anal penetration of cock to ass. Not one talks about any oral penetration, cock to mouth. What they talk about is deep kissing, moans being heard in the backrooms, not even seen. In other words, it was all light S&M acts in these reports. Now this is the Mineshaft. I can't speak about the baths and other places. I never saw them. But the Mineshaft report was posted with great publicity on the door, with TV coverage. The precinct captain was there, even Mayor Koch made an appearance. I was watching on TV with the owners. As I say, nothing, not one real sexual act was mentioned because it was really about taxes, because the owners had this tax situation.

> [In the perfect storm of taxes and AIDS, Wally told me off camera:
> "By 1984, the year before we closed, profits dropped so sharply

that the [straight] owners called me in, and my staff, one by one, saying we were skimming the cash register. I told them AIDS was killing their customers."]

TIMECODE: 29:56

Jack Fritscher: So why do you think this self-policing gay group had an agenda to shut down the Mineshaft? What was their motivation?

Wally Wallace: The same as always. The gays are always embarrassed by the leather community. They don't think we represent them well. They are embarrassed that we exist in the same world. But shouldn't we be embarrassed by men who pose as women? To get personal for a minute. A lot of people think I am anti-women, anti-drag queen. As a human being, I am not. We each explore our own territory. If they don't infringe on my territory, I don't infringe on theirs. I think some of the leather women are wonderful, but I don't want to have sex with them or go to bed with them. I'm a gay man. I like men.

Jack Fritscher: Erotic psychology is rarely politically correct.

Wally Wallace: When it comes to talking S&M techniques with women, I'm all for it; but I think we can have our separate playrooms. At this moment, I'm glad to see all of us seem to be getting together. But in the past, it has been the women who have been as alienating as the men. And, of course, these leather women are looked down upon in their lesbian community in the same way leathermen are in the gay community. The S&M women's groups are outcasts in the lesbian community. I'm glad to see there is a better rapport now between the two groups.

There does seem to be a barrier now between the older leather guys and the young punk gay leathermen, but we shouldn't be apart just because we come in by different routes. We all have to live in the greater world.

Jack Fritscher: Thank you very much.

Wally Wallace: I want to give you some of this stuff [eighty photos for my use with this interview and articles based on this interview.]

Jack Fritscher: This is March 28, 1990.

Wally Wallace: Oh! At one of our Mineshaft Man contests, one of our judges tells me and another judge that he thinks he recognizes one of the contestants [Michael Garrison] as a man who seven years before had murdered the lover [Tom Strogen] of a mutual friend [Rob Kilgallen]. He tells us this during an intermission. So the two of us go to our mutual friend sitting out in the crowd and he confirms this. [The contestant] had murdered the lover, had gone to trial, and three years later he was out of jail, and now, a few years later, was in the Mineshaft Man contest.

Jack Fritscher: *Cruising*, anyone?

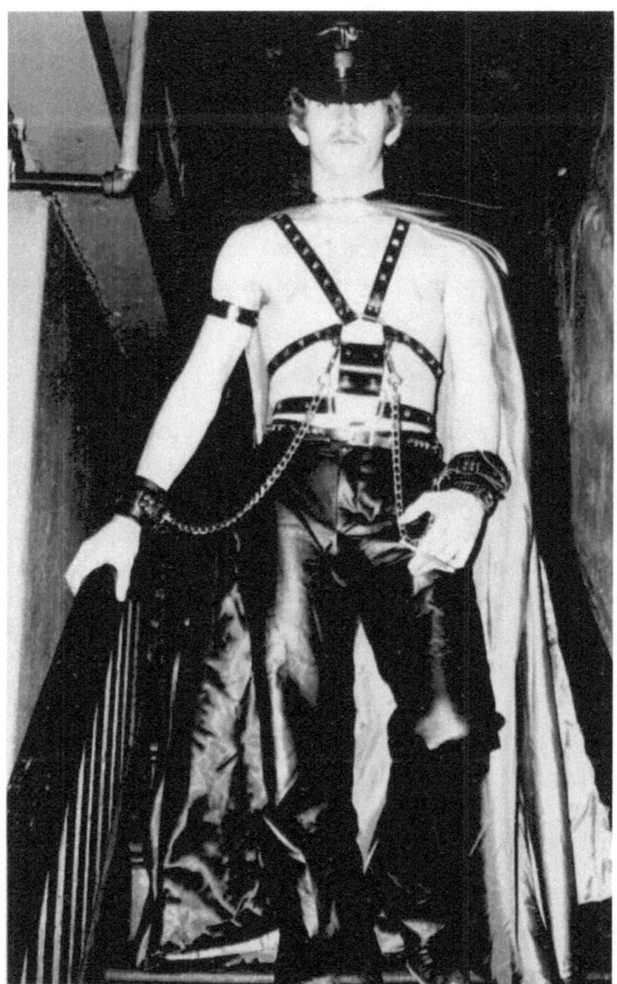

"Dude Descending a Staircase at the Mineshaft," 1980. The basic Mineshaft dress code of boots and jockstrap included fetish variations on kink fashions. Publicity photo attributed to George Dudley for Wally Wallace. Courtesy Wally Wallace.

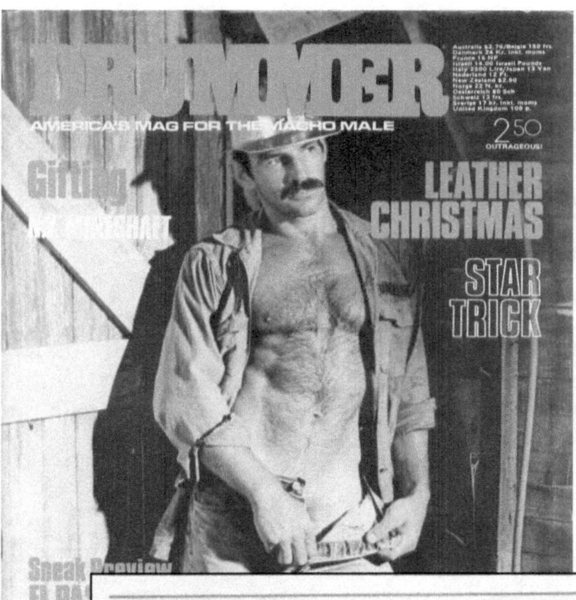

The Mineshaft was headlined by editor-in-chief Fritscher in piss-yellow on the cover of *Drummer* 19, December 1977, pictured here with the first page of the first feature article on the Mineshaft in the gay press.

By Jack Fritscher

Hot spots get too hot not to cool down. So hit them while you can. Like The Mine Shaft in New York, New York. Two floors and a roof of whatever flips your switch. In San Francisco, a friendly stranger asks your sign. In LA he asks what part of town you live in. New Yorkers just do a two-handed fine-tuning on your tits and lift an armpit, either yours or theirs, for openers. That's the Manhattan Hello.

UP A STEEP AND VERY NARROW STAIRWAY

Cab it to The Mine Shaft. It's tucked in among the meat packing houses at the west end of 14th Street. Hang a left to Little West 12th Street. Head on up the stairs. At the entrance, a man checks your membership or issues you a card renewable every three months. For members the door charge is minimal and the stub is

Rob Meijer in interview in his flagship RoB of Amsterdam leather shop and art gallery, June 21, 1989. After his death in 1991, the RoB of Amsterdam group bought *Drummer* magazine in 1992 and published it through 1999. Photo by Jack Fritscher.

ROB OF AMSTERDAM

c. 1940-1991

Leather Fashion Designer

The Man Who Made the Clothes That Make the Man

His Last Video Interview: June 21, 1989

On June 21, 1989, Rob Meijer aka Rob of Amsterdam—who died in 1991, age approximately fifty—took time from his busy Wednesday afternoon to sit for a video interview in his office above his flagship RoB of Amsterdam *couture* shop and art gallery. The designer's company also had corporate RoB franchises in Paris, London, Zürich, Berlin, Brussels, Manchester, New York, and San Francisco. I had first visited Amsterdam in 1969, rooming wantonly above the Argos Bar, but this was different from the wild 1960s. It was Holland at the height of the AIDS pandemic, two months after *Drummer* publisher Anthony DeBlase designed the leather pride flag, three months after the death of leather fashion photographer Robert Mapplethorpe who had shot Rob, four months before the earthquake that destroyed the *Drummer* office, and five months before the fall of the Berlin Wall. Everyone was on edge. Turmoil was in the air.

Rob received me and Mark Hemry, my husband and creative partner of then ten years, because we were from *Drummer,* which was very much a leather fashion magazine. Just two hours before, we San Francisco leathermen had landed at Schiphol Airport. We had been flown in by Roger Earl and Terry LeGrand, the pioneer filmmakers of the 1975 leather classic *Born to Raise Hell.* In 1988, they had shot their film *Men with No Name* in the cellar at RoB of Amsterdam and were back for more Dutch S&M. Because they liked how we directed and shot leather features for our Palm Drive Video studio, they had hired us onto their otherwise European film crew as cameramen to do a two-camera shoot for six S&M video features for their Marathon Studio based in Los Angeles. It was Terry who had convinced Rob to sit for our interview, which Mark shot.

So as a journalist, I made Rob our absolutely first stop in Amsterdam.

Rob was a lively artist who was an amusing and sophisticated man with a jovial sense of ball-busting humor. He was a businessman and sensualist with a wiry dancer's body, sporting black leather gloves with exposed fingertips, drinking Heineken Pilsener from a big green bottle, and chain-smoking cigarettes in a long holder while presiding at his desk, sitting in front of a large potted palm. He was, of course, wearing signature "RoB"—a black leather sleeveless shirt-vest winged with two-inch cap sleeves, epaulettes, a popped collar, and a plunging zipper neckline that was cinched by a wide studded belt over black leather trousers and boots.

He took a quick look at my big black beard and said, "I don't like beards." He was putting me on and creating a bond for the moment. There was lots of laughter during our interview. At first he did not want his face on camera, but slowly, as Rob relaxed, Mark finger-tapped Terry's brand new Sony Video 8 Pro camera, and smoothly edged him into the frame… and Rob smiled.

On May 19, 1992, a year after Rob's passing, Martijn Bakker, the new owner of RoB of Amsterdam, bought *Drummer* and published it from a San Francisco office until the magazine's last issue in 1999.

This carefully verbatim transcription documents an historic afternoon in Amsterdam with one of the great designer artists of authentic leather culture.

Jack Fritscher: Mark Hemry and I landed in Amsterdam this morning, and here we are together in your office two hours later. Thank you.

Rob of Amsterdam: Did you like the RoB Gallery downstairs?

Jack Fritscher: Very much. Your shop is wonderful. Some of the greatest gay artwork I've seen collected anyplace. So many stores have copies, greeting cards, prints, but not the originals you have. I hope you don't mind my saying it out loud, and with respect, that your name is legendary throughout the world. What I'm trying to do is chronicle you as a creator and collector in the context of our recent past now being destroyed by AIDS, because there is a new young generation out there right now in the clubs and bars who came out in the last eight or nine years. They don't know what sex was like before the threat of AIDS. They have no personal idea what the golden age of the 1970s was like. I think the past has no more remembrance than the memory we give it. So I have been interviewing people who remember it, about things that were important to them or helped them create international leather culture, the international art of leather, leather politics, leather image, in short, leather fashion throughout the world. And you have been most instrumental in that.

Rob of Amsterdam: I'm not a good one to talk with about the past because I only think of tomorrow and I don't think about what has been because I find it very unhealthy. To get all those things back in my mind, I don't know if that is—possible.

Jack Fritscher: Perhaps you could just tell us a little about yourself personally. Where you came from…

Rob of Amsterdam: I was born in Amsterdam and had some gay lovers and at a certain moment I met a man who was into the S&M, and he tried to train me as a slave, but it only made me angry, but it got my interest, and he was the first to take me to a leather bar, and I was amazed by the people there and by the way they were dressed, and I found it all very exciting. I was at that time a designer for women's dresses, in the big sizes. And a certain woman said, "Why don't you go and work at home?" So I started my first pair of leather trousers for myself, and took it from there. Then a first customer came, and a second, until I could make a living at it, and then I gave up my job designing dresses. It is very exciting. People only come here to my shop when they are in a good mood, and if they aren't, they don't come. That is ideal.

Jack Fritscher: So the art of your leather, also legendary throughout the world, puts them in a good mood if they aren't already. I've certainly been turned on in the ten minutes I've been here. I want to browse and look at it, want to take it home with me. When did you first open your RoB of Amsterdam store?

Rob of Amsterdam: The first store was opened in 1974. In 1975, I moved down the road where we were all these years, and then the first of November last year we came to these premises, and I think it has been a good move. This is a very beautiful house, and it has lots of space where we can have our big workroom for design and cutting. So we are very happy.

Jack Fritscher: In your creation of leather, have you found that you've helped leather develop its sense of style? I think you have. In every community there is a person, like Rob of Amsterdam or Tom of Finland or Robert Mapplethorpe, who sets a style, sets a mode against which everything is measured. Rather like 1970s *Drummer* helping create the very leather culture it reported on.

[Beginning in 1979, Galerie Rob Jurka in Amsterdam, existing alongside RoB of Amsterdam's RoB Gallery founded in 1978, was the first art gallery in Europe to exhibit a show by Robert Mapplethorpe and to publish a catalogue, *Mapplethorpe Fotos*, dedicated to his work. While Mapplethorpe was still living, one of his last shows was at the Stedelijk Museum in Amsterdam in 1988.]

Rob of Amsterdam: What happened is that I started off making as high quality leathers as possible and that has over the years turned out to be my reputation. In fact, nobody is able to steal this reputation from me and to make it their own, because they think right off that I'm crazy to make such high quality. As soon as they get their fingers on an article or design from me, their first thought is "How can we copy it and make it cheaper?" But your first thought should be "How can I make it better?" So in effect, I don't have any competition. And it is a pleasure to make these things, a pleasure to handle these things, and to meet people who come to buy. In the beginning, I had trouble trying to wholesale it because it was all too expensive; but now most of the shops here sell it more expensive than we do because they don't get a 50% discount. So they have to sell it high. And that's it.

Jack Fritscher: Your place seems more like a gallery than a shop.

Rob of Amsterdam: Yes, that is a thing I don't want so much. I want it in the first place to be a leather shop. For the tourists who stay up late every night, the RoB Gallery is nice in the daytime when they come in to kill the time on their hands. If they want to, they can spend two hours here, but I don't want that art gallery to be the main thing. I'm happy I started it, and I think it has done certain things for the whole gay world, but for me it's not the more important thing. It's time consuming. You do a lot of exhibitions and you don't always sell the art so well. So in effect it has to be supported by the leather.

Jack Fritscher: You plan to continue the RoB Gallery in your shop?

Rob of Amsterdam: Yes, of course. It is said that "Rob himself doesn't make 'made to measure' anymore," and that's just silly—that statement doesn't come out of my mouth. I'm very happy in what I'm doing. My brothers are happy that they are not working anymore, and I am happy that I can continue to do some more work. It is a matter of attitude.

Jack Fritscher: Could you tell me about some of the artists? I notice Tom of Finland has drawn you and Mapplethorpe photographed you.

Rob of Amsterdam: Back in 1978, I had a painting made by an artist, and I wanted to throw a party. I love parties. So I thought, let's make a party for the painting and the second thought was why not give a show? And I wrote a nice letter to Tom. I said, "If you will do an exhibition here of your work, it will be the crown of my work." Of course, Tom agreed. And that's how it started. I had a Dutch photographer on [unintelligible]. And that was the beginning of the RoB Gallery. Then we continued, and I have had some very interesting artists. Some were better than others, but it is very nice to play with.

Jack Fritscher: When did Tom draw you?

Rob of Amsterdam: Tom made the drawing, probably 1981. Yes. 1981.

Jack Fritscher: Eight years ago. Before AIDS.

Rob of Amsterdam: Yes.

Jack Fritscher: You've created a lot of momentum in the last decade-plus, about twelve years, fourteen years, I guess. You've made an international mark. How do you feel about the evolution of leather wear and leather men and leather women? Do you think things have...

Rob of Amsterdam: In the beginning I was worried that it [leather culture and businesses] wouldn't last. And now it is hard to think that it won't exist. I am surprised to see less dyed trousers [blue jeans] worn by the gays. They start to be dressed fashionable, but now they come in their fashionable clothes and say, we want leather pants. I try not to make fashionable things. Everything must be related. I think I have found a kind of secret, how to make a pair of [signature] leather jeans: they fit always very well. And people can walk down the street and people stop them and say, you are wearing Rob's trousers. You can see it and recognize it—mainly by the cut.

Jack Fritscher: Did you wake up one night with that thought in your mind, or did it just evolve?

Rob of Amsterdam: I think I've always been good in my profession and I know how to think. That's the main problem with most people. They don't know how to think. If you know how to think you will achieve, and then there is no problem.

Jack Fritscher: Working with *Drummer* magazine, that's one of the questions I have about gay culture in general and gay leather in particular. Is leather a thinking movement as much as it is emotionally sexual? *Drummer* has a community responsibility to guide readers toward new styles and concepts to realize themselves. For instance, *Drummer* didn't invent Daddies, but in 1979 *Drummer* broke the prejudice against gay men over thirty, praising older men like [rugged pornstar] Richard Locke, and suddenly, the word *daddy* was everywhere. It was a word *Drummer* first heard in the bars and then made fashionable in print.

Rob of Amsterdam: Yes, it is nice to have a daddy. If it is a good daddy, you can learn a lot from him and you can listen to him. As you get older—I'm talking about myself now—I think you get more wisdom. You can do something with such wisdom. Yesterday I had an old friend in, and a few hours later, he telephoned me and said, "I would love to come back and have a talk with you because I admire your lifestyle and I want to get a bit out of my own problems." I think it is nice when people do that privately. It feels better and you can scream harder at them. [Laughter]

Jack Fritscher: Let's say this friend of yours was very specific and wanted to ask certain questions. So out of the experience of your wisdom of a lifetime, could you talk a little bit about what you said to him about what might apply to, or be useful to, other gay men?

Rob of Amsterdam: No. He wanted advice because it was just that he hadn't seen me for a certain time. He never knows if he wants to be seen or does not want to be seen. He is a very intelligent boy. So I don't understand his problems. I think I received you quite unusual when I said that I hate beards. [Laughter] But the moment I see you I know you're okay, I can say it.

Jack Fritscher: Yes.

Rob of Amsterdam: For me that teasing is funny. If you had a different personality, I would probably have a beard ready to stick on you to [indecipherable]. [Laughter]

Jack Fritscher: That's your designer's eye. Add and subtract. What's there, take it away. What's not there, add to it and see how it looks that new way.

Rob of Amsterdam: Something like that. [Lights cigarette] I have customers that I send down directly to the leather shop, and a different kind of customer, not so cool, I ask them to come back some other time. I've put some customers in a corner to make them stand there until the purchase is ready—and they all stand there and take it. Because they want the pants or whatever.

Jack Fritscher: That's wonderful ritual discipline.

Rob of Amsterdam: Yes.

Jack Fritscher: So in a sense, with your own strong male personality, with your sense of Top-ness, you are disciplining them, teasing them, with a bit of S&M they may get off on while you dress them in fetish fashion. You are creating bar styles—evening-wear based on leather sex appeal. They go home to jerk off enhanced in *couture* you've created.

Rob of Amsterdam: And it is beautiful to see someone who has come in a business suit, who has ordered a complete leather outfit and as soon as they have it on, their personality changes 100%. They walk in boots immediately like you should walk in boots. You don't recognize the person. That's beautiful. That change of attitude. I like it very much.

Jack Fritscher: Sort of like Henry Higgins.

Rob of Amsterdam: Yes. [Laughter]

Jack Fritscher: Among some of the other artists, I notice you have a drawing by the Hun downstairs.

Rob of Amsterdam: That's a poster. I had visited the Hun once. But I think in his style he is a bit too exaggerated. He makes things so big you can't fantasize about it. But he has made some lovely drawings that I would like to add to my gallery. Our biggest artist, next to Tom, is Bastille. I'll show you one of his. But the man [Bastille] is so lazy you never get things out of his hand. [stands up and shows drawing.] You see the shine and the shine on the head.

Jack Fritscher: That's beautiful, fantastic.

Rob of Amsterdam: We did a show this winter of his work and it sold very well.

Jack Fritscher: Can you tell me anything about his background?

Rob of Amsterdam: There is an American word for what he does, but I don't know it. [CAD Technology] He draws for people who want to build flats or a building and before a building is built, they need to sell it. So he makes a kind of photographic drawing that you exactly can see. He is one of the best in France for that. If you want a house with a hundred windows, he can draw that.

Jack Fritscher: How old is he?

Rob of Amsterdam: Should I tell his age? Middle-aged.

Jack Fritscher: How long has he been doing erotic drawings?

Rob of Amsterdam: I think all his life. If he only draws buildings and balconies, he gets bored and then he lifts his paper, and underneath it are pornographic sketches in progress. He has a very nice way of thinking and doing it.

Jack Fritscher: He sounds like you designing women's dresses and lifting your paper to draw men's leather trousers.

Rob of Amsterdam: Ah! Then we have had Valvas Barea who is Brazilian, I think. Beautiful pastel drawings. He always does portraits and sometimes gets bored and sick of it and then makes a graphic-looking sex picture which is of very high quality so it is not pornographic. It is an erotic drawing.

Jack Fritscher: I think that is a parallel to what you've done with leather. You've taken the sheer commercial aspects—like an architect who could be just hammering out a building with a hundred balconies—and put an erotic spin on that. When you put the leather boots and leather suit on the man who comes in a business suit, you transform him and out his hidden identity. Your transformation kind of frees him up sexually. That must give you a lot of pleasure when you see a man stand up in leather and stomp out.

Rob of Amsterdam: Yes.

Jack Fritscher: Has anything particularly humorous happened to you in all the years you've been doing this?

Rob of Amsterdam: [Rolls his eyes] I don't know. I'm not a big laugher. I love those people who can laugh with their hands slapping on their knees, but I'm not that type. I take things seriously. But I have had some people who want to be my slave and one in particular asked me, very surprised, "Do you go to the toilet by yourself? I can bring it away for you." Then he wanted to be my slave for three years. I could do whatever I wanted. But then after the three years I had to restore him to society. That's a kind of laboring not for me. It's nice when somebody comes up to you, but…

Jack Fritscher: So you find with your celebrity that you get kind of a fan following, people want to be your slave because you, the private person "Rob Meijer," have become the store "RoB of Amsterdam," so the private side of you has to put up with the courtship of your public self.

Rob of Amsterdam: The only thing I would like to say is that in the early days when I started the shop, things were much more fun, and now the business has grown so big that I have to be serious, and in one way that is a pity. But I still have my memories that I hate, but, you know? I know someone who owned a Picasso and then suddenly sold it and he said, "What nobody can take away from me is 'I owned a Picasso.'" And I think that is quite a nice way of thinking.

Jack Fritscher: It's wonderful you've had these memories and experiences no one can take away from you.

Rob of Amsterdam: The smaller your business is, and in the beginning it was very small, we gave small parties for fifty people, and I had tattoo demonstrations by Mr. Sebastian [London piercing guru and modern primitive, Alan Oversby]. I was the person in Amsterdam who made things happen. Last year, growing bigger, we came out with some erotic [designer] wines, a white one and a red one, with an erotic label done by Eddie Sofoldman [*sic*] who is an American artist, and we launched it with a boat trip. Everybody was there and everybody wanted to be seen and it was very exciting and still people are talking about it. But it makes you tired to arrange those things. Especially when you grow bigger, you have to be more serious. You can't afford mistakes. In the old days, it didn't matter. Now we're big, it has to be a proper party.

Jack Fritscher: That's one of the curses that comes with success. You can have fun at first doing it and then you have to best yourself every time because they expect that of you. I mean, a French *couturier* couldn't have more of a burden put on him than you do.

Rob of Amsterdam: Yes. A good thing for me—since I had been in women's dresses, ordinary dresses for just the ordinary women. The designs were always the same with little changes, perhaps a pocket, the material, the necklines. So I've learned to work in very small steps with details. I make my leather jackets, and it is very rare that they vary a little bit. But variation comes and then I get a kind of new style, which is in fact not a new style but it has something new that it didn't have before. And I like doing it.

Jack Fritscher: All RoB originals. What is your favorite piece of leather gear?

Rob of Amsterdam: I think it is codpiece trousers because they make your dick look the biggest. [Laughter]

Jack Fritscher: That is one of the main contributions that gay leather has given back to the world, isn't it? The Shakespearean codpiece.

Rob of Amsterdam: And I wear my leather wherever I go. To the restaurant or to the theater. When I want to wear leather, I will put it on whenever I want. In Amsterdam I am known for going to the theater in my leather and everybody accepts it. And that makes it easier for another person to put on his leather as well.

Jack Fritscher: Your erotic fashion becomes mainstream. Leather at the opera in New York and San Francisco. Is there any particular thing in the gay world that you wish had gone in another direction than it has?

Rob of Amsterdam: In the first place, I don't think I could do anything about the past. I don't expect much particular change for the future. I expect the leather world to continue to exist because there is nothing to replace it. So if you want to have a good male image, you almost have to wear leather.

Jack Fritscher: You certainly see more and more leather in the straight world as a fashion statement. Leather as a gay style has certainly influenced more people than have other gay styles.

Rob of Amsterdam: The thing is, a gay has to first of all accept himself as a gay. When he has done that and knows he can handle it, it is an easy step to start to wear some leather. Heterosexuals have children, often, and the neighbors and the parents coming in, so for them it is much more difficult for them to come out in that freedom; but the gay has had all the troubles he could have. So it is easy for him to become a leather boy.

Jack Fritscher: It's a surprise to a lot of men that they have two comings out. First is the sexual coming out, and they think that's it. Then after a few years of vanilla sex, things are getting kinkier and then they have a second coming out into all the things that leather symbolizes.

Rob of Amsterdam: And it usually starts towards their forties. That's my opinion. Then they want to have more out of life.

Jack Fritscher: In middle-age, leather is an enhancement of the body. It abstracts, cinches, girdles. You can't go around looking like a twenty-year-old forever—and who wants to? Leather allows a man to be hot whatever decade he is in.

Rob of Amsterdam: I have customers in their sixties. I make them a pair of leather pants, perhaps a bit looser. Things like that. But they look terrific in it. And you wouldn't guess their age anymore.

Jack Fritscher: Leather adds a decade to a man's sex life. Is there any particular political statement made here in Holland by leather? In America there seems to be a tension between the leather community and the vanilla majority.

Rob of Amsterdam: No, I don't think so in Amsterdam. Those that go in their silk blouses to bars will still go on Saturday night to the leather bar in leather. For me, I don't think the leather is necessarily related to sadomasochism, but that has become an official thing.

Jack Fritscher: So a leatherman can be homosexual and masculine, but not necessarily into S&M.

Rob of Amsterdam: I think the group that actually does S&M is very small. Terry [LeGrand seeking private locations for filming] asked me about dungeons, but I don't know them in Amsterdam; but when you see the leather crowd, you should think there are hundreds of them. But I don't know where to find them.

Jack Fritscher: So leather is an expression of a homomasculine lifestyle rather than an S&M style. I think that's rather true in the United States too. We find continual pressure from magazines like the *Advocate* which often runs anti-leather articles because the 1970s publisher wanted gay people to wear suits to be accepted. They don't really approve of leathermen.

Rob of Amsterdam: That happens?

Jack Fritscher: Yes, sensational cover stories, something like "Why I Left the World of S&M Behind."

Rob of Amsterdam: Whatever side you are on, you need each other. They need the leather guys to support their magazine. If you start to scream at each other—No, I don't find that at all a good thing. We are lucky in Holland that we are about the freest country in the world. And we are always accepting people. And it is always the same. A few weeks ago, I appeared on a television program where I was asked questions about these things. It was a complete show about sex and it was called *On Life or Death.* You sit there and answer the questions. Now when I walk down the street, children stop and say, "Oh, I saw you on television," but nobody says, "Ugh, you wear leather." So they accept it and think it is interesting, and most people think it is interesting to know me—which is nice. [Laughs]

Jack Fritscher: So the leather doesn't get in the way, but it serves to set you apart from other people and identify you and it doesn't speak so loudly that it drowns out what you are saying to them when you talk about sex and life.

Rob of Amsterdam: Yes. And then they said, they asked me the question on the television program, did I think it was dangerous for AIDS. All I said was, "Don't forget that if we in the S&M world go to have sex, usually we dress up and don't undress. So with less body exposure, I don't think there is a bigger danger."

Jack Fritscher: That may be true. You made a distinction between leather as a masculine lifestyle as compared to an S&M signal. Where does leather fetish come in? Where two men get together and wearing the leather is part of the sex play, the vision of each other, the creaking of the leather, the smell of it, the feel of it, the sound of it.

Rob of Amsterdam: All you have to do is take your dick out.

Jack Fritscher: And you don't have to shove it into someone else.

Rob of Amsterdam: If you come to an S&M scene, it would be quite unusual—I don't know how to say—for the top to undress. And the other one can be nude and sent to the floor. I think that is the nice thing about it.

Jack Fritscher: I would love to hear you answer this question. I write about and photograph leather culture to cause sexual arousal. That's rather abstract. You are able to work literally hands-on with leather. We consumers buy leather gear and get off on it, but you are able to live one radical step closer to leather by taking a tanned cowhide in hand and fashioning male clothing that causes sexual arousal. What is it, do you think, what is the attraction of leather?

Rob of Amsterdam: I think it is masculinity. Leather makes people look stronger. People love the smell of leather, and it gives them a sexual kick. What I never tell them—and it is even a mistake to tell it now—is what they smell is the dye and has nothing to do with the leather itself. A pair of legs in shiny leather jeans makes the legs beautiful even if they are not so beautiful.

Jack Fritscher: Do you think one of its appeals is that it is an actual animal hide stretched around a pair of legs, beautiful or not so beautiful.

Rob of Amsterdam: I don't think anybody looks at it as an animal hide. They like the look, the touch of it.

Jack Fritscher: So you see the appeal of leather in and of itself. Its texture.

Rob of Amsterdam: Yes, and not related to the animal. Jeans material is tough to touch. It is not pleasant. With leather, your hands just slide over it. That is a nice feeling.

Jack Fritscher: Leather has almost the velvety texture of a dick.

Rob of Amsterdam: Yes.

Jack Fritscher: Because it does pick up body heat and is like a second skin. Do you think there is a bondage link inherent in tight leather that appeals to people on an unconscious level, if not on a conscious level?

Rob of Amsterdam: I think so, because if you have a simple thing, let's say a leather cockstrap, it always brings color to the body, the contrast of its black straps. I like to sell some long belts by which you can do some bondage. I myself admire Japanese bondage because I think it is beautiful, but I don't think it is comfortable. Rope is unpleasant material to have rubbing over your skin, but what I do with the bondage is beautiful—but not pleasant. Black leather gives more than rope and is nicer.

Jack Fritscher: Leather becomes as one with the body whereas rope, as you say, rubs against the body and abrades the body. You are separating leather from S&M—which is revolutionary and good fashion marketing. Do you feel when you are wearing leather that your psychic vibrations are different than when you are not in leather?

Rob of Amsterdam: Don't think so. But me is me, and I don't change no matter what I'm wearing.

Jack Fritscher: Maybe because you have a leather mindset and leather vibrations going all the time wearing leather or not. [Laughter] You are not like customers who arrive in business suits, put on leather, and stomp out the door. You say their aura changes. You say their character changes. I don't want to seem terribly "California," but don't you think you're helping them act out desire by putting them in leather with the freedoms that come with it.

Rob of Amsterdam: Yes. And it makes them happier.

[Telephone rings on the desk]

Rob of Amsterdam: Sorry about that.

Jack Fritscher: And you're famous for your studded hood, which has sort of become your international signature piece, right? Somebody who puts that on is going to feel totally different than he has ever felt in his life.

Rob of Amsterdam: Yes, because the hood weighs three kilos [6.6 pounds]. Because there is leather underneath, it feels very supple and it is an experience to wear it.

Jack Fritscher: So just as you changed women's fashions a bit when you were doing women's dress designs, you kind of help men to change.

Rob of Amsterdam: You better forget about the women. [He laughs.] Another thing, after my television program, people telephoned me to say, "Thank you very much for what you are doing for the S&M world. You make it more understandable and less frightening." I think to be frightened of S&M is ridiculous unless you have a stupid top who doesn't know how to act. For myself personal, the most scene I like is the mind-trip. I like to be clever to people and give them remarks that they are shocked by. I had two guests here and one was a very good-looking boy, but he wants to be a slave. So I am sitting here. Everybody's talking and suddenly I stop the talk and I ask him, "Do you think you are beautiful?" And wanting to be a slave, he wouldn't dare to say he was beautiful. Then the conversation continued, and I said, "Do you think you are ugly?" Now he was *sure* that he wasn't ugly. [Laughter] But that was what shocks people. You don't need ropes and all that. Very nice.

Jack Fritscher: So personally, you prefer the psychological scene rather than the physical?

Rob of Amsterdam: Right. I do tie people up. I do whip people—if necessary. But the most thing what I like is the mind-trip.

Jack Fritscher: Everybody will want to know what is "necessary." [Laughter]

Rob of Amsterdam: Some people only want to be tied up. I've had one person here who really wants to be whipped, really whipped, and I whipped the hell out of him. I shot a movie of that and it is the most exciting film I've ever made because while the man was getting whipped—and I was not very friendly with it—he started to laugh and he laughed and he laughed and he laughed. And it was beautiful. He had a very happy voice: "Ho, Ho, Ho." It was wonderful. Then I really whipped him so hard that his back had streams—how you call?—on it.

And then he said, "I wouldn't mind you doing it another time, but can I bring my photo camera with me because in about three weeks you don't see any marks anymore, but then I will still have the memory in the pictures." I'm surprised because I don't like to be whipped at all. I don't do damage to people—but they always ask for more. Then I come back to it, and all I feel while I am doing it, is that they want to prove that they can take it. It's not about fun or sex. The biggest thing is for them is to think "I must take it and then show my marks and I can be proud that I went through it."

Jack Fritscher: Do you think that's some peculiar kind of religious twist? Like martyrdom?

Rob of Amsterdam: This man I'm talking about is a priest. [Hilarious laughter]

Jack Fritscher: I guess that answers the question. I've always thought the one thing religion and the state have taught young men is that they've got to suffer somehow—enduring hazing in college or the military or prisons to act out the kind of manhood rituals *Drummer* specializes in.

Rob of Amsterdam: One day a customer came in and told me that he was working in a psychiatric center, and I said, "Do you think you have been influenced by that over the years?" And he said, "No," and then ordered a straitjacket. [Amused laughter. Mark Hemry lowers his head to check the camera.] Is the film not going? Am I talking for nothing?

Jack Fritscher: It's recording.

Mark Hemry: I was just checking the batteries. Everything's fine.

Jack Fritscher: You're not talking for nothing, believe me. You're saying such wonderful things here.

Rob of Amsterdam: Good.

Jack Fritscher: What would you say to any man—young, middle-aged, older—who had approached the point in life where he comes to look at, or stand in front of, that Bastille drawing, the rubber hood on the head, the nozzle, a complete bondage scene, breath control?

Rob of Amsterdam: What I usually say is, it might not be your fetish, not be what you are dreaming of, but nobody can deny that it is beautiful, and to me things being beautiful is very important. Looking at such art, some people try to realize those fantasies. With their reactions, you get very bizarre moments, but beautiful moments.

Jack Fritscher: So basically, what you have done, stylistically in leather and in your life, is a pursuit of beauty.

Rob of Amsterdam: Yes. I try.

Jack Fritscher: You can't do better than that. Some people think pursuing beauty is chasing a guy down the street. [Laughter]

Rob of Amsterdam: Do you want some more water?

Mark Hemry: We're fine.

Jack Fritscher: This coffee is good. We've been up for thirty-six hours. If I seem a little punchy, it's because of that. We were crammed into small seats in the back of the plane. Terry and Roger bought the tickets.

Rob of Amsterdam: You didn't sleep at all?

Jack Fritscher: A couple hours. We had to change planes twice. We were on three different planes. They shove food in your face every two hours and start a movie in the middle of the night, but we had books with us and editing to do on a new book. Of course, we crossed on the Summer Solstice which is my birthday, and a short night to sleep. It got dark very late and got light very early. The full moon was beautiful.

Rob of Amsterdam: What direction did you fly in? You came from Los Angeles?

Jack Fritscher: From San Francisco.

Mark Hemry: To New York, then London.

Rob of Amsterdam: That's horrible. You should go New York to Amsterdam.

Jack Fritscher: That's the way we had been scheduled. Then Pan Am in its wisdom changed its mind and everyone going to Amsterdam had to land in London and change. Thanks for asking.

Rob of Amsterdam: Of course.

Jack Fritscher: Regarding the future. Terry LeGrand told me that the future is very important to you because now at the end of the eighties, you are looking to help shape that future. Do you have plans for a permanent RoB Gallery, a kind of historical leather museum of sex, art, and fashion?

Rob of Amsterdam: I don't think so, no. I don't know what to do, but I think the main thing is that RoB [of Amsterdam] should continue on as a business, but a museum? Those things don't work, I don't believe, because you still have to make changes all the time. You change one business for the other. You need a big stock of all kinds of art. I don't know what will happen in the future. I can't say.

Jack Fritscher: Who do you think in the leather world—a name or two—has been very influential to help men express leather masculinity? I would say that you are one in terms of the design and mystique of leather that you have given people in the sculptural, ritual garments that they collect and wear.

Rob of Amsterdam: That is very difficult to answer. There are certain people who have done a lot for the S&M world, but I don't think they have done anything in particular for the leather image. The leather image is created when you go in your own leather gear into the bar on a Friday night, and everybody is standing with his beer. That's what creates the image. But I can't give you any names.

Jack Fritscher: What do you think of all the different leather contests with their remarkable runway fashion shows? Like our "Mr. Drummer" contest. Contestants walk the stage in leather designer outfits...

Rob of Amsterdam: ...being beautiful.

Jack Fritscher: Yes, and then they act out their S&M fantasy scene.

Rob of Amsterdam: Do they have to do an S&M scene?

Jack Fritscher: It's customary. And often quite beautiful. The producers and audience kind of expect Leather Fantasy Theater. You clarify the idea that wearing leather does not necessarily mean S&M. So a man could enter the "International Mr. Leather" for the IML runway contest and never whip people or tie them up, because that is no longer what being "International Mr. Leather" is about. Your clarification is helpful. Just because I see a hot man in leather, it doesn't signal he'll tear my tits off.

Rob of Amsterdam: [Arched eyebrow] Do you have sensitive tits? [Laughter]

Jack Fritscher: [Playing meek] Yes, your Top-ness. [Laughter]

Rob of Amsterdam: Good.

Jack Fritscher: I really appreciate the honesty you've displayed today. I know you're busy and have to get back to your work. But with all your experience, is there anything you would like the world at large to know about?

Rob of Amsterdam: Nothing in particular. What would I say? I hope that there will be for a long time people in leather, but that's nonsense and doesn't relate to whatever.

Jack Fritscher: When did you personally first put on your first leather in connection with sexual games?

Rob of Amsterdam: My own leather?

Jack Fritscher: Tom of Finland told me years ago that his leather fetish surfaced when he was four or five years old when he found himself drawing pictures of policemen in tight pants chasing robbers in big boots and tying them up.

Rob of Amsterdam: No, no. I think I started in 1973 when I made my first pair of leather pants, which were much too tight, so that I could only stand in them. I couldn't sit. But from that moment on, I really enjoyed it, especially in the bars, with the leathermen standing around. It was beautiful and at long last I had found men.

Jack Fritscher: But as a boy you never experienced leather?

Rob of Amsterdam: No. And I don't so much believe in all that. I find it nonsense.

Jack Fritscher: What particular style of man appeals to you? The Greg Strom bodybuilder type? Or a more average type? What kind of body do you think is best enhanced by leather? What do you prefer to see?

Rob of Amsterdam: I think a good body is best enhanced with leather. But another part of it is the character of the person. He makes his leather work. If he is intelligent, he knows what to do with it. I think it is more that.

Jack Fritscher: But personally, would you rather see a bodybuilder in leather or…

Rob of Amsterdam: I find bodybuilder figures horrible because their necks are always too heavy and then their shoulders drop down like a bottle, and that I find terrible.

Jack Fritscher: You find them difficult to drape.

Rob of Amsterdam: Also that, but they don't look beautiful. I've had bodybuilders here and I know how to handle them, but if you point at their arm, immediately the muscle flexes. They must always make sure there is a mirror around so they can look in it. Then they are happy. And I think all those shoulders going down is not very beautiful. Bodybuilders' legs are nice, I think, because they don't go out of shape. They look heavy.

Jack Fritscher: One last question. Your tattoos. Were they done over a period of time?

Rob of Amsterdam: Mr. Sebastian did them. One was done by Mad Dog [Robert Roberts] from San Francisco.

Jack Fritscher: Who did the eye?

Rob of Amsterdam: The eye was Mr. Sebastian. He lives in England and he is famous for his tattoos. In the beginning, I had contact with Mr. Sebastian and then he came here twice a year for three weeks to do tattoos.

Besides being important for the world of leather, I think I've been important for the world of tattoos because I think I have been able to lift the art of it out of a kind of cheap way of decoration. In my time [when he was tattooing], people came in Rolls Royces. One had a little swallow on his ass. My quality has been very important so that people from the highest place in society would come to me because by me they would get a good tattoo. The atmosphere was there in my shop, but it was not like a tattoo parlor, which is usually dirty and unpleasant. And I think for that I have been very important.

Jack Fritscher: Was that early on when you had your leather parties?

Rob of Amsterdam: That was in 1974-75.

Jack Fritscher: So at the same time you were introducing your leather clothing line, you were introducing tattoos. What about piercing? I noticed that downstairs there was…

Rob of Amsterdam: I myself am fairly interested in piercing and I like to do it on people. It is nice, and I always say, "You'd better come here and know that it is done as good as possible. Unless you like to have someone fuck around with piercing, where their hands are not clean and where they get excited and get carried away and just do something without being clean." The main reason I do piercing is that I don't want other people to fuck up.

Jack Fritscher: One thing readers of this interview will want to know is, what is your favorite body part to pierce? [Laughter]

Rob of Amsterdam: The favorite places to me are tit piercings and a Prince Albert. I think every man should have a Prince Albert. It's exciting, it's great, and when it's in, you will never take it out because you are very happy with it.

Jack Fritscher: People I've talked to have said it enhances masturbation.

Rob of Amsterdam: It enhances masturbation, and it gives you a kind of tingling extra feeling, and I love it.

Jack Fritscher: How do you feel about your influence. You yourself have changed some of our sexual ways of coming on to each other, of people getting more into their personal body adornment, of more people wearing leather, of more people getting tattoos, more people getting pierced.

Rob of Amsterdam: I think what I've done makes people freer, and that freedom makes them do things.

Jack Fritscher: But do you think they are moving into these more aesthetic enhancements of the body in order to move away from unsafe sex and still have a wonderful time psychologically and physically? Your devotion to leather, tattooing, and piercing is furthering a new style of sex fetishism for gay pop culture, especially as the 1980s are becoming the 1990s. You mentioned my beard. I could never have had this big beard as a leather fetish style back in the 1970s because with all the Crisco, after fifteen minutes at the baths, my beard would have gone up in flames. [Laughter] Now with AIDS, many other men in San Francisco, the bears, also have big beards.

Rob of Amsterdam: Do you know that it is beautiful to burn hair?

Jack Fritscher: I…have…heard…people…say…that.

Rob of Amsterdam: And I'm not talking about your beard. [Laughter] But I have rubbed people in oil, just a little bit, and then set a match to it and it becomes like fireworks, phtttt! It's beautiful, and it doesn't hurt, but it scares them a lot.

Jack Fritscher: Just a little surprise for them.

Rob of Amsterdam: [Leans forward with his elbows on his desk] I think we are there.

Jack Fritscher: I think we are there. So nobody ever comes in to see you and goes out the same?

Rob of Amsterdam: I hope. [Laughs]

Jack Fritscher: He either changes his clothes or changes his mind. Or has his mind changed.

Rob of Amsterdam: Yes.

Jack Fritscher: Thank you so much for your time.

Rob of Amsterdam: If it gets printed in *Drummer*, I would like a copy.

Jack Fritscher: Definitely. I shall do that. Could we take a couple of pictures of you?

Rob of Amsterdam: Of course. Perfect.

Jack Fritscher: Thank you very much.

Terry LeGrand and Roger Earl asked Jack Fritscher and Mark Hemry to shoot local-color exterior shots for *Bound for Europe* as pictured here filming atop an observation platform built at Brandenburg Gate on the West Berlin side of the Berlin Wall for Westerners to see over the Wall into East Berlin. West Berlin, July 1989. Photo courtesy of David Pearce.

Street scene; RoB of Amsterdam flagship leather shop and art gallery, June 21, 1989. Photo by Mark Hemry

Ed Parente, 1982. His stylish drawing for Wakefield Poole's film *Boys in the Sand* in 1971 was the first gay display ad to be published in the *New York Times*. Photo by Jack Fritscher.

Parente Plexiglass. A delicate bouquet of 18 male fingertips cast from life, with butterfly, 1982. Photo by Mark Hemry.

EDWARD PARENTE

1941-1992

Wakefield Poole's *Boys in the Sand* and the NYT

Raised in Queens, Long Island, Ed Parente (March 11, 1941-November 19, 1992) was a fine artist and sculptor who attended Parsons School of Design. He created the signature poster and graphics for his longtime friend Wakefield Poole's ground-breaking *Boys in the Sand* (1971). Known for his pointillist technique, his stylish line drawing for the film was the first gay display ad to be published in the *New York Times*. They met on Fire Island and became, Wake said, "instant friends."

In 1969, he starred in Poole's ten-minute film *The Gift* at the same moment his first solo show opened at Cannabis Gallery, 295 Mercer Street, New York. In 1971, the Earth Gallery, now evaporated from Manhattan, was selling his psychedelic lithographs of astrological signs to "delight the 70s acid-tripper in you." One of those cards—the moustached gladiator standing on a beach—became the ad for *Boys in the Sand*. He also sold his work, including his "pre-futuristic primitive" disco feather masks, and sculptures of found animal skulls adorned with leather and feathers, at Ballardos Glassware shop on Christopher Street.

Famous on the sands of Fire Island Pines in the 1960s for netting butterflies for his delicate boxed sculptures, he shaped his twin sister's face into his plaster-cast work. To this day I own and love several of his sculptures. One is a bouquet of eighteen white-plaster male fingertips, each standing two or three knuckles tall, with a single yellow butterfly specimen perched on the tallest finger. The other is a white-plaster mask of his sister's face wrapped in white silk and creamy lace which Ed found blowing down Castro Street. I named the sculpture "The Dead Bride" as a kind of empathetic homage in honor of all the women whom gay men loved but could not marry. Both are encased in Parente's signature Plexiglas boxes.

As a graphic artist supporting Poole's San Francisco career, he moved to the City in 1975 where as a smoldering five-foot-six Italian sensualist, he was a gloriously stoned habitue of the Barracks bath where for two years without speaking we fucked like destiny every time we saw each other.

Then, one night after those years of hot scenes, we were kicked back sharing a joint on the stairs, and spoke for the first time.

"Hi, I'm Ed Parente."

"Hi, I'm Jack Fritscher."

"All my friends have been telling me I should meet you."

"All my friends have told me I should meet you."

We laughed and bonded instantly as friends and never fucked together again.

And then we found that for years we had lived around the corner from each other in upper Noe Valley. I lived at 4436 25th Street where I edited *Drummer* magazine and he lived at 403 Hoffman Street which doubled as his working studio and open gallery. So began our at-home social visits. That was the way glorious anonymous sex worked—until it became personal friendship that was just too incestuous in our hot little crowd.

My longtime friend from 1973 and housemate on 25th Street, the *Drummer* photographer Jim Stewart, the late author of the gorgeously nostalgic memoir *Folsom Street Blues*, wrote in his gay history column in the *Bay Area Reporter*, May 14, 2014: "You never know what, or who, you might find at a flea market [in Alameda on May 14, 1977]. We found Michael Monroe and Ed Parente. Ed was gathering vintage doll parts for his sculptures. He'd pull off the heads, sometimes the limbs, put them in his rucksack, then toss the remains in a handy trash can. He paired his flea market trophies together with butterfly wings and nature's random ephemera in Lucite boxes that were featured at high-end galleries in the tonier parts of the City."

In the 1970s, Ed exhibited at San Francisco's first new gay art galleries: Oscar Streaker Robert Opel's Fey-Way Studio in SOMA; *Erotic Hands* pornstar Richard Trask's atelier, The Wizard's Emerald City, on Market Street; and Wakefield Poole's Hot Flash of America on Market at Castro which hosted the first exhibition of his disco masks behind Plexiglass titled "Boxes." In the 1980s, he also exhibited his masks and faces and totems and fingers to crowds at the Church Street Fair, the Castro Street Fair, and the Folsom Street Fair. In summer 1984, when the first gay-owned financial institution, Atlas Savings and Loan, opened its 18th Street branch in the Castro, 4128 18th Street, it courted customers by exhibiting his work.

He designed the Pegasus-motif invitations, posters, and pop-art tin-can gift sculptures for Michael Maletta's Creative Power Foundation's legendary "Night Flight," San Francisco's first mega-party which he co-produced as New Year's Eve 1977 welcomed 1978. To market his art, he and Tom Sandburg founded the greeting card company Cold Shower Press.

His much published work appeared in *Drummer* magazine. He is referenced in Wakefield Poole's autobiography *Dirty Poole: A Sensual Memoir* (2011), in Jim Tushinski's documentary *Dirty Poole* (2011), and in the history book *Gay San Francisco: Eyewitness Drummer* (2008).

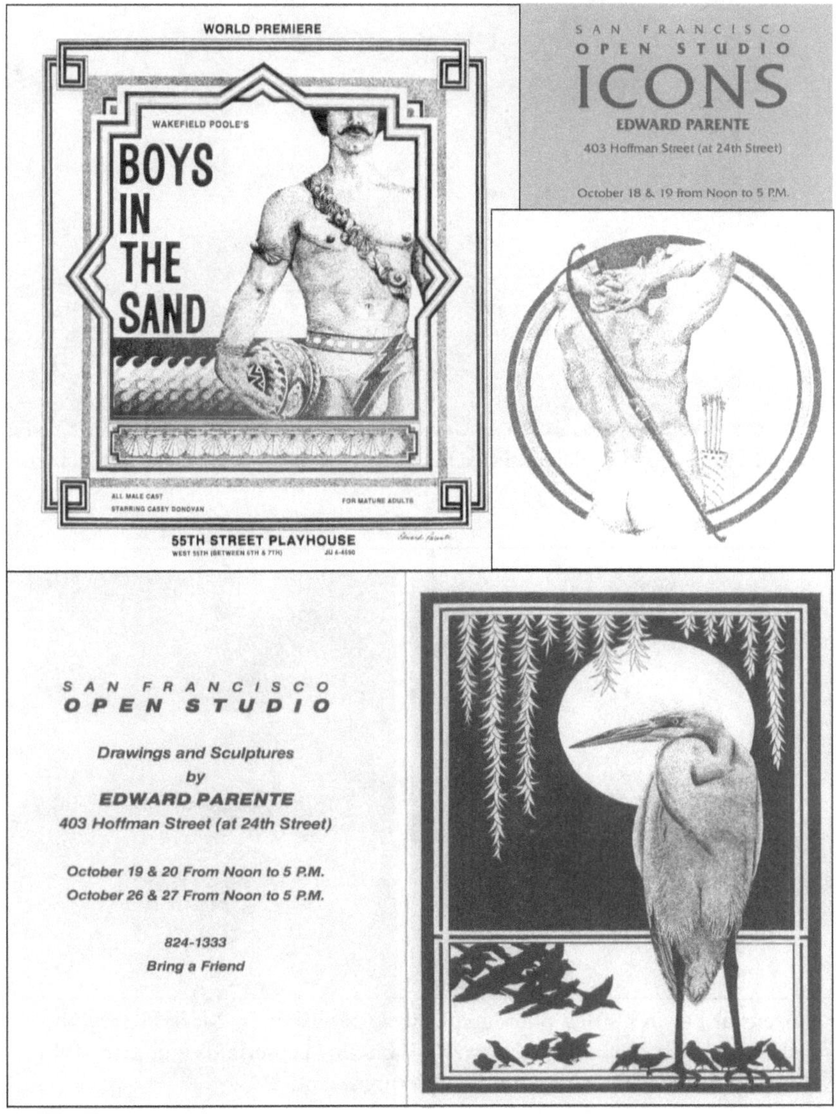

David Hurles (Old Reliable), Fritscher-Hemry house, 1981. Photo by Jack Fritscher.

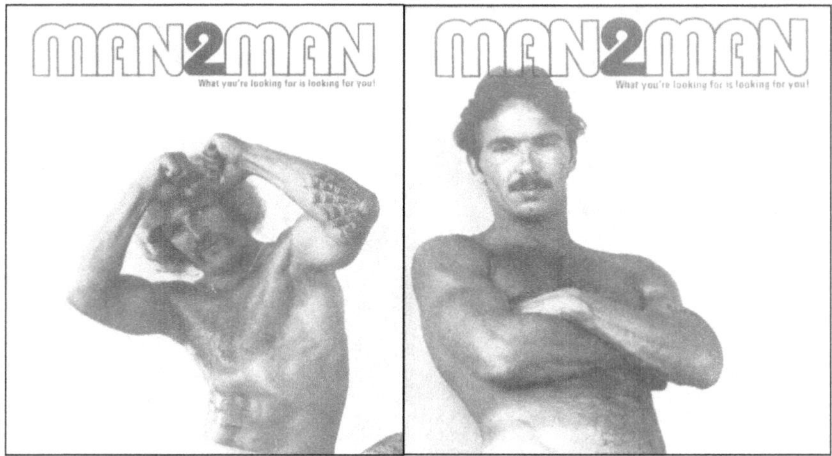

Dozens of David Hurles' photographs were published by Mark Hemry and Jack Fritscher in *Man2Man Quarterly*, including centerfolds and three 1981 covers of *Man2Man*, issues 4, 6 (not pictured), and 8.

DAVID HURLES

1944-

TERROR IS MY ONLY HARDON!

The Homosurreal Life of the Artist-Director of Rough Trade S&M Verbal Abuse Films

---

TOPS AT THE BOX OFFICE

From 1970 to 1995 in San Francisco and Los Angeles, David Hurles directed nearly 300 feature-length films (90-120 minutes) that at $59 each entertained thousands of fans, and grossed a fortune through Old Reliable mail-order sales that as Mass Media far exceeded walk-in ticket sales at brick-and-mortar porn theaters.

David Randolph Hurles, admired by passionate film fans, is a West Coast creative genius, born in Ohio in 1944. Fascinated in 1963 by John Rechy's expose of hustlers in *City of Night*, he started his career in June 1968 on Polk Street in San Francisco shooting his first pictures of his first model, Richard Jalakas, whose wife was in hospital giving birth. In 1969, at the famously gay Sloane House YMCA in New York, he met two "gracious" Mafiosi who bought his photographs for adult book covers and playing cards. For a few months, he worked for one of the first full-frontal publishers, DSI Sales in Los Angeles, before moving to start the 1970s at physique photographer Howard Lynn Womack's Guild Press in Washington, D. C. Womack, the publisher of *Grecian Guild Pictorial*, hired the baby-faced David as a handsome assistant who had been photographed as a flexible auto-fellatio model by San Francisco porn-loop filmmaker Hal Call, the legendary publisher of *The Mattachine Review*. Womack so appreciated David's even more flexible mind, personality, and talent that he welcomed him as apprentice, photographer, and friend working at Guild Press.

In 1972, when the federal government arrested Womack for pornography, David testified as one person who was both model and photographer.

He became the star witness defending Womack against the government's key charge that erotic models are by definition sexually exploited adults. The judge called David an excellent eyewitness who testified uniquely about the quality of human life and dignity possible in front of and behind the camera. He and Womack won the case that helped pioneer the long legal road that allowed the American porn film industry to flourish in that first Golden Age after Stonewall.

Womack was so grateful that he helped fund the startup of Old Reliable Tape and Picture Company. "Old Reliable" is street slang for a penis that always functions. The title is a sex pun promising potency on screen and in the viewer's hand, as well as good business practices assuring clients wary of mail-order fraud.

By 1975 in San Francisco, Old Reliable was shooting still photos and Super-8 movies of hustlers, and directing verbal-abuse soundtracks starring rough-trade drifters, ex-cons, and rent boys on sixty-minute audio-tape cassettes which he sold mail-order. His muse and business model was pioneer Los Angeles filmmaker Bob Mizer who became David's longtime mentor and friend. In fact, when Mizer, who had founded Athletic Model Guild studio in 1945, died in 1992, David wrote one of the most touching and informative obituaries one friend has ever written for another.

David and I met in the post-Stonewall Dreamtime of 1976 when he was thirty-two and I was thirty-seven. We became instant platonic friends who collaborated on projects and once bought a house together. I drove him to bodybuilding contests and boxing championships where we watched firefighter Dan White win his last Golden Gloves bout before he assassinated Harvey Milk and Mayor George Moscone. Because I was the founding San Francisco editor-in-chief of *Drummer* magazine, David trusted me, after he first doubted me, when I told him my *Drummer* readers would love his blue-collar photography and nasty audio tapes, five of which I transcribed and edited for publication. Living South of Market near Folsom Street, David was a versatile entrepreneur, creating a museum's worth of black-and-white 5"x7" photographs, color transparencies, Super-8 films, 400 audio recordings, and feature videos of backstreet boys working out of the Zee Hotel, 141 Eddy, in the red-light district of the Tenderloin; the Old Crow hustler bar at 962 Market Street; and, after his move to Hollywood, the Spotlight dive bar at 1601 N. Cahuenga Boulevard.

His roughnecks were graduates of American oil rigs, trailer parks, carnival midways, bus station toilets, and juvenile reform schools of the redneck South. He favored white trash as well as aggressive blacks and sultry Latinos. He told me: "I would rather sniff the armpits of a tough young Mexican boxer after a fight than climb between clean sheets with a Colt model." He employed, for cash money, more than 500 vagrant and sometimes homeless street people in this order: straight, bi, and gay. He shot men of all types and races as long as they were tough, had attitude, could smoke cigars, box, wrestle, kick, spit, jerk off, and talk abusively directly into the camera. Gay magazines rejected Old Reliable's frightening work with these S&M-tweaked delinquents who were way outside the respectable queenstream. However, as editor and talent scout for *Drummer*, I spied he was in gay media something quite new that was akin to Weegee and Diane Arbus. He was an edgy artist whose homomasculine art it was an honor to introduce and publish in *Drummer* 21, March 1978, perhaps the best-ever single issue of *Drummer.*

David invented Old Reliable all by himself, but *Drummer* boosted his brand nationally and internationally—exactly as its covers, centerfolds, and reviews helped popularize filmmakers Roger Earl, Wakefield Poole, the Gage Brothers, and Mikal Bales of Zeus Studio. The first mention of Old Reliable in *Drummer* was my "Prison Blues" feature in *Drummer* 21, March 1978, in which he told me: "I'll let you in on a little secret of why I like what I like and do what other guys only beat off to thinking about doing with bad boys. I'm like every other sexual specialist. I'm 80 percent impotent unless I get sex my way, unless I'm with these ex-con biker boys. Prison turns out some of the best trade in the country." To create a sequel to that prison feature article, I produced an additional transcription of his audio-tape monologue, "Scott Smith: Heavy Rap with a Solitary Ex-Con" followed by his audio tape "Ex-Cons: We Abuse Fags." in *Drummer* 24, September 1978. It was the issue made famous by the Robert Mapplethorpe cover photo of a "Dirty Biker for Hire" near whose cigar-smoking face was the cover headline announcing Old Reliable's "Ex-Cons" which shouted in shocking, big, bold, red all caps: "WE ABUSE FAGS!"

Old Reliable was a hit. *Drummer* readers ate him up. He became an immediate member of the *Drummer* Salon of writers, artists, photographers, and filmmakers. His photographs in 1978 created more sensation than Mapplethorpe who wasn't famous until the mid-1980s. His outlaws scared men into orgasm. In his brochures, he quoted *Straight to Hell* publisher Boyd McDonald's caution to his mail-order customers: "Never invite them into your lovely home."

He was an authentic *auteur* director who lived the life he filmed. In 1969, he was first arrested in a male house of prostitution in Los Angeles, and went briefly to jail. After his second 1972 arrest—four times in one week—by the San Francisco police, he used his mugshot to score "street cred" with his models. He seemed so addictively driven to his jailbirds by fear and lust that my job as a journalist was to re-characterize his dark sex psychology and pitch it as risky fun. For a lark of camp, I mimicked *True Confessions* magazine. To title one of my articles about him, I made up a *faux* quote he never said in our thousands of nightly telephone conversations, although it has since become a famous and quintessential summation: "Terror Is My Only Hardon," *Man2Man Quarterly*, Issue 8, October 1981.

After his arrest by the SFPD, the *San Francisco Chronicle* reported on Saturday, February 12, 1972, with the headline, "Vice Squad's First Gay Film Bust," and the text, "Vice squad officers have scored another first with the first arrest here on charges of producing obscene homosexual movies. Officers of the Bureau of Special Services went to the Dave Hurles Photo Studio, at 531 Howard Street, yesterday and arrested the operator, David R. Hurles, 27....In the fully equipped second-story studio, police found four water beds which were apparently 'props' in the films. Hurles was booked at City Prison on a warrant charging him with producing and distributing obscene material and for conspiracy [as well as, according to the police report, "oral sex perversion" and "crimes against nature"—all eventually dismissed]. Captain Gerald Shaughnessy called him the 'main producer of homosexual films in San Francisco.' Bail on the warrant was set at $625." Noting that filmmaker J. Brian of Calafran Enterprises was also arrested in those raids, David told me that the SFPD seized all of his prints, negatives, transparencies, films, and paperwork, among other things, and that the court denied him any recovery of his seized materials. On August 8, 1979, he called from another jail, and Mark Hemry and I bailed him out later that night.

David always shot on location, and that location in San Francisco, when we met, was his living room at 10th and Mission, conveniently across from the Doggie Diner. He was a street photographer who rarely left his flat in the single-room occupancy building he managed in trade for rent. Side-stepping a touch of agoraphobia, he paid the street to come to him. Casting was easy: a sexual pyramid scheme. He paid one hustler to refer two others who would refer four others who all had learned the prison wisdom that divorced women and queers are easy marks. So the Doggie Diner was to him and his models what Schwab's Drug Store in Hollywood had been to director Mervyn Le Roy who mythically discovered Lana Turner sitting at the ice cream counter sucking a soda straw in 1937. Even though the furniture and lamps in his flat were second-hand from the Salvation Army, he was more than once bound with duct tape and choked or held at knife or gunpoint by his models. In my 1981 interview, "Call Him Old Reliable Because He Is," he told me: "This Salvation Army junk hardly tempts anybody. This illusion keeps me safer, although there is the constant problem of the video cameras and recorders, the still cameras, the audio-tape recorders, the tape duplicator, and the color TV. My work requires electronic equipment and, of course, that is high on the burglary-robbery hit list. So far I haven't gone down in a hail of hot lead."

That real-life danger David injected directly into his duo and solo films of men aged eighteen to thirty-five. He directed so that his viewers, and *Drummer* subscribers, could enjoy the vicarious thrill of having dangerous rough trade look directly into the camera and verbally abuse them. He created metacinema in which the film was as much about the danger of his making the film as it was about the model. That direct eye-to-eye and mouth-to-ear connection between model and viewer was his genius breakthrough. He made his models become *present* to the viewer. That was how he re-invented gay film's passive point of view of watching models who, like fish in an aquarium, never acknowledge the viewer. Directing this kind of presentational "acting," he broke the Fourth Wall of the screen.

He assaulted his viewers who were eager to pay to be topped the way masochists seek sadists. He directed his aggressive models to push themselves into his camera on its tripod. He anticipated the way tough hustlers later on YouTube and Skype push their performance art directly into the viewer's face. He helped introduce the homomasculinity of straight blue-collar sex appeal into the casting and content of gay cinema. His down, dirty, and authentic films of real bad boys pushed viewers existentially beyond the golden bromances portrayed by gay actors in the macho movies of Roger Earl and the Gage Brothers.

His queer eye for hypermasculine men offered homomasculine men an alternative film esthetic, made way for the outré Mapplethorpe who collected Hurles' *Basic Black* series, and changed the way masculine-identified gay men gazed at themselves and the objects of their desire. He wrote in 2008, "I recall Jack bringing his friend Robert Mapplethorpe over to meet me in 1978, before he was touched by fame. I was especially delighted when Robert asked to buy some black-and-white prints of a favorite Old Reliable model, 'Mongoose.' I declined any payment, rewarded instead by the pleasure of sharing the joy these photos obviously brought him."

On June 20, 1982, we conferred in his Hollywood apartment about the feature essay, "Old Reliable: A Legend in His Own Time," in which he said: "A couple of my boys live in bushes which makes them homeless. I really get off on natural smells, sweat, and sweaty T-shirts, and uncut cock that showered yesterday. But I am turned off by filth. Why do poor boys always have stinky feet? As a rimmer, I prefer clean assholes. The balls can smell any way they want as long as they're bouncy. Many young men have used my shower to clean up. It's one of my social services."

"Do you have sex with the pricks you photograph?"

"Yes. 99% of the time. It is part of the deal, although if they're real good, sometimes I'll give them a few extra bucks."

In September 1988, I recommended his casting, style, and methods in my "Solo Sex: Who's Who In J/O Video" in *Drummer* 123: "Old Reliable's videos are like a symphony in three movements. First, the always-muscular young thugs strip off their clothes, oil up their naked bodies, and grind out tough muscle poses. Second, because they all inevitably know boxing and karate, they flex and shadow-box with the camera, free-styling into kicks and punches and hot licks, inter-actively right into the camera lens, which means, right into your face, fucker! Third, they lay back on Old Reliable's trademark couches on Old Reliable's trademark towels for an Old Reliable trademark cumshot. Video fans can carbon-date Old Reliable's videos—and his success—as his couches and tables change from early Salvation Army to West Hollywood glass and chrome."

His legend was minted when, in 1983, David said, "The French are coming with a camera crew to interview me about my work." Mais oui! The French knew his IQ. I found David, who quoted Soren Kierkegaard and Wilhelm Reich and W. H. Auden in his catalogs, to be very Jean Genet, very Pier Paolo Pasolini. He wrote about his *video verite*: "My work is not about sex. It is about life." He dared living at the real edge, and the real bottom, of sexual society glamorizing and romanticizing the very kind of tough top boys who had threatened him as a bottom boy himself, the kind of bullies who would wrestle and punch and choke, and be bad, and hurt you, the way they murdered film director Pasolini in 1975. Growing up in Ohio, David had a sweet mother whom I have hosted and photographed in my California home. Yet the bullying he took from rough boys in Cincinnati seems almost too perfectly on-brand with his Old Reliable concept to be true, but it is. He told me in "Call Him Old Reliable": "When I was a kid in Cincinnati, I wrestled with tough kids and didn't get hurt. They respected my brains. I respected their strength. I could watch fights without taking sides. Boys told me their secrets. Today they still do. On screen. And off. I was free back then to not be one-of-the-boys while enjoying all the protection and privilege of being with the tough guys. Sounds like my situation now. "

By May of 1980, David, who could take a beating from a boxer, was so bruised by vanilla magazine editors rejecting his photographs that he grew hesitant to edit his first video featuring several models solo. So Mark Hemry and I abducted him gently from his flat in a scheme that involved his model "Gentleman Dan," with girlfriend Carla, driving him to our home where we "locked" him in our bedroom with two primitive VCRs and told him he could not come out and eat supper until the edit was done. The rest is history.

He once told me one of his favorite videos, one of the ones that made him proudest, was *I, Rick* which earned him an Adult Video News AVN "Best Director" nomination, and that his favorite model, lensed repeatedly, was "Gentleman Dan" who for years, in prison and out, was his big romance—and was allegedly the model who in January 1980 gave David his very first video camera which had fallen off a truck, still in the box. Earlier in 1970, another special "boyfriend jumped off the Golden Gate Bridge," David said, "on Christmas Eve—so I'd always remember him." Once when a model flaked, he cast me with one of his Mexican convicts to record a duo prison-themed audio tape. Later in Los Angeles, he handed me his video camera and asked me to shoot two huge-hung hillbillies for him. His gesture was a personal and professional compliment inviting me to work inside his process. That's how I shot the only Old Reliable video Old Reliable did not shoot: *The Adams Brothers.*

Old Reliable videos are ground-breaking and historic as erotic jerk-off material as well as *video verite* documentary films. Like an anthropologist studying a certain class of males in a certain place at a certain time, he chronicled real-time street hustler delinquents who were paid to spill their guts after a lifetime of people telling them to "shut the fuck up." I'm nostalgic that, as part of our collaboration, he often gave me for my birthdays hustlers fresh out of prison or the military like "Mike Glacier," "Mike B," "Jose," and "H. D." who, after I bought him a new pair of Redwing boots, stole my belt buckle—as required by his DNA. His model "Barry Hoffman" was the muscular blond hustler who inspired the character of the hustler "Joe Buck" in James Leo Herlihy's novel and movie *Midnight Cowboy.*

Some think I returned his erotic gifts by making David Hurles the model for the virtuoso pornographer, Solly Blue, in my *Some Dance to Remember: A Memoir-Novel of San Francisco 1970-1982.* The truth is that to create the gonzo world of Solly Blue I had source material from my own experience running my own erotic video company, as well as in my familiarity with director friends such as Roger Earl, Wakefield Poole,

J. Brian, Bob Mizer, Mikal Bales, and Lou Thomas of Colt and Target studio. The fictitious amalgam of Solly Blue is not the real David Hurles who read the novel before publication and liked it so much that he helped me find a publisher, and then wrote a wonderful review he published on Amazon. One can, however, "read" his life into that fiction. He is the dearest friend. In 2008, he toasted our ancient friendship with his introduction, "A Thousand Light Years Ago," for my pop-culture history book *Gay San Francisco: Eyewitness Drummer*. Photographer Jim Stewart, who introduced David and me in 1976, profiled David and our San Francisco *Drummer* Salon in his book, *Folsom Street Blues: A Memoir of 1970s SoMa and Leatherfolk in San Francisco.*

In 1992, David drafted his memoirs as an unpublished work, on blue paper with a red-comb binder, titled *No Title Necessary: A Few Notes, Comments, and Observations*. He gave me a copy for safekeeping in my archives along with his collection of letters hundreds of convicts sent him from prison. His memoir consists of typed, sequential human-interest notes for each Old Reliable video feature with anecdotes about the shoot, the model's rap sheet, and his apartment-studio, along with autobiographical reflections on his own philosophy as a director. As an intimate eyewitness to so much of him personally and professionally, I can verify the actual behind-the-camera comedy and drama that surrounded David and his wilding boys.

Afternoons at his flat in San Francisco or in his one of his penthouses in Los Angeles—where he sat sipping endless Coca-Colas—were a fascinating revolving door of hustlers stopping by to introduce another hustler for a finder's fee, or to hang out killing time, or to twist his arm for cash to buy their girlfriends tampons—with fries and a Big Mac. One afternoon, David invited me over to meet a convict two-days out of San Quentin where David and I were once given a very serious off-limits conducted tour described in "Prison Blues." The convict, who arrived towing his new Baby Doll girlfriend, had been an "incident photographer" who had smuggled out a stiff stack of a hundred black-and-white 8"x10" crime scene glossies he had shot inside San Quentin of inmates immediately after their being beaten or tossed off an upper tier or killed by other inmates. The photos were unlike anything civilians ever see, and the ex-con with his stolen goods was disappointed that David and I agreed there was no legitimate market where he could peddle such pictures.

Collectors and completists wishing to sample David's nearly 300 films can find a treasure trove of his video stills in his years of monthly mail-order brochures, and in the on-going series of his seductively written and lavishly illustrated *Old Reliable Video Catalog.* His *Catalog* #2, January 1995, advertised, "Over 500 photos of almost 500 men in 170 videos." Most often, he simply titled his films with the featured hustler's name: *Champ, Cholo, Miracle Man, Rabbit, Tico,* and *Five Days with Phil.* He frequently kited fun flights of fancy with titles for his anthology collections like *Entrees from the Cafeteria of the Damned* and *Arkansas Luggage* which was sex code he coined for uncut hillbilly foreskin. Finally, becoming an acquired taste among savvy editors who realized his pictures sold their magazines, he also offered select photographs in trade for advertising in periodicals from *Drummer* to *Skinflicks, Skin, Just Men, Inches, Straight to Hell, California Action Guide,* and *Man2Man Quarterly.* His masculine photos helped shape the editorial look of twentieth-century magazine erotica. When I was editor of *Man2Man* in 1980 and 1981, he supported my startup and helped create that magazine by permitting his photos on the front and back covers of issues 1, 3, 4, 5, and 8 with another dozen in the interior and centerfold spreads of issues 2 and 6. Finding our work compatible, magazine editors at Mavety Media Group's Modernismo Publishing often paired the gray text of my sex stories alongside the dramatic black-and-white of his photographs.

In chronicling him in gay pop culture, I have devoted many column inches to his irresistible work and personality: "Old Reliable: The Company Dirty Talk Built" in *Skin* 2 # 5, 1981, page 30, alongside my companion feature articles, "Bob Mizer's AMG Duos" and "The Spotlight: Inside an LA Hustler Bar." I also profiled him in "Terror Is My Only Hardon: Old Reliable Speaks" in *Man2Man Quarterly,* Issue 8, October 1981, pages 24-32; and in "Old Reliable Confesses" alongside the Q&A interview, "Old Reliable: A Legend in His Own Time," with forty-eight Old Reliable photos in the *California Action Guide,* Volume 1 #3, September 1982; and in "Beauty and Terror: The Art and Trash of Old Reliable" in *Skin* 4 #3, 1983, page 10.

Two coffee-table photography books of his work have been published: *Speeding: The Old Reliable Photos of David Hurles,* (2005) and *Outcast: David Hurles Old Reliable in Living Color* (2010). Finding *Speeding* too small a sample of his far-ranging work, he wrote me, on its title page, the kind of existential note, with italics, that a pioneer survivor might send: "Although this book covers little, it confirms that I was *there.* Indeed. I *was* there."

Box-office receipts are a measure of success in porn as much as in Hollywood. David, cycling through thirty years, made two or three enormous fortunes of cash and condos which he earned and lost living in Los

Angeles after he sped into the fast lane of Santa Monica Boulevard's faster hustlers, one of whom late one Saturday night totaled David's brand new Corvette, crashing it through a curbside telephone booth. Unperturbed, David sometimes quoted, in his words, "two great philosophers": Miss Peggy Lee who sang, "Is That All There Is?" and Auntie Mame whose *carpe diem* was: "Live! Life's a banquet and most poor suckers are starving to death!"

In the 1990s, David told me a sad tale worthy of a Tennessee Williams' short story like "One Arm" or "Desire and the Black Masseur." He said that in 1991 a model had kicked him in the head, rupturing his eye socket bones, giving him double vision, ruining his camera eye, and effectively ending his career. He told the model, "I'm going to pass out. Stay till I wake up." Penniless but inventive, he changed his style. He perched his autofocus camera on a tripod to shoot with a new point of view that was as dispassionate as a hidden security camera. Instead of him shooting solos of others, his camera shot long-take duos of him *with* others. They were endgame videos, private reserve videos few have seen, in which his streaming parade of tricks lays him belly down on the bed.

Unable to use a still camera for production photos, he used video frame grabs in 1995 to illustrate the five titles of his new duo series, *In Private*, in his "Bonus Video Brochures" which whispered like a flasher in a raincoat: "Originally, these private tapes weren't for sale...Not everyone was aware of them....They offer maximum excitement from a minimalist point of view....How the sex moves the viewer, in the end, depends upon the angle from which it is experienced. There are 10 different sequences on each 75-minute tape. Some of the men preferred to remain anonymous... No story. No script. No acting. No kidding. No fancy camera angles. No Hollywood editing."

His shadowy frame grabs, printed the size of a postage stamp, reveal to those who know his body, his profile, and his tattoos—one of which I gave him for his birthday—that it is he himself, the director, who has become the actor, in a sexual power exchange of role playing straight out of Genet's drama, *The Maids*.

Because of Andy Warhol's *Empire*, *Sleep*, and *Chelsea Girls*, there is filmic heritage in the minimalism of his tripod-mounted camera eye. The static camera intensifies the voyeurism of looking frankly at the existential action in which the director, who famously always remained off-camera, becomes the horizontal receptacle for the seed, anger, and violence of his rough trade. His oeuvre had been solo videos, and these end-of-career duos, which he sent to me, seem kind of a delicious and perversatile victory lap of a sadomasochistic race that started years before in Cincinnati. The transfer of seed is the transfer of life. In gay psychology, are his final videos *Baby Jane* horror films? Or are they absurdist comedies of the physical humor of fast entrances, faster exits, and slamming doors in a French sex farce? The first time we met in 1976, David announced without irony, "There are no old gay directors."

On February 9, 2007, David sent me a copy of *Speeding* with his note written in black ink on the title page: "To Jack, My sometimes long-lost friend, a man who knows firsthand the intrigue, excitement, and also disappointment making pictures can arouse. You've seen my work firsthand as it happened for thirty years, *and* created your own. You are truly a man of unlimited ideas—and when you reacted or made suggestions, they were always positive and encouraging. You know some of these men—good and not good. Your constancy has been a support always. Even though there's no point in wondering what more we might have done, we did what came our way, and that was plenty. With love, David R. Hurles. Thanks."

Near the same time, on January 31, 2007, my friend and frequent house guest, the British art critic Edward "Ted" Lucie-Smith introduced me to his friend, Dian Hanson, the Erotica Editor at Taschen in Los Angeles, who had told him that without success she was searching for the reclusive Old Reliable to publish his photos in her upcoming *Big Penis Book*. During a two-hour phone conversation on February 1, I convinced David that Dian was so perfectly credentialed and suited to his work that he should at least talk to Taschen's star editor on the phone. More than royalty payments for his film stills, David needed the place Dian might secure for him in the canon of gay art history. When he agreed to meet her at his Hollywood walk-up, he made one of the best decisions of his life, and it saved his life. The *Big Penis Book* brought him back to consciousness with fans, critics, and serious art collectors.

Continuing pro-active for David's legacy, I suggested to Ted in an email on December 27, 2007, that he include Old Reliable in the exhibit he was planning for the Leslie-Lohman Gallery in New York: "David has work available, and he is desperate for money. He called me four weeks ago to tell me goodbye because he was wanting to 'end it all,' and he said, I was the only one who ever loved him." Ted replied, "David Hurles is certainly an idea. Charles Leslie loves things raunchy. But the money could be a long way off in January 2009." On May 15, 2008, Ted wrote, "Dian joins with you in urging me to use David Hurles. However, there is one sticking point: I don't want, or have time for, any hassle. Can you perhaps deal with him for me, when the time comes?" On June 7, he decided: "Let's forget the boy Hurles. Life's too short."

Literally too short. Late on the night of October 5, 2008, David, home alone writing the overdue preface for *Outcast*, suffered a stroke. Lying on the floor, he was lucky to be rescued by the arrival of his ex-con assistant, Mykey, to whom he had entrusted a key. In gratitude, David dedicated his book *Outcast* to Mykey. Just twenty months into their friendship, Dian stood by him in critical condition in ICU and held his hand as he went in for surgery to relieve pressure on his brain. In 2008, disabled and fostered by Dian, he retired to a Los Angeles eldercare home where he continues to abide in 2022.

In January 2010, I curated the Old Reliable film photographs for Chuck Mobley's SF Camerawork Gallery exhibit: *Autobiography of the San Francisco Bay Area, Part 2: The Future Lasts Forever.* In June 2010, Dian Hanson and John Waters curated the exhibition *Outsider Porn: The Photos of David Hurles* at New York's Marianne Boesky Gallery. Late in his own life, John Waters wrote his personal take on the importance of being Hurles in *Role Models.* To this day, David treasures the memory of his friendship with Gore Vidal who, like Waters and Mapplethorpe and Susie Bright and Joe Gage and Paul Reubens aka Pee-wee Herman, was a fan.

In 2016, the Tom of Finland Foundation inducted David into its "Artists Hall of Fame." His work.is curated in the permanent collection of ONE National Gay & Lesbian Archives.

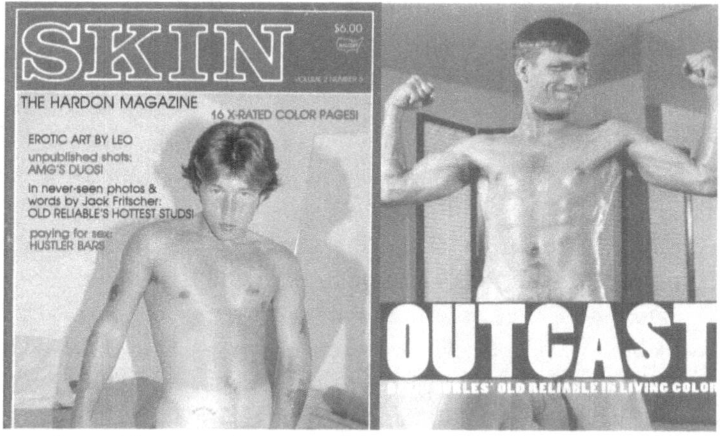

During the Golden Age of Gay Magazines (1975-1999), only the edgiest like *Drummer* featured Old Reliable. *Skin* Cover Photo: "Old Reliable's Hottest Studs in never-seen photos & words by Jack Fritscher." *Skin*, vol. 2, # 5, Sept. 1981. Hurles' photobooks *Speeding* and *Outcast* followed in 2005 and 2010.

DAVID HURLES

1944-

CALL HIM "OLD RELIABLE" BECAUSE HE IS

"Streetboys, ex-cons, and hustlers are my only hardon," David Hurles says. It's 1981 in Hollywood. We've been close friends for five years. He is internationally famous as the photographer and video director of his Old Reliable Studio. The art of his radical erotica is so much his personal vision that guys often refer to him as "Old Reliable." "Nothing beats," he says, "looking up at a tough young streetwise punk straddling my chest, flexing his muscles, and talking nasty to me. Sure, it's dangerous. Nobody in his right mind should bring rough trade into his house and put himself in a compromising situation. I've been raped at knifepoint and robbed at gunpoint. I've been stripped naked by a 19-year-old blond ex-con who fucked me till he got off, and then duck-marched me around my apartment with the palms of my hands on my shoulders prison-style while he made me rifle my drawers for cash."

Old Reliable is in his early thirties. He's a cherubic brown-blond, blue-eyed junk-food addict who rarely ventures out of his Los Angeles apartment. He hardly needs to. In 1975 he invented the better mousetrap, and the world beat a path to his door. "Judy Garland and me," he says. "This is the apartment-hotel where she used to bring the rough trade she liked to have fuck her senseless. Ain't Hollywood grand? LA may not be the center of the universe, but it sure is the center ring of the circus."

Reliable rises to pour more Coca-Cola. The Coke always goes in the glass before the ice: it foams less.

"I must be crazy to be in the business I'm in. If the Moral Majority, which is neither, doesn't get me, then the hustlers will. But then my business is my pleasure. How many guys can honestly say that? To be perfectly real with you, in a world that grows increasingly unreal, I must tell you: Terror is my only hardon. I used to think this was weird; but lately the headlines and movies prove that terror sells. And what sells in America is always what excites people the most. America's into terror. Think of the

American hostages in Iran, movies like *Jaws* and *Halloween*, the election of any Republican. It's an axiom of art: the mix of beauty and terror."

Attractive danger is Old Reliable's product. He recruits tough street males to make audio tapes for mail-order sale to an international clientele of men who prefer, in their wise concern for the safety of their persons and possessions, not to hit the bricks themselves to pick up a piece of lower-class trash who will do anything they want—or he wants—for fifteen bucks on up. Enter Old Reliable and reality. Old Reliable refuses to script his authentic tapes. He turns his boys loose with a blank audio cassette. What they confess to and brag about is the stuff wet dreams are made on. Lots of gay men, with a yen for nasty talk, enjoy beating off listening to Old Reliable's straight men admitting, in slow southern drawls and "dude" street lingo, that they're fuckin' righteously into abusing fuckin' fags.

Once a man discovers the performance-reality that Old Reliable produces, he becomes a sucker for these hot social documentaries that ivory-tower academics would give their right nut for. Reliable realizes the socially redeeming value of his work. But that's accidental to his purpose. His reason for being, he realizes, happens when a guy listens to these tapes on his car stereo, on his cassette player next to his pillow, or on his Walkman while sitting in a sleazy neighborhood on a bus bench watching the danger-boys cruise temptingly by. Sex, Old Reliable figures, ought to have a verbal soundtrack.

"I'm an outlaw," he admits, "artistically, politically, even philosophically." Reliable is attractive enough to make a pickup in any gay bar in the world; but he frankly eschews sex with gays. He prefers sex with men. Not that he feels superior to gays. "It's ironic. Just as the media accepts the word *gay*, homosexuals realize that *gay* has reduced itself to mean little more than the lifestyles of the disco clone and the political activist. That does not, by any stretch, represent the extraordinary range of queerness." He smiles. "I think it was better before we divided ourselves into rich gays, poor gays, city gays, female gays, etc. I think it was better when we were all just outlaws."

Knowing the danger of Old Reliable's lifestyle, the very lifestyle that gives him access to a reality that is the heart of the contemporary young urban male American experience, one wonders about the chances of his longevity. Are his forays into the hustling *demimonde* a kind of living by the sword you die by?

"I'm homosexual," he says. "But like many queer men these days, I find homosexuality is more than designer jeans and Lacoste polo shirts. Maybe I'm reactionary."

Actually, his erotic tapes are an art form reminding gay men of the kind of men they originally came out for—before studios like Colt laundered masculinity into a spruced-up parody of mannikins and modelles.

"Few men alive, I dare say, ever came out to go to bed with gays. Men come out to bed other men. Heterosexual is not better than homosexual. Yet if you check out, and really listen to, the so-called gay values of who's so-called *hot*, you see that the straighter the guy's appearance the bigger the throb. That says everything about what gay guys deep-down want. That says everything about the deep-down levels at which I mine my work. Sometimes guys buy my tapes and get scared."

Old Reliable believes in being careful of what you wish for, because he finds you usually get it.

"When I was a kid in Cincinnati, I wrestled with tough kids and didn't get hurt. They respected my brains. I respected their strength. I could watch fights without taking sides. Boys told me their secrets. Today they still do. I was free back then to not be one-of-the-boys while enjoying all the protection and privilege of being with the tough guys. Sounds like my situation now. I used to get my pals to wrestle. Crotch-to-crotch. Stripped to shorts. Twelve-year-old cocks curiously against each other. One guy, when we weren't wrestling, was always strutting and telling me how tough he was, and how he could really whip me if he wanted to. When I think about it, those experiences were like a dry-run for the way my sex life and my art life are today. Maybe that's the point and secret of my tapes: LA reality isn't too far from Cincinnati fantasy."

Old Reliable is generous to his boys. Sometimes to a fault. They call him "Dear Old Dad" and he melts. A hustler gets fifteen to twenty-five bucks for sex, another ten or fifteen for the sixty-minute tape, another twenty or so for photographs. That's sort of the standard package. It varies greatly with the look and talent of the toughie. Some guys return for free. Some, for bigger bucks.

"These young men serve themselves up *à la carte*." Old Reliable spreads some of his distinctive camera-verite pix across his blond-veneer coffee table. His eye sports a small mouse: a black eye. His lower lip is slightly puffy. "Kenny, last night, for instance, came over for twenty bucks' worth of fun. Let me say that Kenny was my type and cheap at twice the price. I offered him during the scene another ten for some attitude-posing. Another five for his fancy presentation of his butt for some fancier rimming. And so on." Old Reliable smiles like a cat accustomed to eating canaries. "By this morning, Kenny had earned himself $85."

Old Reliable hardly minds paying for it. His auditions of these boys assures Old Reliable customers that they're getting "The Real Thing." No wonder he keeps a refrigerator stacked full of liter bottles of nothing but Coca-Cola. For every true artist, his work must also be his life.

"Hollywood," Reliable says, "is the city of performances. Everybody here is paid to perform. I pay to go to a stage play where actors strut their stuff for a group. So what's different about paying my little street actor Kenny for a one-on-one performance? It pays his rent. It keeps him from robbing somebody." He looks around his apartment.

Outside, a Southern-California fountain, reminiscent of grander Hollywood times, babbles under a motionless palm. "Of course, they always sooner or later rob me. That's one of the reasons I rarely go out. Everything in my apartment turns over, through burglary, at least once a year. Am I complaining? Hardly."

Old Reliable's fifth-floor apartment is early St. Vincent de Paul. Fans of his photography can watch his possessions change as they study the backgrounds of the pix of his young studs. The lamps, the couches, the chairs, the sheets are all familiar.

"This place is not exactly my choice of style," Reliable says with no apology in his voice. He's not a queen living the designer life. "Most of my customers live in very nice middle-class homes. I had," he confides, "three address changes from my customers in Washington, D.C., for instance, just as President Carter left office. Anyway, if a man lives in a comfortable home, he can't bring back a street hustler where everything they see is temptation. This Salvation Army junk hardly tempts anybody. This illusion keeps me safer, although there is the constant problem of the camera, the tape recorders, the tape duplicator, the color TV, and the video camera and recorder. My work requires electronic equipment and, of course, that is high on the burglary-robbery hit list. So far I haven't gone down in a hail of hot lead."

One wonders if Old Reliable's customers realize the extent of the dangers he faces to produce his erotic art. That knowledge that the danger is as real as the tapes, that none of his work is scripted, might add to the erotic, exotic intensity of smoking a joint, greasing up the palm, and turning on the tape cassette.

Old Reliable founded his cassette mail-order trade in the middle of the night. This was before home video. Erotic films in the 1970s were silent, and he thought to give sex a voice. He sat up in bed, sort of like movie star Al Jolson saying the first line of dialogue in the first talking movie in 1927: "You ain't heard nothin' yet!"

"Actually," he says between answering the constantly ringing phone, "I always got turned on at the baths back then listening to men fuck and moan in the next room. I jerked off hearing my roommate getting into S&M and fisting. I loved the panting, crunching sound of myself and my partner wrestling. And I could, and can, cum listening to a hustler or straight man tell about his exploits: fighting, doing sex, rough-housing, keeping cool in the slammer. Sex isn't silent. Sex involves all the senses. I like the sight, taste, and smell of action. So why not the fucking sound of it?"

Old Reliable's style is the style of men he recruits: a direct drive to real, painful, penetrating, curled-toe orgasm. The men he photographs and tapes are from the lower class: outlaws, young men from broken families, reform school, prison, drug addicts, bikers, all of them living day to day, often on the street, or with whoever will take care of them, male or female. Most identify themselves as straight.

Old Reliable's style is also the style of the men who buy his tapes, men reacting, perhaps subconsciously, to their privileged upbringing. Like Old Reliable, who dares to extend himself out into the mean streets to front for them, they have, if their purchasing power is any statement, similar tastes. "I like," Old Reliable confesses, and the truth of all this is in his work, "the smell of sweat, armpits, cock, asshole, and balls. I like muscular, hard bodies. I like men doing things that our middle-class parents always thought of as dirty: spitting, cussing, even fucking women. Sex is beautiful and compelling, but I prefer it on the seamy side. I would rather sniff the armpits of a tough young Mexican boxer after a fight than climb between clean sheets with a Colt model.

"For my tapes, I basically use men who haven't grown up with middle-class restrictions. I encourage them to be as honest as they can. I let them say whatever spills out of them—from nice to nasty. They tend to tell secrets and spill their guts all over the tape. Most of it is what some people regard as seamy, not just sexual. Some talk of violence and hate and prejudice, of sins venial and mortal, of omission and commission. Most of them are pretty worldly whether they're 18 or 38, What is *dirty* changes a lot and keeps changing."

What Old Reliable ends up with on his erotic tapes is something really important and unique in contemporary American popular culture.

"What you hear on my tapes is more than suck and fuck and rim. It's also sweat, piss, hardcore masculinity, strength, attitude, lack of pretension. These men haven't been conditioned the same way as their listeners. Most of them love the chance to say anything they want, and for money, and they come off with a seething intensity that can't fail to move the listener."

Old Reliable knocks down neat the last of his glass of Coke.

"How often," he says with all the passion of an artist with a vision, "do we get to hear someone say what he really thinks and feels? The men of these tapes can do just that—because I release them from any judgment on what they say. After they leave my apartment, after I get a little ripped and listen to the tape, I just share the street-gifts life sends to me."

He smiles his deceptively boyish smile.

"I'm sharing people who don't always wear clean underwear," he says, "with those who do."

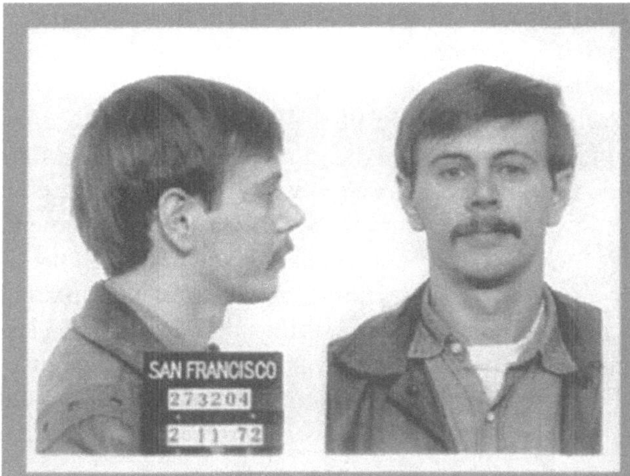

After David Hurles' second 1972 arrest (four times in one week) by the San Francisco police, he used his mug shot to score "street cred" with his hustler ex-con models.

Jose del Norte, Old Reliable model photographed on set at David Hurles' studio for the Palm Drive Video shoot, *Illegal Alien Blues*, Hollywood, 1986. Photo by Jack Fritscher published in *Drummer* 155, May 1992.

David Hurles carefully curated his actors and videos in his annual Old Reliable catalogs which in themselves are art objects documenting the gay history of Old Reliable Studio. The cover shown is *The Old Reliable Collection Catalogue: On the Record*, September 1994.

Jack Fritscher and Thom Gunn, Folsom Street Fair, San Francisco, 1996. Photo by Edward Lucie-Smith.

The Letters of Thom Gunn, Selected and Edited by Michael Nott, August Kleinsahler, and Clive Wilmer (2022).

THOM GUNN

1929-2004

On the 90th Anniversary of His Birth, a Memoir of the "Leather Poet Laureate" of Folsom Street and His Pop-Culture Life in San Francisco

Thom Gunn and I first met fifty years ago, as noted in his diary, in early November 1969 when he was on a reading tour and I was an assistant professor in the English Department at Western Michigan University in Kalamazoo. I had found his poetry while browsing in Barbara's Bookstore in Chicago's Old Town in 1967. Scanning the virility of his texts with gaydar, I also studied the one photo I found of him in a leather jacket on the back cover of *My Sad Captains.*

I appreciated his photogenic bone structure and studied his face for the gay cast in the eye that gay men seek to identify each other. The very title *My Sad Captains* is gayer than *Billy Budd*, and sounds like a gay torch song sung by Judy Garland. I figured he was gay, and more than gay. He was a brother leatherman whose inclination framed his poetry. In one of his many notebooks later archived at the Bancroft Library at UC Berkeley, he wrote: "I say that S&M is a form of love. I think it is, but I don't think that goes quite deep enough."

Introduced at 8 PM by faculty poet and professor John Woods, Thom read in a lecture room in newly opened Brown Hall that seated fifty—and that night was standing room only. My friend, the author, poet, and MacArthur Fellow Stuart Dybek, and I had attended graduate school together at Loyola University of Chicago and were both teaching creative writing at the time. I began at WMU in 1967, and Stuart in 1968. I was out, and the straight Stuart and I had many gay friends in Chicago. We figured Thom was, in the polite term used then, a "homophile" person of interest, but tried not to project fanciful autobiography into his poems when such a thing was considered defamatory. The Stonewall Riot had happened only five months before, and few outside New York had yet heard of it.

Having spent May 1969 cruising in London on mod Carnaby Street, and at the Coleherne leather bar in Earls Court, I knew a Teddy Boy from a forty-year-old Leather Boy who was born two years before the slouching James Dean whose cool he was channeling. James Dean's middle name was Byron, courtesy of his mother who loved poetry and died young when Dean was a boy. Thom as a young teen lost his mother to suicide, and like Dean coped with her exit by turning to the arts. "Maybe I'm so cool," Thom wrote, double-daring himself to face death, that "I could out-stare her [Medusa]" and her powers over life and death. Like Dean, he found solace in literature and performance.

Thom revealed the mask that let his creative self stand beside his personal self in *My Cambridge*: "Viewing myself as an actor trying to play a part provided rich material for poetry." Thom, who created many photo collages of multiple faces on his study walls over the years, included the famous Dennis Stock photograph picturing James Dean wearing glasses and reciting from his fellow Hoosier's folksy book, *The Complete Poetical Works of James Whitcomb Riley.*

The appealing actor, dead young like Byron, Shelley, and Keats, dead before rock stars died, meant a great deal to Thom and me, and to men of our post-war consciousness. Frank O'Hara wrote several poems about the discipline and disorder of Dean. Controversial French philosopher Edgar Morin took a deep dive into the actor in "The Case of James Dean" which was the title essay Thom read in the 1958 issue of the *Evergreen Review* that pictured Dean on the cover, with hustler John Rechy excerpted in the same issue from *City of Night* bragging and complaining that he was followed by the "shadow of James Dean because of the movie." Warhol silk-screened Dean. Lou Reed cited Dean's gender-fluid imprint on drag artist Jackie Curtis, who "thought she was James Dean for a day" in his song "Walk on the Wild Side," produced by David Bowie. Because we all thought we were James Dean, my own essay crushing on Dean was published in 1962.

So I was curious to check Thom out when the elegant John Woods introduced him to an audience that included W. H. Auden expert Edward Callan who saw Thom as an heir of Auden, and celebrity poets Herb Scott and Conrad Hilberry whose students at Kalamazoo College interviewed Thom for their literary magazine, *Cauldron*. Of average height, Thom carried his speed-lean body with a kind of aw-shucks diffidence, and confidence. His aura was handsome and, to me, sexy, including his picket smile of clean British teeth. One must sometimes contemplate the poet's mouth.

He had carefully groomed and accessorized himself with gay signifiers. He combed his healthy black hair in a brush cut, and wore one gold earring, which was unconventional then and there. He wore that earring in his left lobe, and hung his ring of keys on the left side of his leather belt. In the semaphore of leather culture, the right side signals a bottom man and left says the man is either a top or negotiable. He wore black Levi's 501s with a red bandana handkerchief in his left back pocket and black cowboy boots with a blue denim shirt open two or three buttons down his skinny chest inside his signature black leather jacket that he kept on for the first half of the reading.

Midway through his performance, as part of the show, he bantered with the audience while he removed his jacket under which he was wearing a black leather vest. His shirt sleeves turned up twice at the cuff exposed a black panther tattoo on his right forearm. My longtime friend Samuel Steward, an intimate of Gertrude Stein and Alice B. Toklas, was also known as both the writer "Phil Andros" and the tattoo artist "Phil Sparrow" who had personally inked a black panther on James Dean's forearm which Dean covered with pancake makeup for filming. Sam told me that the black panther tattoo was popular with sailors and bikers up through the 1960s until the rise of the Black Panther Party.

Thom looked like the incarnation of one of his leather poems the way Edward Carpenter said that Walt "Whitman as a concrete personality entirely filled out and corroborated the conception of him which one had derived from reading *Leaves of Grass*." In the arc of popular culture, we were old enough to be 1950s beatniks who evolved into 1960s hippies who morphed into 1970s leathermen. Thom's presentation was gentle, unassuming, the kind of cordiality suitable to an international poet entertaining a literary crowd in the Midwest. Performing poem after poem, he read for about an hour and was met with a standing ovation, and then answered a few questions.

As soon as I could make my way to the little stage which was no more than the platform dais where I stood teaching American literature six times a week, I reached out to greet him. I was also up to dress code in my own black leather jacket tailored like a Levi's denim jacket by Taubers of California in San Francisco. After watching him chat with faculty and students stargazing at him, I said, and I remember the dialogue planned like a bar pickup line while watching him read: "I like your leather jacket." He said, "I like yours." I said, "Who did your tattoo?" He said, "Lyle Tuttle." I said, "Cliff Raven did mine." The month before, Lyle Tuttle, tattoo artist to San Francisco leathermen, had been on the October cover of *Rolling Stone* while the gay Cliff Ingram, who was taught tattooing and re-named Cliff Raven by Phil Sparrow, was inking leathermen in Chicago.

I then introduced him to my new lover, David Sparrow, a twenty-four-year-old leatherman who was drop-dead handsome. I was thirty, and we were both chicken to Thom who was forty; but he was far from "the fallen rake" in middle age in his poem "Modes of Pleasure." David and I had met only four months before in July 1969 and were a committed couple until 1979, and friends till his death from AIDS in 1992. Thom liked that David had hustled and knew his way around substances. Because I found Edna St. Vincent Millay's "Passer Mortuus Est" ["The Sparrow Is Dead"] usefully coincidental in my imagining of my handsome "petulant" Sparrow, "my erstwhile dear," I wondered if Thom—who liked bad-boy types, and liked David a lot—found his surname of coincidental use in the poem he wrote three months later, "Sparrow," in "Three Songs." But then, sparrows figure so frequently in his poetry.

Thom looked relieved at finding fraternity on the road. He was a bard and sex tourist in search of "funny discreet understandings." He wrote that phrase in his diary to describe how he and David and I had negotiated our tryst. His pattern on his junket was the usual gay quest to find sympathetic company in the gay student or gay professor he could latch onto to survive the evening reading and faculty after-party.

David and I walked Thom to my 1969 Toyota Land Cruiser, a purposely macho vehicle used as bait in cruising, and drove off to the reception at the home of a professor of children's literature. The party was a mix of faculty and students talking to Thom who listened and smiled. After an hour or so, he nodded a high sign, and whispered, "Let's smoke a joint." I grabbed David's elbow, and the three of us disappeared into the bathroom. Smoking the joint launched a three-way bonding made all the more exciting because we were a trio of outsider men discovering each other in an otherwise straight soiree of very nice people drinking mulled wine on the other side of the door.

We became instant mates. He smelled clean and tasted like cigarettes which at that time did not bother me—as did later his substance use which had prematurely wrinkled his thin skin years before he died, with methamphetamine in his system, at age seventy-four. He wrote a very short poem, "Listening to Jefferson Airplane," in response to Grace Slick's lyric that "Some pills make you larger, and some pills make you small." In "Street Song," he mentioned shopping for Methedrine, hash, and "… Keys lids acid and speed." Thom was always one smart party drug ahead of everyone else.

Our organ recital in the bathroom was an interlude of twenty minutes. When we came out of that water closet, no one noticed; or, if they did notice, they didn't know what "it" was that happened if it was anything; and they said nothing because it was too soon in gay liberation to know what to say. And they were too liberal to care. Times were different then. Freer. No one would dare do that today. That's how cool universities were back in that liberated day of campus revolution. It was not *post hoc ergo propter hoc*, but soon after, my department named me assistant professor with tenure.

During this visit, at my home, I showed Thom a painting done by my immigrant acquaintance Otto Stauffenberg, a cousin of Count Claus von Stauffenberg whom Thom had called "honour personified" in a poem in *My Sad Captains* for his brave attempt to assassinate Hitler with a suitcase bomb in 1944 when Thom was turning fifteen. Thom wanted to meet the ancient Otto (1888-1977) who was an artist in residence at the Kalamazoo Institute of Art, but his itinerary was too tight. To this day, I wonder if he might have found a new poem in the immigrant German painter.

From my first acquaintance with his poetry in 1967, I had a queer literary detective's interest that was italicized because of his subtle gay content whose dark eros he softened, I thought, for literary consumption that was then still rather homophobic. In his crossover from the tight metrics of his first British poems to the California freedom of his later, he was slowly defrosting his stiff upper lip to write more boldly about gay sex the way the gay Countee Cullen had boldly pioneered emerging "Negritude," his term, in his Harlem Renaissance poems. However, few if any of Thom's lines, composed laterally amidst poetry's San Francisco Renaissance, beat with the bumptious rhythms of "Homotude" that drove the jerkoffian beat of the erotic poetry later favored in *Drummer*, the international magazine that was a bible for leathermen.

Erotica is as essential to gay culture as rap is to black culture. Thom dared sensuality, but seemed to shy away from the unpasteurized sexuality awakening in gay literature and pop culture. As the 1960s became the 1970s, times were changing. E. M. Forster's long-gestating *Maurice* written in 1913 finally found its first publication in 1971, the same year Thom's magical *Moly* was published, and two years after Thom read that November night in Michigan.

At age forty, Thom—like his genius friend, the British leatherman-biker and neurologist Oliver Sacks, who in the 1960s was interning at Mount Zion Hospital in San Francisco and hanging out at the Tool Box—was a half-generation earlier on the gay scene than the younger people who began their version of modern gay liberation at Stonewall. His poetry, like the cool leather photography of his peer Robert Mapplethorpe, who also did collages, seemed formal, restrained, and clever, but not the kind of art that rouses the reader to orgasm. He lived in a gay culture where gay art came to pride itself on being erotic and confrontational. So why so little frank Anglo-Saxon vocabulary and action on his pages?

It was as if he himself was under a discipline to compose courtly love poems within the conservative specifications of proper literature for his literary audience when he might have also penned more frankly gay colloquial poetry in touch with the real-life vernacular of his gay pop-culture audience for whom eros is the vulgate soul of gay arts, and the barbaric yawp of same-sex orgasm is most often the existential point. But maybe it's better not to explain too much. If only he had celebrated the raw erotic haptics of gay sex with the same heart-stopping frankness with which in 1992 he tolled the raw sorrows and grief disorders of AIDS in his most famous book, *The Man with Night Sweats.*

In the way playwright and poet Thomas Lanier Williams changed his name to "Tennessee," William Guinneach Gunn, whose mother's family name was Thompson, changed his name to Thompson William Gunn out of which he designed a marquee name that would have suited a porn star. The name-framing poet, a genius at connotation, traded on "Tommy Gun," the assaultive slang for the famous Thompson Sub-Machine gun he saw carried by American soldiers, whom he adored, in the world war. "Thom Gunn" could have been as revered in gay pop culture as the "poet laureate of leather" as was our mutual international friend, "Tom of Finland," the "artist laureate of leather" who drew his erotic art in touch with the common gay man. Like Mapplethorpe, Tom of Finland used paradigms of erotica to create his stylized identity archetypes of homomasculine men and their cool *couture.* I once wrote that it's likely few have ever pleasured themselves over a Mapplethorpe photo.

Might the same be said of a reserved Gunn poem in a subculture worshiping hot porn? Can intentionally provocative erotica be foreplay, entertainment, and art? Is orgasmic triggering a literary talent? Is any art form more sensationally and beatifically interactive than erotica and its synonym pornography? Is that sacred erotic transaction between poet and reader even meaningful outside the queer eye? Thom's erotic modesty may have little consequence to some old-school scholars, but it means a lot in the gay measurement of queer authenticity.

I mention this because as editor-in-chief of *Drummer* magazine in 1977, I found an appetite in gay popular culture hungering for literary erotica that didn't insult the intelligence of readers. The marvel was how the artist Thom, the son of two disciplined journalists, kept producing fine poetry from the conformist 1950s up through Swinging 1960s and 1970s and the *fin de siècle* AIDS emergency. If the immigrant Thom whose legal status was "permanent resident" had not re-invented himself as a true San Franciscan, if he had not been inspired by sex and drugs and cruising and plague, how different his poetry would have been. Writing about our then current moment, he stood up as artists do in a community to make sense out of change. He was an HIV-negative artist who chronicled the plague in much the same way the HIV-positive Mapplethorpe documented the 1980s.

My Sad Captains should be the title of the inevitable biopic Hollywood or the BBC will make of Thom's life. That title intones Whitman's "Oh Captain, My Captain," as well as Scott Fitzgerald's *All the Sad Young Men*, which, quoted by Thom at the beginning of Part 2, was a heterosexual romantic lament compared to Thom's homosexual existential concerns. Thom's texts, even while modest about sex, were difficult to present to university students in the 1960s and early 1970s because his poetry, as enigmatic as is all poetry to freshmen studying Literary Interpretation, was doubly perplexing to straight students. Classroom discussions of his content, as with Whitman's, led to teaching moments about gay realities in a mainstream culture adjusting to emerging gay liberation.

Thom's name and legacy might have been saluted earlier and deeper inside the ecosystem of post-Stonewall gay American popular culture that was slow to acknowledge his midcentury poetry as well as the international and local literary company he kept in the gay capital of San Francisco that made Cupid boss.

Even so, the summer after Stonewall, editor Daniel Halpern headlined Thom in the first issue of *Antaeus* with fiction by Paul and Jane Bowles; poetry by John Fowles, Lawrence Durrell, Tennessee Williams, Lawrence Ferlinghetti; and an interview with Gore Vidal. However, inside the gay ghetto, it took till 1977 for the national gay magazine, *The Advocate*, with its politically correct bias against the leather lifestyle, to cover Thom with an interview by Tony Sarver, perhaps because it took that long for his American poetry to come out of the British closet.

Thom had been famous for thirty-four years when the first gay literary prizes, the Lambda Literary Awards, were founded in 1988. It was only in 1992 that *The Man with Night Sweats* earned his first nomination for a Lammy, but he lost to Academy-Award-winning poet Edward Field's *Counting Myself Lucky*. Not until 1995, when he was sixty-six, did his *Collected Poems* win the Lambda Literary Award for Gay Men's Poetry. In 2001, Thom won the Triangle Award for Gay Poetry from the literary gatekeepers at the Publishing Triangle. It was only in 2005, the year after his death, that the Publishing Triangle marketing group paid him the honor of changing that trophy's name to the Thom Gunn Award for Gay Poetry. Why did the Publishing Triangle wait? It wasn't for death because it also named an award for the living Edmund White.

Among the postmortem considerations of Thom, two invocations touched me. In 2009, poet Randall Mann wrote *Breakfast with Thom Gunn*. In 2012, Christopher Bram, whose novel *Father of Frankenstein* became Bill Condon's Oscar-winning screenplay *Gods and Monsters*, channeled Ralph Waldo Emerson's *Representative Men* and Lytton Strachey's *Eminent Victorians* and included pertinent mentions of Thom in his *Eminent Outlaws: The Gay Writers Who Changed America.*

Thom crossed the Atlantic and double-crossed the conventions of poesis. He kept his cool dodging labels, and never weaponized his poetry for gay pop-culture conquest and coverage. He never swanned into a bar playing the poet to get laid. The year before he died, Thom told Robert Potts in *The Guardian*: "I don't expect my friends to read me. Most of the people I know have heard I'm a writer, but are not very interested."

"COFFEE ON COLE": PRIVATE LIVES AT THOM'S COLE STREET COMMUNE

After Thom and I met in Michigan, we became friends in San Francisco the way writers become friends. We bonded as mates in a homomasculine version of homosexuality, which also animates the fraternity in his poetry. Homomasculinity is Whitman's Calamus emotion applied to masculine-identified gay men bonding together not in separatist, sexist, or racist patriarchy, but in the humanist best that men do, avoiding toxic masculinity ideology, and living the best of natural manhood. Thom's friend Wendy Lesser, founding editor of *The Threepenny Review*, wrote in her essay, "Thom Gunn's 'Duncan'": "He [Thom] was always the most masculine of men. There was nothing 'sissy' about his homosexuality, as he might have put it—no desire to imitate the female of the species, no particular bond with the feminine."

When David Sparrow and I moved to San Francisco, Thom and I kept on keeping on via telephone and bars and coffee shops, as was the custom then, which he later pictured in his clever "Coffee on Cole," but not at his home with his partner Mike Kitay first on Filbert Street and then later on Cole Street or at mine with David Sparrow on 25th Street because we were social not domestic friends. "South of Market Street" bars, aka

SOMA bars, like Febe's, Folsom Prison, the No Name, the Ramrod, the Ambush, the Eagle, and the Lone Star were our Café Les Deux Magots. There was a nonstop gay party going on in the 1970s that started with celebrations in gay bars worldwide on the symbolically sexy date, 6/9/69, nineteen auspicious days before Stonewall. We figured we could always become domesticated later when we were older.

He wrote in "Lines for a Book," "It's better / to go and see your friend than write a letter." It wasn't cool back then to ask about another man's private home life. Thom was genuinely contented with the long-term safety and security and love in his domestic life which gave him the communal home of men and privacy he needed to create in his study and bedroom. Surviving his father's cold shoulder, his mother's suicide, the London Blitz, two years in the British army, immigration, and the deaths of friends from plague, he seemed to live a charmed life. With Kitay, he had the gay male equivalent of "happy wife / happy life" which he saluted in "The Hug," his lovely Valentine of a sudden moment of domestic intimacy.

Sowing wild oats in the 1970s in the carefree window between penicillin and HIV, leathermen rarely cared to know anyone's domestic drama because too much personal pathos broke the fourth wall of the carefree sex opera. One of the joys of John Doe/John Doe serial sex was anonymity. His poem, "Wrestling," praises the joys of anonymous sex. The artist Ed Parente and I had brokeback sex a dozen times during two years at the glorious Barracks bathhouse on Folsom until, during one exceptionally perfect night, post coitum, we sat on the stairs and introduced ourselves and moaned with laughter because for years his friends and mine had told each of us that we must meet. We became friends, but never balled again because personal information killed the buzzed-up Platonic Ideal of the Hard Man neither of us was in real life outside our thrilling anonymous sex. For reasons such as this incestuous short circuit, Thom tended to keep his bar life with middle-aged leathermen fairly separate from his sex life with young men.

The main caution that blocked us from developing a closer friendship was his drug use which unnerved me. Addiction made him a dangerous friend. His home-commune roommate Bill Lux noted Thom's three-day sex and crystal-meth binges. I knew that William Burroughs lived his whole long life on heroin, but still. Whatever was going on with Thom's "fiercely attractive" house guests who were trying "to stick their needle in my [his] arm" in his poem "In Time of Plague," I wasn't interested in either a soap opera or a situation comedy with older men and younger hustlers shooting up—even though each roommate "cooks one night and each cooks well."

When Thom died, the headline on his obituary written by Edward Guthmann for the *San Francisco Chronicle* read: "A Poet's Life. As friends died of AIDS, Thom Gunn stayed healthy—until his need to play hard finally killed him." The medical examiner's report said he passed from "acute polysubstance abuse" including alcohol and heroin. Wendy Lesser praised Thom for not being a "careerist," telling Guthmann that Thom's "poems about death, particularly 'Elegy,' will be read as long as people read poetry in English."

THOM'S SHORT STORY IN *DRUMMER* MAGAZINE

Meanwhile, *Drummer* was helping create the very leather culture it reported on. In 1978, when a gay book selling 5,000 copies was considered a bestseller, *Drummer* had surged to a monthly print run of 42,000 copies which, with a pass-along rate of at least one more reader per copy, was a potential audience of 80,000. So I suggested introducing several of Thom's poems to drum up publicity for him with new readers. In the 1960s, good authors who once knew better words saw the pop-culture value of four-letter words and crossed over to publishing in men's mass-market lifestyle magazines that paid better than literary journals. Jack Kerouac, Gore Vidal, Norman Mailer, and Gabriel García Márquez wrote for *Playboy.* Tom Wolfe, Terry Southern, and Tennessee Williams wrote for *Esquire.*

But Thom blinked about the aspirations of *Drummer*, perhaps on principle against writing "occasional" poetry, perhaps for the sake of protecting future awards and grants, or perhaps because he could not see the perfect destiny of his canonical poetry reaching its most appreciative end-user audience in a gay men's adventure magazine that during twenty-four years of publication was curating a new street-view canon of erotic writing. *Drummer* was named out of Henry David Thoreau whose marching to one's own drum we quoted on every masthead, with Walt Whitman always in mind: "Your very flesh shall be a great poem."

This situation arose twenty-two years before Thom matured fully into the matter and form of *Boss Cupid* that sang free with a vivid California frankness *Drummer* would have lapped up. Maybe he thought his imported mid-century literary restraint might not pass hardcore erotic muster with unrestrained smart-ass leathermen subscribers who were the wised-up sons of the bikers he limned in his 1957 poem, "On the Move."

He crafted that poem around "Black Denim Trousers and Motorcycle Boots," the 1955 hit song by Jerry Leiber and Mike Stoller, that played for years as an identity anthem on leather-bar juke boxes. In his 1957 poem, "Elvis Presley," he wrote about pop-culture derivations in terms of Elvis, and, I think, himself: "Distorting hackneyed words in hackneyed songs / He turns revolt into a style…" As if anticipating the storyboards of Hollywood biker-movies spawned in the 1960s by *The Wild One*, he kick-started this motorcycle poem, "On the Move," with a shimmering long shot of vaguely Nazi leather bikers riding "on motorcycles, up the road, they come:…bulges…goggles…gleaming jackets…damned…half animal…self-defined."

That poem of scooter trash manufacturing "both machine and soul" was also sparked by brutalist motorcyclist Marlon Brando who was the butch version of the sensitive James Dean. Brando, the original-recipe "Boss Cupid," was the atavistic leather biker with a thousand pounds of hot-steel combustion power thrusting between his thighs in *The Wild One*. That film of biker identity and independence was based on the 1947 Hollister Riot that was for bikers what the 1969 Stonewall Riot was for queers.

When Dean went to meet Brando for the first time, he duded himself up in the same off-the-rack leather jacket, boots, gloves, and cap Brando wore in the film. Thom's subtitle for "On the Move" was the determined "Man, You Gotta Go"—a line declaimed by Brando in *The Wild One*. Thom's phallic images of centaur-bikers are sourced similarly in that movie: "…the Boys /…their hum / Bulges to thunder held by calf and thigh." A flirtatious girl named Mildred asks Brando, "What are you rebelling against?" Brando sneers: "Whatcha got?"

Our rebel readers, who were also boning up on the straight biker magazine *Easyriders*, would have cheered, not challenged, a Top Gunn for writing a really rockin' "unsettled motorcyclist's vision (of his own death)" or two. Thom had a fluid homosurreal point of view that made him able to write as top, bottom, or versatile—precisely what master, slave, and mutualist readers wanted and expected. In "Jack Straw's Castle," like a boy sitting in the curving infinity between facing barbershop mirrors, he wrote his trilocation of his astral self: "I am the man on the rack. / I am the man who puts the man on the rack. / I am the man who watches the man who puts the man on the / rack."

I had thought to pair four of his poems with four Mapplethorpe photographs the way I had written four poems in *Drummer* 30, June 1978, to caption four photographs by Arthur Tress who later lensed portraits of Thom and me separately in 1995 and 1999. I was planning my

"Mapplethorpe issue" in September's *Drummer* 24 to introduce Robert to international leather readers, and thought to showcase Thom at the same time. I felt he might be open to it because with his brother Ander Gunn he had created the book *Positives* in 1966 which was a collection of his sibling's photographs each captioned with a poem. I did not know then what years later in 2003 he told my neighbor Chuck Forester in "Re-Experiencing Thom Gunn": "The book [*Positives*] includes 'very little great poetry, and I was never sure if I was writing poems or captions.'" A picture worth a thousand words can easily overwhelm a short poem. Perhaps he simply did not want to play second-fiddle and caption yet another photographer in *Drummer* 24 or the artists in my special September 1978 arts issue, *Son of Drummer*.

The poems I considered publishing were his then most accessible to general readers. "My Sad Captains," with its reckoning of sex partners past, was to be the first poem as well as the feature title of the poetry photo spread, followed with the born-to-lose biker boy's initiation in "Black Jackets"; the homomasculine uniform fetish in "The Corporal"; and the tattoo ritual in "Blackie, the Electric Rembrandt."

Having just commissioned Robert to shoot a bespoke cover for *Drummer* 24, *Authentic Biker for Hire*, to introduce his work, I pictured Thom writing a bespoke poem more explicitly erotic to match the new 1970s sophistication around the art genre of pornography. How wonderful the synthesis of Thom and the *lingua franca* of leather culture if he had written "a *Drummer* poem." As editor, I thought he had a tongue for the territory.

In "At the Center," he wrote an LSD love poem to the mind-altering ambience of Folsom Street whose sex-magic mystique was illuminated nightly, he lyricized, by the beacon of the huge Hamm's Brewery sign, with its giant sparkling rooftop beer glass, a holy grail, a totem for Thom, fourteen stories high, lit by five thousand golden bulbs continually filling and draining like a water-sports trophy cup.

He was a fan of *Drummer* and sometimes commented on writing or illustrations he enjoyed. So he was tempted, but he was conflicted like my dear James Purdy, whose agent did not want Purdy's work in the new erotic magazines. We were all assessing the meaning and value of the gay culture we were inventing in that first decade of liberation after Stonewall. The first slick gay magazines with subscribers only just started up around 1975, and gay book publishers around 1984. So why couldn't Thom's words have been stirred into *Drummer* the way Robert Duncan stirred up Thom's texts in his 1972 sequence "Poems from the Margins of

Thom Gunn's *Moly*." Duncan thought that one's writing should arise out of one's reading which is a creativity similar to one's writing rising out of one's orgasm. Thom, a visionary drug-tripper, huffing hallucinatory amyl nitrite while making notes and manhandling himself, sometimes wrote nude in a jockstrap penning popper-unlocked glyphs and lines of poetry.

Then something curious happened, perhaps because Thom wanted to sample the force field of being published in *Drummer,* which published fantasies to help readers deal with adversities caused by homophobia. *Drummer,* for instance, spun the cold fear of cops into hot cop worship that relieved some of the anxiety of gay PTSD.

The public poet had a private urge toward fiction. As an undergraduate at Cambridge in the 1950s, he wrote three experimental novels, and in San Francisco in the late 1960s, he drafted an unpublished erotic story, now in his archives, called "San Francisco Romance."

Shortly after I kited a soft pitch for his poems, an envelope with no return address arrived at my desk with a typed manuscript for a short story titled "Star Clone" which I published alongside photos by Robert Mapplethorpe and drawings by Rex in *Son of Drummer.* I illustrated "Star Clone"—which focused on cop worship—with drawings of my longtime friend, Dan Dufort, the leatherman, and Gay Games physique winner who had posed for Los Angeles artist Ralph Richter.

The short story's byline cited the author as "Sam Browne" which was also the name of a much fetishized black leather belt, a regulation police/military belt with a narrow leather strap passing from the left waist up diagonally across the chest and over the right shoulder. There was a measure of internal evidence in the story that Thom could be the author. He had written in "Blackie, Electric Rembrandt" about a young man, getting tattooed with stars, becoming "starlike." However, still respecting what was left of our gentlemanly discretion of the midcentury, and in keeping with the tacit balance of our relationship, I did not push the point of authorship, and was happy to publish the sci-fi story whose hook was akin to the dial-up teleportation of sex partners, like a foreshadowing of Grindr, in the 1976 British film *Logan's Run.*

I figured in our gentlemen's agreement that Thom knew that I knew what he knew what I would suspect about authorship, and he trusted I would do right by his story and not edit a word of it. He was fully aware that *Drummer* had published fiction by our mutual friend, gay literary pioneer Sam Steward, who had helped Alfred Kinsey with his culture-rattling book, *Sexual Behavior in the Human Male.* That book alerted the nineteen-year-old Thom in England to sex in America. In 1948, the same year Jack Kerouac coined the phrase "Beat Generation" which alerted Thom to San Francisco, Kinsey's book topped the bestseller lists alongside a literary novel that also raised consciousness about American homosexuality, Gore Vidal's *The City and the Pillar*.

When I was playing literary detective years later, my friend the late Robert Prager—an open-hearted starving artist who lived in a tenement flat he called a gallery at 568 Natoma Street in the heart of the leather district South of Market—wrote to me on June 14, 2013:

> My filing system still hasn't recovered from the disaster it suffered the last time I moved. My question concerns *Son of Drummer* which it appears was published in 1978. I'm looking for the Table of Contents. [There wasn't one.] This is because Thom Gunn wrote a story that was published in it under a pseudonym. At his last poetry reading at the Main Library, I waited until all the poetry mavens had their books signed and Thom and I were alone. Then I brought out my copy of *Son of Drummer* for him to sign his short story. This was the one time in the 8 years Thom and I were friends that he was genuinely angry at me. He was worse than angry. He was furious. "Who else knows about this? Did you tell the guys at The Magazine about it? [The venerable gay archive store "The Magazine," 920 Larkin Street, San Francisco, owned for fifty years by author Bob Mainardi and historian Trent Dunphy] Did you tell your writer friends?" Thom wanted to know how I found out about this in the first place. He forgot he told me himself a few years earlier.
>
> "I thought you said you didn't care about your literary reputation," I taunted him.
>
> "I don't, but that would be like feeding people false information."
>
> After the thing at the Library was over, Thom and I automatically started walking to the Hole in the Wall Saloon. His anger didn't start to subside until after we had crossed Mission Street.

Six days later, on June 20, 2013, Prager wrote:

> You're right. "Star Clone" is the story Thom Gunn was ashamed of. As I recall it, there's a remodeled South of Market building in the story [a flophouse sex hotel] called "the Arnett."

The "Arnett" reference is to Thom's druggy pal, artist Chuck Arnett, one of the co-founders of the Tool Box bar, and a frequent contributor to *Drummer*. Thom's "My Sad Captains" could also serve as the forever caption for the powerful leather mural Arnett, collected by Andy Warhol, painted on the wall of the Tool Box.

That bar and that mural of leathermen silhouettes became world-famous five years before Stonewall in the June 24, 1964, issue of *Life* magazine which was like an engraved invitation to closeted refugees everywhere on the globe to migrate to the sanctuary of San Francisco where Thom, resident for ten years, welcomed the new talent with a gimlet eye.

In terms of gay spaces like leather bars which are universally black-painted rooms lit with red bulbs, it is worth noting the rise and fall of the Tool Box which was Thom's local pub as soon as it opened in 1961. When the Tool Box at 4th and Harrison was bulldozed for urban renewal in 1971, photographer Mike Kelley (two e's) shot an eyewitness black-and-white picture of the one last standing wall—that "Arnett mural wall," that monochrome cave painting, standing cool, tough, and unbowed over the romantic ruins that were not unlike the bombed-out ruins the teenaged Thom saw during the war. For two years, at the corner of Fourth and Harrison, drivers coming down the off-ramp from the freeway were greeted by Arnett's somber dark shadows, each twenty feet tall, those Lascaux cave drawings of Neanderthal, primal, kick-ass leathermen.

In 1975, David Barnard, a 1960s friend of Thom and a dancer with the San Francisco Ballet (as was Arnett), raised funds for his startup dance company, the No Theater, by publishing Kelley's photo as a collectible postcard titled: "The Wall, 1975: Chuck Arnett's Tool Box Mural." Kelley's photo, with Arnett's archetypal dozen of Boss Cupids, could cover almost any Gunn book.

Prager concluded:

> When I met Thom, he told me that when he decided he wanted to try being a writer, he wasn't sure if he wanted to write poetry or prose. This would have been during the early 1950s. I don't think this story is the kind of prose Thom meant.

"STAR CLONE" INTERNAL TEXT EVIDENCE OF GUNN AUTHORSHIP

"Star Clone" is a 1978 sci-fi story taken from "federal files," set five years ahead in a futuristic 1983 San Francisco, and narrated by "Joe Robson," age twenty-eight, whose name is also the name of two popular British footballers of Thom's childhood. Coincidentally, the year before this story was written, Robson Books published Thom's time-bending reminiscences of his school days in *My Cambridge*. For sex adventuring, Joe Robson subversively re-purposes his dead father's secret invention, a Transistor, that opens the "Transistor Time Travel Portal" that is Alice's Looking Glass tricked out in leather drag and narcotized by Grace Slick.

Drawn by news of poet Lawrence Ferlinghetti founding San Francisco's City Lights Bookstore in 1953, Thom in 1954 immigrated into the American leather scene, just as postwar pop culture changed. He arrived one year after Marlon Brando's *The Wild One*; and one year before Elvis's first hit which led to his poem, "Elvis Presley"; and one year before James Dean's death on a highway near Salinas, two hours south of Thom in San Francisco, hearing the news on his transistor radio. The invention of those tiny transistor radios freed rock-and-roll rebels from the big furniture radios dominating their parents' living rooms, and introduced portable music to gay beaches everywhere.

To travel ten years back to the Folsom Barracks of 1973, Joe retreats to his soundproof playroom with its fetish-gear closet and a mirrored fourth wall that serves as the portal in "The small and exclusive apartment house where he lived, 'The Arnett,'...built inside the carefully restored frame of a men's bathhouse that had been gutted by fire some years earlier."

Here, the author of the story is prescient about the inevitable: the Barracks did indeed burn down in the shocking Folsom Street fire of July 11, 1981, just as the news of gay plague first hit the headlines. Joe takes "a capsule of the latest illegal erotic drug...known on the street as Itch...a development from the drugs MDA and MDM." In his Castro Street poem, "In the Post Office," Thom identifies sexual tension as an "itch."

Trips on a micro-dose of those two drugs lasted approximately as long as the trip permitted by the Transistor that Joe's father had limited to two-hour tours traveling only one or two weeks into the past or the future. In real-life San Francisco, this smooth drug cocktail was popular with leathermen who wanted to launch short early-evening trips, to go up and down with enhanced sex experiences on week nights, and still wake up fit for work the next day.

Joe has planned his virtual-reality "...trip into the past, as an exercise in sexual nostalgia: he would return to the bathhouse before its burning and spend two hours terrorizing the studs of ten years ago. He had worked out the layout in relation to his apartment with enough accuracy to ensure that by placing the Transistor about four feet from this side of his wall he would emerge into the corridor of the second floor of the bathhouse in 1973."

This is the same taxis and kinesis maneuver, measuring rooms at home to match rooms at the Barracks, that Thom does creating the virtual reality in his mind's eye in "Jack Straw's Castle."

In short, Joe is staging a Mirror Fuck, the narcissistic ritual of solo role-playing to transform one's plastic self into alternative, idealized, erotic selves through fetish costume and shadow lighting while posing alone with pills, pot, and poppers in front of a mirror.

The wishful author describes his avatar Joe grooving on his ideal self. "He took in what he saw—the big well-built body with the baby face, the short blond hair, the transparent blue eyes...."

Quintessentially, the leatherman he depicts is very much the leatherboy drawing that years later was commissioned for the cover of *Boss Cupid*.

In a way, this is Thom's "theory of poses." He wrote in *My Cambridge* that he liked masks, literal and metaphorical, for role playing. Joe decides not to wear a mask while his visitors arrive each wearing "a black leather mask with slits for eyes, nose, and mouth."

The story also references Jean Cocteau's film *Blood of the Poet* in which the artist is transported through a mirror to a hotel as bawdy as a bathhouse.

In *Passages of Joy*, Thom wrote that sex, music, and men helped him lose himself. Joe takes "a last appreciative look at himself in the mirror before...adjusting the timer to the year, day, hour, and minute of his arrival in the past. He took in what he saw." His Mirror-Fuck reflection, the narrator writes, "made a great image for beating off in front of."

Then suddenly, in a revealing ritual of homosurrealism that perfectly fits its poet-author, Joe tries to leave self behind, as Thom wrote in *Passages of Joy*. Instead, Joe's sense of self divides into the first of two masked visitors who are his self, two versions of his self, making for the same configuration of three selves as in Thom's man on the rack who puts the man on the rack who watches the man put the man on the rack.

Being topped by a California Highway Patrol cop in leather, and by a logger, Joe endures and enjoys a vivid ordeal of S&M toys and tortures detailed with enthusiasm and authenticity by the story's sadomasochistic author, Sam Browne/Thom who—no doubt, turned on, as noted, in the jockstrap he wore when writing nude, and masturbating to masochistic visions while writing erect—says about male rites of endurance, "He rode the pain like a man." Erotic literature begins with one stroke of the penis.

Joe in an ecstasy of self-examination wonders with pleasure if he is suffering a kind of revenge torture with whips, needles, and catheters. "It was only a few days since Joe and a leather buddy had a sixteen-year-old hustler stretched on it [a ladder used as a rack] for a long afternoon. They found him in Levi's and engineer boots on a street corner downtown, doped out on one of the new erotic drugs, and figured that this was an unparalleled educational opportunity for the kid."

The two men know Joe so perfectly well that he asks at the end of the story: "Are you humans or robots?" The question, asked during the Age of Clones, suits Thom's sense of sarcasm, popular in 1970s bar culture, questioning whether "S&M" leathermen were "Sadist and Masochist" players or just "Stand and Model" poseurs.

When the cop removes his leather mask, he answers: "I'm just you, Joe Robson, a week in the future...And he's you too, but *two* weeks in the future." When the logger then peels his mask, the author states it's "Joe's face duplicated again." Joe asks, "But whose idea was it?" The logger gives Joe an answer that is as perfect as any answer six characters in search of an author could give Pirandello: "Yours, of course."

SIX DEGREES OF SEPARATION: ROUGH-TRADE VIDEOS

Thom and I shared genial respect. I knew who he was. He knew who I was. In his poem "Carnal Knowledge" in his first book, *Fighting Terms* (1954), he had written the copacetic base line that nurtured equanimity man to man in his diversely layered, and very intuitive, relationships: "You know I know you know I know you know." What was spoken and what was left unspoken was always agreeable.

From 1985 to 1995, I directed and photographed many leather and fetish feature videos spun out of *Drummer* for my boutique studio, Palm Drive Video, for palm-driving men. One day, opening mail, I discovered an order from Thom for four titles. It was cool he liked my offbeat movies. He enjoyed homomasculine porn and collected his spank bank of VHS cassettes at home to use as educational television to warm up visiting young men, like the sixteen-year-old tied on the ladder, who for money and drugs and daddy issues chased older men, a fetish identity category first identified in the pages of *Drummer* 24, September 1978.

In those days, we were all tribally incestuous, sexually and creatively, well within the six degrees of separation. In that *Drummer* 24 feature, for instance, I wrote against ageism in praise of the thirty-seven-year-old pornstar Richard Locke, the legendary Daddy, who soon became the lover of Thom's true-true-true friend, Allan Noseworthy—with whom I had worked producing the Creative Power Foundation's *Night Flight* party in 1977. In 1984, Thom invited Noseworthy, dying of AIDS, into his home for hospice care until the desperate night Thom whisked Allan to the Emergency Room. Gunn scholar Michael Nott observed that Thom wrote an elegy for Allan that was the first poem in what became *The Man with Night Sweats*. I checked the Palm Drive files, and Thom had ordered several films, including two starring mutual friends. I immediately called him and told him I would comp him any videos he wanted.

In his virtual treatment for a film, *The Man with Night Sweats*, Thom, the homomasculinist, "adored / The risk that made robust / A world of wonders in / each challenge to the skin." From the PDV catalogue, Thom selected tough-guy solo films featuring rugged men dominating and exciting the viewer with verbal abuse spoken directly into the camera. He was masochistically thrilled by ruffians who made him cum. In "Lines for a Book," he wrote this line twice: "I think of all the toughs through history / and thank heaven they lived, continually."

Like E. M. Forster who took up smoking because his rent boys smoked, Thom, nearly always photographed with a film-noir cigarette, had a personal smoking habit that grew into a fetish in the 1950s imitating Marlon Brando and James Dean and continued because the young street trade he liked smoked and bonded in masculine identity over cigarettes—"Got a light?"—as did Robert Mapplethorpe, who smoked Kool Menthols because Kool was the brand favored by young black men.

A WALKING TOUR OF THOM GUNN'S SAN FRANCISCO

It's easy to map a "Walking Tour of Thom Gunn's San Francisco." He used SOMA's Folsom Street as his main drag. In "Transients and Residents," he wrote that signature line: "I like loud music, bars, and boisterous men." For sex, he went cruising north across the Market Street divide from South of Market in nearby neighborhoods like the druggy Tenderloin and the draggy Polk Street. He knew the City and celebrated its street grid in "Night Taxi." Randall Mann in his venerational eightieth birthday salute to Thom, "A Memoir of Reading," in the *Kenyon Review* quoted San Francisco poet August Kleinzahler who edited the 2007 book, *Selected Poems by Thom Gunn*. Mann says that Kleinzahler "…in his lovely essay on Gunn, wrote, 'To travel with Thom was to participate in an erotic mapping of San Francisco out of the bus window.'"

Thom had a taste for young skateboard hustlers. He universalized rough street trade from Rome to home when he rhapsodized about Caravaggio's "insolent young whores," "pudgy cheats," "sharpers," and "stranglers" in his painterly open-form poem, "In Santa Maria del Popolo," the first entry in *My Sad Captains*.

He cruised Market Street for the rent boys working inside the dark shadows of the Old Crow bar, and posing outdoors on the sidewalk, framed, as if in a huge Caravaggio canvas *vivant*, against the big plate-glass windows of Flagg Brothers Shoes, a triangle building that stood on the corner of "Market at Turk"—which is the title of one of his Market Street poems. His "San Francisco Streets" mentions Flagg Brothers and ridicules Castro Street for being too middle-class.

Wearing the mask of Verlaine, with a salute to Alfred Jarry's *Ubu Roi*, he wrote the hustler-bar poem, "Shit: An Essay on Rimbaud," and cruised Polk Street, called *Polkstrasse*, where at the southeast corner of Sutter Street his young rim-ram beaux "with sweet sticky ardor" loitered against the moody display windows of the sweet little lighting shop at 1201 Polk whose sign over their heads read "Any Object Made into a Lamp." The Flagg Brothers building at 950 Market, now torn down, was featured in the film *Interview with the Vampire* by Anne Rice whose more erotic work was separated out, as Thom's could have been, from her "literary" writing and excerpted for publicity in *Drummer*.

Thom, who had endured the universal gay legacy of scally schoolmates bullying him in Britain, carried the internalized PTSD of his boyhood masochism into his endless itch for American rough trade and for the rough-trade photos and videos of David Hurles whose mail-order company, Old Reliable, eroticized angry bully boys who, speaking and spitting directly into the camera, were speedy, rude, trash-talking young graduates of the best reform schools in America.

On October 2, 1997, Thom sent me an envelope including a postcard with a leather photo by Kim Hanson from the SoHo Galleries, 1216 Valencia Street, San Francisco. He wrote: "Dear Jack, The parcel of goodies [four Palm Drive Video features] arrived yesterday. Thank you! Enclosed is what I think I owe you—if I'm out, let me know and I'll send you the rest/ Best, Thom." I tore up his check.

The candid photo that my frequent houseguest, British art critic Edward Lucie-Smith, shot of Thom and me together at the 1996 Folsom Street Fair captured our mellow friendship. I drove Edward aka Ted to the Fair to meet Thom in front of the Powerhouse bar, which years before had been poet Ron Johnson's No Name. Thom and Ted had first met when both poets were angry-ish young men in the gritty postwar Austerity Britain of the 1950s. We found Thom in a casual group of our mutual pals surrounded by a milling crowd of 400,000 leatherfolk, many of whom had grown up reading Thom and *Drummer*. Thom at that moment had been published for forty years, and *Drummer* had been in monthly publication for twenty-one years.

As eyewitness to the access offered by the Folsom Fair mixer, poet Kevin Killian (1952-2019), co-author of *Poet Be Like God: Jack Spicer and the San Francisco Renaissance*, recalled how at the Fair he first met Thom leaning with the sole of one boot propped up flat against a lamppost—much like the photo of Thom on the cover of *Letters of Thom Gunn*, edited by Clive Wilmer, Michael Nott, and August Kleinzahle. Folsom Fair, San Francisco's version of Burning Man, was what it always partly is: an annual health-and-safety check-up in broad daylight of us pallid creatures of the night.

For a dozen years, I shot street-fair video documentaries, my visual journals, that show the gone-with-the-wind leathermen and local-color Thom reveled in. To keep Thom alive and accessible on screen, what a heritage kick it might be for a new-generation queer film student to cut a fifteen-minute montage flick with Thom, unseen, speaking a voice-over from existing audio recordings matched with video footage that illustrates the *mise en scene* of specific poems like "At the Barriers."

It was fascinating to watch my friends, Thom and Ted, two senior Brit poets abroad in America, checking each other out, Thom was sixty-seven. Ted was sixty-three. Later, Thom said something nice about Ted; and Ted cocked an eyebrow's worth of attitude about Thom "from Cambridge." Ted later told author William Wootten for *The Alvarez Generation*: "We Oxford poets had an inferiority complex about our Cambridge contemporaries. The chief cause was Thom Gunn....[who had] a bully-boy strut."

However, on that day, together, full of chat, they represented a literary reunion from 1950s London when, with Ted Hughes, Philip Larkin, and others, they were part of "The Movement" that preferred poetry sensual in content and traditional in form. By the 1970s, *Drummer* readers preferred writing sexual in content and free in form.

OUR WEEKEND TRIPPING AT "THE GEYSERS": THE BIRTH OF A POEM

In Thom Gunn's lifelong diary begun when he was fourteen, he noted that on the weekend of July 15-16, 1972, he and I with David Sparrow and several mutual friends took a magical mystery tour to the dynamic Geysers, the world's largest geothermal field—famous for its run-down hot-springs resort in the Mayacamas Mountains, seventy miles north of

San Francisco where for 12,000 years the Pomo, Wappo, and Miwok peoples had built steam baths. For a hundred years, the Geysers's natural steam and mud baths had been a vacation draw for rich nineteenth-century San Franciscans, and for authors like Bret Harte and Mark Twain and Jack London who wrote about the area. The site became popular with hippies in the 1960s before shutting down in the early 1970s.

We were there, romancing its ruins, in its last days before nearby utility companies and cities began disposing of their wastewater by piping it in to vaporize it deep in the geysers which were running out of steam. As an immigrant living successively among immigrant Beats in North Beach and immigrant hippies in the Haight and immigrant leathermen on Folsom Street, Thom was sensitized to cultures evolving around him. He responded on drugs—pot, acid, mescaline—to the lingering presence of the Native Americans who had lived at the Geysers which, in decline for years, was no scrubbed Swiss spa. No health department would have approved.

Over the years, the Geysers slid down hill socially and literally till all that we hiked into with tents and sleeping bags and coolers of campfire food was the small mountain stream with its shallow wading pools, the thermal mud-wallow baths, and the ghost-town remains of a weathered wood building on whose unpainted barn-interior framing, at night, sat hundreds of hippie-dippie candles swirling smoke into a psychedelic light show around a hundred moonbeams shafting down on naked bodies through punctures in the roof.

Bike runs—motorcycle rides for weekend outings in the woods, much like Brando's "Hells Angels" bike run to a hick town in *The Wild One*—were very popular ways to get out of the City. So a group of us, all friends together from Folsom Street, decided to drive to the Geysers to camp out, trip a bit, and get in touch with nature and the cosmos in a kind of back-to-basics homomasculine sex party and psycho-active religious experience.

That first weekend after the long Fourth of July weekend, David and I drove together, but I can't recall if Jim Hart and Roy Siniard and Jack Garcia drove their bikes or a truck, or how Thom, who owned a motorcycle, traveled with us. He may have climbed once again into the Land Cruiser with David and me. Years later in 1990, Thom told me that Roy Siniard, crippled by unbearable arthritis, committed suicide. For us nighthawks, daylight in the foothills of Gold Country was a shock, a sunburn, and a picnic.

I shot seven frames of a roll of 35mm color transparencies of some of us wading naked in the pools of the stream. Out of discretion, David and I did not shoot Thom, who was a public person privately high on acid. Actually, it's a wonder any pictures were shot at all. We were almost too blissfully stoned to focus. Film was expensive to buy and difficult to develop because of photo-lab censorship in the years before Harvey Milk opened his Castro Camera shop in 1972.

In the 1970s, cameras were not cool because of entrapment, blackmail, and privacy. One camera could empty a gay bar in an instant. Shooting people who were gay and spaced out was a bridge too far in that period before glossy gay magazines of the mid-1970s liberated us by printing pictures not of models (which had always been done), but of newly uncloseted leathermen who looked like, and often were, the readers. *Drummer* made graphic Whitman's class-defying passion for erotic bonding with ordinary men. When I finished shooting that roll of thirty-six exposures two weeks later, the developed slides of that weekend returned imprinted "August 1972."

Off camera, Thom, chatting, nude, hung nicely, and uncut, mixed in, and together we wandered, wading with strangers, naked up the creek, "with tan black and pink, firm shining bodies," smelling the rotten-egg sulphur of percolating little cinder cones. At night, under the stars, in the wooden barn filled with candles, and the "drifting fume of dope," we gay men, we "bearded boys," sank into the hot mud watching the other mostly straight males and females watching back. Primal in the mud, we had a hippie openness to all comers, joining in, sharing a joint, flirting, sniffing poppers, playing with strangers, as Thom did with "pubescent girl and bearded boy," falling back into the thermal muck, feeling divine under the stars, him writing: "I am raw meat / I am a god."

Thom was forty-three. I was thirty-three. We admired the lovely next generation of young American males and females playing it cool in California—with all that liberated "mystique" means, especially to a poet who rejoiced that America "changed everything for me." Tripping in our altered minds at alpha level, the mind's most creative level, we sat side-by-side communing in the mud, the stream, and the hot sun on the creek bank. Thom with vine leaves in his hair, and a pencil in his hand, was a hippie holy man changing the water of words into the wine of poetry. He subverted Alfred, Lord Tennyson's love-me-tender lyric, "I am part of all that I have met," into the love-me-tougher haka, "I am part of all / hands take / hands tear and twine."

Jonathan Levin noted in "Thom Gunn," *British Writers: Supplement IV*, 1997, that "The Geysers" is "a four-part poem about community, formed largely by the mutual pleasure people take in nature and in each other."

As a professor teaching literature in 1972, I appreciated my eyewitness front-row seat, and my sleeping bag next to him, that long slow weekend observing the magic of his being and becoming, watching the poet with his sleight of hand divining runes of mud, flesh, and stars. The *mise en scene* I was reservedly documenting with tiny frames of film, he was documenting with the largesse of his poetry. Soon after, he wrote "The Geysers," that enigmatic recital of our, or more properly, his, sensual weekend that for him was so transfiguring; but what's a poet for if not that?

THOM'S LOCAL PUB. BARS AS ART GALLERIES

In our Folsom Street Bloomsbury, South of Market, the leather crowd played musical bar stools in search of creative sex and fetish. Over the years, Thom parked his bike in front of the dozen leather bars up and down the Miracle Mile of Folsom Street where from before the Gold Rush to the 1960s itinerant working men, sailors new in town, merchant marines, and military men during the world wars holed up in the flophouse hotels and boarding houses that we, in our turn, gentrified into our gay bathhouses and bars. In the 1906 earthquake, hundreds of single men died South of Market, some trapped in the wooden wreckage begging to be shot before the advancing fires reached them. That haunting inheritance of proletarian beauty and terror underscored our gay role-playing at being roustabout bikers, construction workers, cops, sailors, soldiers, and other Village People.

When Thom arrived in 1954 at the height of the anti-gay witch-hunt led by the cross-dressing gay traitor J. Edgar Hoover (Director of the FBI from 1924 to 1972), he mingled with Beat poets who, in new reporting by historian Michael Flanagan in "Beats, Bohemians, and Bars," had been socializing at saloons like Vesuvio where Jack Spicer served up Lorca poems, and Gino & Carlo's in North Beach, and Jose Sarria's drag bar, the Black Cat, 710 Montgomery Street. Thom also gargled at the Gangway, Tony Tavarossi's Why Not, and Jack's on the Waterfront, a leather bar (1952-1963) located along the Embarcadero skid row near the east end of Folsom Street.

As gay identity bars emerged, Thom became a fixture at the Tool Box co-founded in 1961 by Chuck Arnett, a former swing dancer from the national tour of *Bye Bye Birdie*, whose popular drawings, like his hypodermic

Santa Fix for the Fey-Way Gallery Christmas party, introduced the needle to South of Market Street sex. Thom was also a familiar face at Febe's leather bar founded in 1966 by his pal, fisting pioneer Jack Haines, who also founded the crystal palace of the Slot Hotel, for midcentury gents like Thom who were teenagers on the cusp of coming out in the 1940s. Thom turned twenty-one in 1950 and moved to the Bay Area to take on his creative writing fellowship at Stanford when he was twenty-four.

Febe's and its Museum of Unnatural History, outrageously extant at 1501 Folsom Street from 1966 to 1986, was named after the magical Goddess of the Dark Moon, and was famous for enshrining artist Mike Caffee's literally iconic statue, the *Leather David*, which, sculpted from Sam Steward's original pitch to Caffee, was like a plaster "Boss Brando."

The affable Caffee, who dropped LSD at parties with Thom, put boots, Levi's, and a leather cap and jacket on Michelangelo's *David*. Camp or not, copies were on sale upstairs over Febe's in the sex-toy and popper shop, A Taste of Leather, owned by the biblically named Nick O'Demus. In 1970, when my monthly rent was fifty dollars, I thought twice about buying a plaster copy that cost $125.

Thom had been in the city fifteen years when such incoming leather gentrification changed the light-industrial area South of Market. During the 1970s, the sheer numbers of bohemians arriving in the slums of SOMA turned the Folsom leather bars into art galleries with monthly shows and poetry performances no straight gallery would handle. In its arts' patronage, the Ambush bar, for instance, mailed out engraved invitations for its launch party for two of my leather-fiction books based on *Drummer*. In 1978, Thom was a guest artist in attendance when *Drummer* leather poet and Oscar Streaker Robert Opel opened the first gay gallery in San Francisco, Fey-Way Studio, where he was murdered in 1979.

Thom's pub crawl in the 1970s included the Folsom Prison at 1898 Folsom; the No Name at 1347 Folsom (later called the Brig and the Powerhouse); the Balcony at 2166 Market Street; and the Ambush at 1351 Harrison, a more relaxed hippie-leather bar popular for its art shows and pinball machines that inspired his "*Bally Power Play*" which was coincidentally illustrated by San Francisco leather artist Rex in his pointillist drawing (dated 1/26/79) of four brutalist leathermen standing around a pinball machine in the Ambush.

After the first Lone Star bar at 7th and Howard was destroyed in the 1989 Loma Prieta earthquake, Thom hung out at the new Lone Star founded, at 1354 Harrison Street across from the Ambush, by original Rainbow Motorcycle Club (RMC) member, Rick Redewell. In *Boss*

Cupid, Thom assessed the blue-collar bears throwing their weight around with curvaceous avoirdupois as the new fetish in his poem "Front Bar at the Lone Star" first published in the *New Yorker*, May 18, 1997.

In "Front Bar," the elder-biker Thom, observing bikers gaining weight, declared his appreciation of the Lone Star where body diversity was a welcome new turn-on well beyond the Castro clone look: "Fat flesh egg / 400 lbs. of him / set firmly on / the toothpick stool. / Fat, fat."

New words, he recognized, shifting beauty and "melting contempt," like *chubby* re-imagining *fat*, can change a liability like weight or age into sex appeal. "Styles change / The democracy of it: / eventually everyone / can hope for a turn / at being wanted."

He also partied at the CMC Carnival, the annual autumn bacchanalian party, beer bust, and wild orgy of group-sex on drugs at Seaman's Hall in SOMA where Los Angeles leathermen flew up *en masse* to fuck with San Francisco leathermen.

The CMC Carnival, a wall-to-wall *pissoir*, begun in 1966 by Thom's friend, Jack Haines, was run by the California Motor Club until closed by the City in 1979. I think the CMC chose Seaman's Hall, 350 Fremont Street, to gayify Ken Kesey's "Acid Test" parties, which Thom and Haines attended, in Golden Gate Park and the Longshoremen's Hall in North Beach in 1966. The CMC Carnival was the inspiration for Thom's poem, "Saturnalia."

To illustrate the homomasculine fraternity around the bars, I published a Robert Pruzan photo of Thom standing outside the Ambush with Robert Mapplethorpe and photographer Crawford Barton in *Mapplethorpe: Assault with a Deadly Camera* (1994). Their clothing shows the diversity of fetish costume: Thom in Levi's jean jacket, Robert in tailored leather jacket, and Crawford in denim military shirt. Thom's look in that photo typifies his bar-days demeanor as a keen-eyed artist who was an embedded poet a decade older than most of us who did sex in public places unlike him who liked to find younger playmates for stoned sex performances in private places during his fifty years on the scene.

In the bars, he was in various combinations friendly, stoned on grass, beer in hand, tripping on acid, ready with a laugh, and always in control of himself. With dry British humour, he could confide deadpan comments with trademark smirk and squint.

Thom was a lucky sybarite who never looked like he suffered unwillingly for his art. Despite Dean and Brando, he was no romantic cliché of the tortured gay poet. He was a realist well met who got what he wanted and needed and gave as good as he got. Odd that some of his British critics, left behind looking in the rearview mirror, felt that young Thom followed his cock and moved to San Francisco and fell apart as a poet when, in fact, he kept his act together and grew his eloquent style. Did Foucault, born three years before Thom, fall apart being fisted on Folsom?

In his poem "A Map of the City," Thom states with "delight" that he would never have the "risk" of living in "luminous" San Francisco "diminished." He acted out that delight when, in pose and virtual mask, he faced the camera of Arthur Tress. In that comical 1995 photograph, an ironic, camp, and shirtless Thom sits at home cuddling to his chest a life-size ceramic "cookie jar" shaped like the head of the Man in the Moon with its lurid wide-eyes and a rampant tongue, slurping from the corner of its mouth, licking at Thom's tit. The walls behind him are papered with a collage of photos he cut from magazines featuring male faces and nude torsos and most notably Warhol's muse and superstar Joe Dallesandro.

One of his favorite bars, and mine, was the early 1970s No Name bar managed by poet Ron Johnson and his lover, photographer Mario Pirami, whose work I published on the cover of *Man2Man Quarterly* to which Thom subscribed. When Thom arrived in San Francisco, two years before Allen Ginsberg debuted *Howl*, at Jack Spicer's 6 Gallery, the bar buzz among the oft-censored Beats was about the Mattachine startup of its hands-on zine, *One: The Homosexual Magazine,* which the Post Office had just declared obscene, prohibiting its delivery by mail as a way to censor and suffocate the free press of gay citizens.

Thom fancied samizdat poetry chapbooks and underground gay zines like *Man2Man Quarterly*, Bob Mizer's *Physique Pictorial*, Richard Bulger's *Bear*, and especially Boyd McDonald's *Straight to Hell.* He also attended the two multi-media "Happenings" Ron and Mario and I produced for the participating sex-scrum crowd in the No Name in the summers of 1971 and 1972.

Thom and Ron, as famous poets important to one another, both writing while carousing in San Francisco, shared a special regard in person and in their letters. Ron Johnson (1935-1998) authored many books of poetry including his masterwork, the ninety-nine-part metaphysical poem, *ARK.* Thom wrote: "I have always thought Ron Johnson a terrific poet: everything he has written has surprised and delighted me." As did we all back then, they likely had sex on their first meeting in the 1960s after the free-love fashion of the time. Once that fundamental bond was established, our friendships, often with Ron as social secretary, entwined in our affectionate little leather fraternity of writers and artists and photographers.

For instance, in 1988 when elusive poet and RMC member Jack Sharpless died from AIDS, unpublished at thirty-eight, Ron reshuffled our grief by editing the 1989 anthology, *Presences of Mind: The Collected Books of Jack Sharpless* which was endorsed by Robert Duncan, Robert Creeley, and Guy Davenport. Kevin Killian wrote about Sharpless and our SOMA salon that "Ron Johnson and Thom Gunn both loved him." Thom's archive at UC Berkeley contains a file pertaining to Sharpless.

"LEATHERHENGE" STONE MONUMENTS OF THE LEATHER HISTORY ALLEY & CULTURAL DISTRICT

San Francisco is a fishing village with an opera where everyone knows everyone else. Thom was known as a poet by people who never read poetry. He was a famous name, but not a famous face; so he had some protection in public from starfuckers. To some locals he was a cult figure, but he seemed mostly just another leather guy like Ron Johnson who few knew, or cared, was also a celebrated poet.

When Thom walked into a bar, he bought a beer, and leaned up against the cardboard beer cases stacked like perimeter benches against walls around the pool table. Because he was not cruising so much as socializing, he was soon met by a pal or two. In the 1970s, before the Republicans defunded and dumbed down American education to kill critical thinking, many guys in the bougie leather scene were conversationally interesting because in schools they had been privileged to learn some credential other than cocksucking.

Thom kept a low observant profile in the theatrical hallways at the drug den of the Barracks which he wrote about in his homosurreal poems "1975" and "Saturday Night." In "The Corridor," he embraced such public voyeurism as a sexual pleasure that is also a social learning experience. His teleporting poetry makes me wish to be where I no longer am, and readers to wish for a trip to the scene they missed.

When angel dust (PCP) was the drug of choice, he monitored wild acts of homosurrealism similar to mime Leonard Pitt performing in the Barracks corridors costumed as a French Maid flicking naked sweaty men with a feather duster, sending them up with his question, "Wanna get dusted?"

He soaked up the power of a muscleman idol standing naked on a toilet sink, posing hardon for two dozen kneeling men worshiping his golden calves, thighs, and torso like a C. B. DeMille movie.

He marked the vitality of hungry hunters cruising through the crowded corridors of open doors, peering into each "discrete" room, as he wrote in his poem "1975," to pursue "drug-and-wrestling buddies" like fabled wild man Fred Lee in his chamois-skin Tarzan loincloth. Thom was one of the many men fascinated by sportfucking roughnecks like the lean-muscled Fred. Voyeurs stood in the hall outside Fred's room jostling and jerking and hoping to be next, held back by the single chain Fred hung across his open doorway. Every six weeks, he flew down from working on the Alaska pipeline to take on city-boy challengers—who every time they lost a wrestling match had a funny feeling that they won.

In 1976, in the virtual reality of "Jack Straw's Castle," Thom, like Joe Robson in "Star Clone," pictured the overlay "room on room on room" configurations of both his commune-home and of the maze-like hallways at the communal Barracks bath. His rooms were either "boudoir or oubliette" inhabited by transient "dream" men with "too much of the phantom to them." From my three hundred visits over nine years of play at the Barracks, Thom's "Jack Straw's Castle" seems an almost Dada vision of the Barracks he recalled while lying abed, himself dusted by angels, on psychedelic PCP.

Like the use of the gay identity words, *leatherman* and *bear*, Thom's animal imagery characterizes bathhouse primates orgying in pig piles, "buried in swine," as he wrote in *Moly* that is filled with "the nightmare of beasthood" and dogs and toads and "putting pig within" human skin.

Signs and omens of our evolving liberation fomented in the psychedelic poet's mind. Because the bars and baths filled up every semester break and summer with university professors on vacation or sabbatical, our running joke was about scholars doing research on their knees at the tubs. As a teacher, Thom enjoyed the down-low invasion and conversation of hot high-brows who raised the IQ of Folsom Street, until a hotter lad rolled by on a skateboard.

When visiting New York, Thom spent long nights at the mind-blowing Mineshaft club—the Barracks' twin—in the Meatpacking District of the West Village, writing about the "meat" and "meat district" in his incarnational poem, "The Menace," which could have been retrofitted into *Drummer* for its ethos perfectly describing homomasculine role-playing: "He is not a real soldier / but a soldier / inducted by himself / into an army of fantasy / and he greets another.... / We play without deceit / compressing symbol into fetish."

In San Francisco, he kept up with the ever-changing SOMA leather bars as well as the Balcony bar on Market Street near the Castro which he mentioned in "Another All-Night Party." The word "Balcony" was pronounced "Baloney" because of the cheap-meat pun, but mostly because the "c" had fallen off the bar sign nailed on the mansard awning over the front window, and for the sake of the joke and publicity was never repaired.

In 2010, when the San Francisco Planning Commission set out to designate SOMA as a gay cultural district, Western SOMA Task Force planners Sandra Soto-Grondona and Paul Lord, because of *Drummer*, sent me an email requesting input about who and what might be included. I submitted a dozen friends' names, among them: Thom Gunn, Ron Johnson, Tony Tavarossi, Cynthia Slater, Catholic leather priest Jim Kane, *Drummer* publisher Anthony DeBlase, and *Drummer* itself. In 2018, the City designated SOMA as a Leather and LGBTQ Cultural District.

Creating a "Leatherhenge" for pilgrimage, the District installed an artwork titled "Leather Memoir" on the ancient, and sacred, late-night cruising ground of Ringold Alley, at 9th Street, where, before the plague, motorcycle headlights steering slowly swept like prison searchlights across the *tableaux vivants* of wild outlaw leathersex between parked cars and up against chain-link fences. The design features bronze boot prints set in the sidewalk surrounded by twenty knee-high granite stones, with each bronze and each stone engraved with an honoree's name. Thom is boot print 22.

Having written since the 1960s about pagan folkways, I find it a nod to the sex and magic of S&M that the granite markers were carved from the City's recycled curbstones — many trod by Thom — because, traditionally in ancient pagan lore, crossroads were marked to curb and guide travelers with just such priapic herms and cairns, rectangular standing stones often topped with erect phalluses, to curb, guide, and define the pale, who was in the pale, and who was not.

TWO ARTISTS IN FINALE: MAPPLETHORPE AND GUNN

In 1979, I put Robert Mapplethorpe and Thom Gunn together over beers at the Eagle leather bar on the corner of 12th Street and Folsom. I had known Thom for a decade and was in the second year of a bicoastal affair with Robert who was eager to meet up with him. They were two cool artists who seemed instantly amused, wary, and mutually respectful. Robert, tutored by Patti Smith, had developed a graphic sensibility around Verlaine and Rimbaud, poets whom he could not photograph, and an urge to shoot Thom, whom he could, because as poet and celebrity, Thom was a perfect fit for his *oeuvre.*

Robert, often thinking of scoring literary "captions" for his images, would soon provide eight of his photos to illustrate a facsimile edition of Rimbaud's *A Season in Hell.* Imagine if Robert had illustrated a similar deluxe book of poetry by Thom who also embraced Rimbaud in his poem, "Shit." Such a book, in fact, might still be considered for the two artists who dramatized themselves as pagan leathermen. Robert photographed himself as the goat-footed Pan with horns in his curly hair, and Thom wrote in "Rites of Passage," his opening poem in *Moly*: "Horns bud bright in my hair. / My feet are turning hoof."

Robert was seventeen years younger than Thom and seeking to make his mark. He was more interested in shooting Thom than knowing Thom, and Thom was more interested in knowing Robert than being shot by Robert. The next year, Robert photographed Thom, and was always complementary whenever Thom's name was mentioned. That same year, San Francisco photographer Robert Pruzan lensed Thom and Robert standing together in the afternoon sun outside the Ambush bar during its April opening of a photo exhibit by Crawford Barton, one of whose books was *Beautiful Men.*

For time travelers to the past, as in Thom's story, "Star Clone," Barton's candid daylight photographs of 1970s gay life on Castro Street are time-portal illustrations of the men, faces, and places that inspired some of Thom's Street-View poems, and, if any book of his poems—that need no illustration—were to be illuminated to help entertain the reader, Crawford Barton's street images really should be considered for their apt fit.

Robert in New York sent Thom in San Francisco a copy of his portrait via gallery owner Edward DeCelle, in care of his Lawson DeCelle Gallery at 80 Langton Street in the SOMA leather district. Thom liked the suave cool of the photo which his publisher showcased, six years after Robert's death, on the cover of Thom's *Collected Poems* in 1995.

Thom's reciprocal poem about Robert, "Song of a Camera," which he dreamed up while Robert was shooting him, seems more about Robert's knife-like collages than his photos because Thom viewed Robert's process of assemblage as art akin to the linguistics of constructing a poem by adding "adverbs to verbs" bit by bit.

Without being compromised by mainstream appreciation, both artists achieved artistic, critical, and financial independence in the straight world which caused some jealousy within politically correct gay culture that was often suspicious of success outside the gay ghetto. Thom was an eyewitness at the 1990 Out/Write writers conference in San Francisco, May 3 and 4, when the crowd of authors booed keynote speaker Edward Albee for daring to say the gay literary ghetto was stifling to talent. In his letters, Thom, who also expressed reservations about the gay sensibility, had written as early as 1963 that Albee was the best dramatist in America since Tennessee Williams—who likewise succeeded beyond the gay ghetto.

Robert never received any grant or government money while alive. He earned his own way on his talent, selling his photographs while funded by his lover Sam Wagstaff. Thom supported himself with studying and lecturing at Stanford University (1954-1958) and at the University of California Berkeley (1958-1966 and 1973-2000) and with scholarly work such as his name-brand anthology *Ezra Pound Poems Selected by Thom Gunn*. Support also came through major literary cash awards from the Guggenheim, the MacArthur Foundation Genius Grant, and the David Cohen British Literature Award.

Regarding that potential book collaboration between Thom and Robert? Back in those early days of gay lib, everyone pitched a book to everyone else. Imagine Robert, who by then knew of Thom's poems framing his brother's photos in *Positives*, pitching Thom a collaboration titled *Negatives*.

In a letter dated July 2, 1984, the hesitant Thom wrote that while his verses in *Positives* were written to match the photos, he feared Robert's specific pictures would "interfere with the generality of the poems."

Robert was constantly pitching writers. In 1978, when he pitched me, he was immediately concerned that his photos top my text. An early manuscript draft of the book we began, titled *Rimshots*, is in the Mapplethorpe Archive at the Getty Museum Research Institute along with Robert's photo of Thom who wrote that the Getty Museum was the place he liked most in Los Angeles.

On December 6, 1990, Thom, assisting with research for my memoir of Robert, sent a copy of *Passages of Joy* from Cole Street to share his poem about Robert, writing all too modestly, "See page 45, but I don't expect the poem will be much to your purpose."

He also included a copy of sex-radical Boyd McDonald's popular zine, *Straight to Hell: The Manhattan Review of Unnatural Acts*, which was read for years by fans like Gore Vidal, William Burroughs, Allen Ginsberg, Tennessee Williams, Christopher Isherwood, Felice Picano, and John Waters. So Thom was in good literary company when McDonald re-printed a headshot of a bearded Thom being quoted in the San Francisco

Sentinel in which he said: "Personally, I have been far more influenced by the wit and style of *The Manhattan Review of Unnatural Acts* than I have been by the tiresome campiness of Ronald Firbank, who is usually taken as one of the chief exemplars of the aforementioned gay sensibility."

From inside the gay ghetto, an editor's note at the conclusion of Thom's satirical squib said, "As I don't know from poetry, I inquired about Thom Gunn, an Englishman now living in San Francisco. A professor who is an *STH* subscriber assures me that Gunn is highly regarded."

At the end of Thom's note to me, he wrote: "The date on the *STH* in which R. M.'s [Robert Mapplethorpe's] interview takes place is MCMLXXVII, but, as I say, I think it wasn't published until 1978. X Thom."

As Thom would have turned ninety in 2019, I turned eighty, not keeping still, writing about him. "One," he wrote, "is always nearer by not keeping still." I treasure that he signed his notes to me with an old-fashioned "X" for kisses. So warm. So cool. So unforgettable.

Drawing by Los Angeles artist Ralph Richter picturing Gay Games bodybuilding winner Dan Dufort in this illustration for Thom Gunn's attributed short story, "Star Clone," in *Son of Drummer*, September 1978.

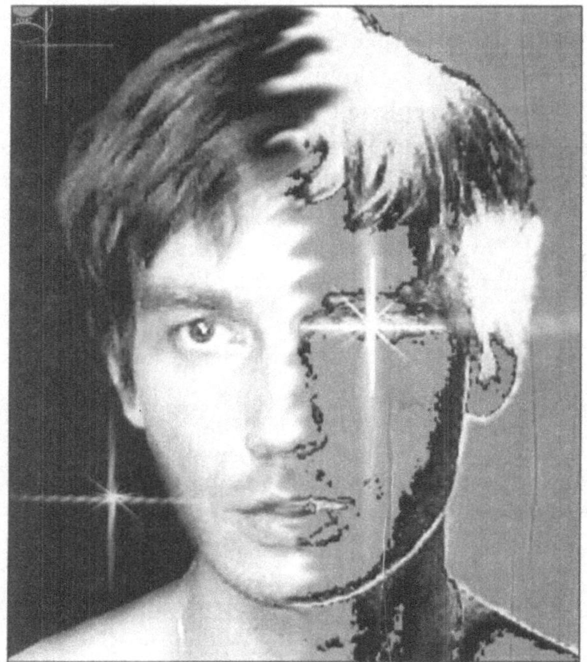

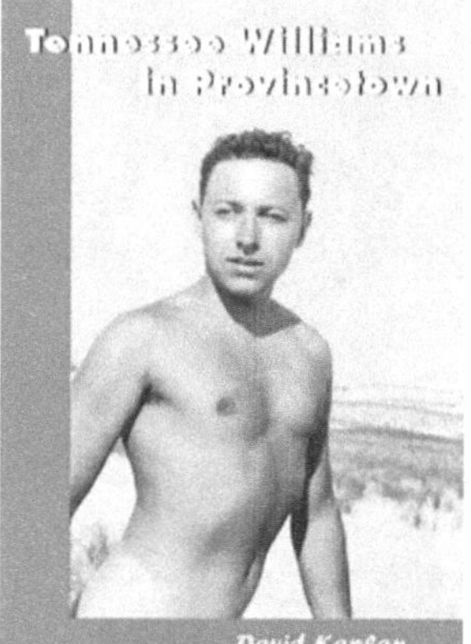

The 9/11 World Trade Center attack closed *Something Cloudy, Something Clear* leaving this *Playbill* abandoned in the deserted lobby at the Theater at St. Clement's.

Six years after 9/11, Director David Kaplan, cofounder of the Provincetown Tennessee Williams Theater Festival, published his immersive book of local color, *Tennessee Williams in Provincetown*, revealing new context and concepts about the four summers Tennessee spent in P-town writing first drafts of plays in the early 1940s when Joe Hazan shot him nude on the beach.

TENNESSEE WILLIAMS

1911-1983

"We All Live on Half of Something"

Playbill Essay for the New York Art Theater Production of *Something Cloudy, Something Clear* A Play by Tennessee Williams, Directed by Anatole Fourmantchouk, Theater at St. Clement's

Author's Note. My essay, "We All Live on Half of Something," here redux, was published in *Playbill: On Stage*, September 2001, for the New York Art Theater Production of *Something Cloudy, Something Clear.* A Play by Tennessee Williams. Directed by Anatole Fourmantchouk. Theater at St. Clement's, 423 West 46th Street.

Director Fourmantchouk, defining his unique production, gave me the typed pages of his script and explained: "The New York Art Theater is working from a copy of an original uncensored and unpublished version of the play."

This *Playbill* issue was distributed to audiences during early September previews until the run was abruptly stopped by the World Trade Center attack on 9/11. In the troubled urban aftermath, the play returned for opening night on September 20 and closed on October 1.

* * * *

There exists a famous 1941 photograph of a fit Tennessee Williams, 30, striding the beach, stripped to the waist, and wearing a sailor's white bell-bottoms. Such portrait of the artist as a young man makes Tennessee poster-boy for his autobiographical play, *Something Cloudy, Something Clear.* Set on the shifting sands of time in the Provincetown dunes, this 1941 postmodern memory play is more personal than a writer's riff on Luigi Pirandello's 1921 modernist *Six Characters in Search of an Author.* Pirandello's characters struggle like the characters in *Cloudy/Clear* and complain that they are the incomplete faces of an author who can't finalize the play for which they were invented.

In the several drafts of *Cloudy/Clear*, the very "august" Williams, an author in search of himself, duplicates and names himself as "August" after the equinox month of shooting stars during which this romantic summer-place drama occurs—and in homage to August Strindberg whose streaming *A Dream Play* he admired. The twin character framed as Tennessee/August is so personal in this "august portrait" that it may as well be played naked—as August is, at the end of act one, when he says, "Present and past, yes, a sort of double exposure."

This is an opportunity to get into the moving parts of a master playwright's head. Tennessee Williams has always been his own best script doctor. In 1941, he wrote his first draft, *Purification*, set on the Provincetown wharf where he met his golden lover for the summer, Kip Kiernan. Inspired and bedeviled by Kip's unrequited love, he soon rewrote and re-titled his second draft of their affair, *Parade, Or, Approaching the End of Summer.*

In 1962, he titled his third version of *Purification/Parade* as *Something Cloudy, Something Clear.* In 1981, the first production of that unpublished script was directed by Eve Adamson for the Jean Cocteau Repertory Company and supervised by Williams himself Off-Off Broadway at the Bouwerie Lane Theater. It was the last Williams play produced in New York City during his lifetime. In 1983, he died by accidental suffocation, age 71, choking on an inhaled plastic cap from a nasal medication bottle in the Sunset Suite at the Hotel Elysée in Manhattan.

The play's present force, coming from the past, thrusts formatively into the future. Five hundred years from now, actors—genetically wired to his texts in the manner of Marlon Brando, Vivien Leigh, Elizabeth Ashley, Vanessa Redgrave, and Anna Magnani for whom he wrote *The Rose Tattoo*—will be performing his plays, because Williams writes his words to and for the actors. Good actors play a script the way musicians play a score: live and perhaps differently each time. Once more, with feeling. In *Cloudy/Clear*, Williams, folding time, announces his double-exposure frame of remembrance of things past: "Life is all—it's just one time. It finally seems to occur at one time."

Poetically, the geography of Tennessee Williams' body is the horizon of this unabashedly gay-themed play. The author's eyes, hidden in real life by dark glasses, are title and central symbol: his left eye, cloudy before age 30 with a cataract (of lust, he said); his right eye clear (with love, he also said).

He wrote of Kip Kiernan in a 1940 letter to Donald Windham, "I lean over him in the night and memorize the geography of his body with my hands." Sex becomes the poetry of memory. Williams, always aggressive sexually, idolizes the Platonic Ideal of the perfect lover even as perfect young bodies romantically decay. Kip has brain cancer; Clare, an anagram of *clear*, clear as a conscience, has half a kidney; August has one white eye.

Kip needs brain surgery to recover his health. Violet in *Suddenly Last Summer* demands unnecessary brain surgery to silence Catherine's truth about cannibalism: "Cut this hideous story out of her brain." Williams, haunted by his sister Rose's surgical impairment by lobotomy, gave one of his short-story collections about broken bodies and souls, struggling with one arm tied behind their backs, a title of disability: *One Arm*. This anthology title of existential amputation and loss is repeated in his prison death-row short story, "One Arm," and in his screenplay, *One Arm*. In addition to his plays, he wrote eight original screenplays: *The Glass Menagerie*, *A Streetcar Named Desire*, *The Rose Tattoo*, *The Loss of a Teardrop Diamond*, *The Fugitive Kind*, *Boom!* (*The Milk Train Doesn't Stop Here Anymore*), and *One Arm*.

Gorgeously doomed, Williams' creatures live as erotic castaways. They seek SOS rescue on the proscenium beach which the author warns in *Suddenly Last Summer*, *Night of the Iguana*, *Milk Train*, and *Small Craft Warnings* is a dangerous place for poets and priests and women. If aliens knew of Earth only from the plays of Tennessee Williams, they'd judge the planet to be a tropical rain forest, a ruined Garden of Eden, filled with overheated men and under-ventilated women. So integral is Williams in popular culture, his dramas like *Un Tramway Nommé Désir*, *Un Deseo de Nombre de Tranvía*, and *'N Tram Genaamd Begeerte*, continue to play globally in dozens of translations. The 1951 film of *A Streetcar Named Desire* is number 45 on the American Film Institute's list of Top 100 Films. The San Francisco Opera commissioned an operatic version of *Streetcar* that premiered in 1998.

These lost souls find God in the convergences of sex and in the violence of the natural universe. In *A Streetcar Named Desire*, Blanche is the desperate descendent of the desperate Scarlett O'Hara by way of origin, sensibility, and casting. Frantically seeking rescue by a gentleman caller, she declares a magical main theme in Williams' dramas, "Suddenly there is God so quickly." Maybe. But what if he is the vengeful God of the Encantadas? In *Suddenly Last Summer* when Sebastian freaks out in a sex-panic, he screams, "Complain? To the Manager? What manager? God?"

Will God rescue us or not? Williams is ambivalent about theological rescue, about salvation itself, which Big Daddy in *Cat on a Hot Tin Roof* rails against so hysterically. Sometimes God is found suddenly in love, sometimes in violence, sometimes in sex, sometimes in absentia. The long-missing father in *Menagerie* "was a telephone man who fell in love with long distances." God is something cloudy, something clear. The only theological certainty Williams wrote in his *Memoir* is "God don't come when you want Him but He's right on time."

In *Cloudy/Clear* Williams turns his *affaire de coeur* into a queer *cri de coeur*. Because Tennessee grew up as a nelly boy beaten up by a sexy bully boy named Brick Gotcher, he rejected the masochism of effeminacy and built his esthetic of masculinity romancing ideas about straight men. His play hangs its heart on a quintessential gay fantasy: the impossible petard of loving and being loved by a straight man.

In Lord Byron's 1824 poem, "Love and Death," the windswept poet—beloved by Williams who resurrected him in his 1946 *Lord Byron's Love Letter* and his 1953 *Camino Real*—loves a young straight soldier who does not love him back. In August's unrequited love for Kip, Williams dramatizes homosexuality's Catch 22.

If a straight man reciprocates, what is the meaning of *straight*? Brick, the temporarily disabled football hero, querying homomasculine intimacy with his buddy Skipper, tackles similar tensions about the nature of male love in *Cat on a Hot Tin Roof*. Where does Tennessee begin to transgress, or not transgress, queer politics?

With his alpha-male protagonists, he distanced himself from drag, swish, and camp which he called degrading forms of self-mockery. Is Blanche the closest he ever came to coding a drag queen? During the 1956 Broadway revival of *Streetcar*, he told his star and dear friend Tallulah Bankhead, whom he had in mind while creating the role, that she was the worst Blanche he had ever seen because she, as a gay icon, camped up the sensitive part to play to her cheering gay fans.

In Stella's "Stanley," Williams and Brando launched a new postwar torn-T-shirt standard of masculine beauty. Their rough-trade blue-collar male sex appeal sold tickets and liberated pop culture's gaze at men in the conformist 1950s via Marlon's sweaty factory worker in *Streetcar* and his Hells Angels biker in *The Wild One* which unreels as if it were Stanley's backstory. Even today, years later, personals ads in the gay press cry out from the heart for authentic "straight acting, straight-appearing." But what is that? Blanche queries Stanley: "Straight? What is straight? A line can be straight, or a street, but the human heart, oh, no, it's curved like a road through mountains."

That oh-so-declarative sentence of sexual politics is so at Williams' short hairs, he re-quotes it exactly in his *Memoirs*. Even so, as with an original all-male Shakespeare production in 1605, Williams greatly approved of an all-gay, all-male, but non-camp, non-drag staging of Gertrude Stein's *Four Saints in Three Acts.*

Does anyone in the audience care about the politics, theology, or esthetic of Tom/Tennessee, the person, the isolato, all alone in his room? Or is it all about Stanley and Blanche and Maggie and Violet Venable and the Princess Kosmonopolis, characters chewing scenery for a packed house? "His plays have their own reputations," wrote Williams' biographer, Lyle Leverich. Is it worthwhile knowing how the author was dumped? By Kip Kiernan for a woman. By the critics grown brittle to his poetic passions.

Hot for twenty years on Broadway and in Hollywood, Williams was cast away in the 1960s when critics moved on to the next Fifteen Minutes of someone else. His plays and movies became box-office disappointments like the 1966 film *This Property Is Condemned* and the 1968 *Boom!* Nevertheless, he kept writing and revising. As a positive result, his canon remains in constant motion on, off, and far from Broadway. Annually, his plays—whose titles alone sell tickets—top the lists of any year's most revived dramas. *The Glass Menagerie* is the straight play most revived on Broadway during the last seventy years.

In the early 1940s, MGM hired Williams to write a screenplay for Lana Turner. When he wrote *Girl in Glass*, MGM hated it and fired him. When re-worked, *The Glass Menagerie* became a Broadway hit. MGM had to bid for film rights to a property it once owned, and lost to Warner Bros.

In *Cloudy/Clear*, Williams articulates his anger at market-driven artists' concessions to bad taste to sell tickets. He writes of the "exigencies of desperation" and the "negotiation of terms." The theater, he said, is "little sentiment and all machinations." In his *Memoir*, he writes of suffering depression and scoring "uppers" from "Dr. Feel Good" in "the disastrous decade of my sixties." Witnessing his stress in commercial theater, his own mother said, "Tom, it's time for you to find another occupation now." He described her as "a little Prussian officer in drag."

Despite his addictions, he tried to keep his unclouded voice clear. Personality cannot be replaced. He declared in his *Memoir*: "The individual is ruthlessly discarded for the old, old consideration of profit." What other American dramatist, age 65ish in the mid-1970s, was rebel enough to read his own poetry free to all—no charge—at the 92nd Street Y? What to producers was money, and today is politics, were to him heartfelt themes in the universal human condition.

The ravenous Sebastian Venable in *Suddenly* was eaten alive trying to write his poem of summer. "Fed up with dark ones, famished for blonds…

[Sebastian] talked about people as if they were items on a menu. That one's delicious-looking." Cannibalism may be Williams' metaphor for what he calls "the cruel exigencies of theater." Cannibalism is what critics, producers, and agents do to artists, what straight society does to queers, and what gay culture does to its own.

The dramatic-poet Williams never impedes narrative or character by explaining the metaphor of "cannibalism." The audience is left properly to its own magical and critical thinking. Perfect. Entertainment gives you what you expect and does not disturb you. Art snaps you around with disruptions you don't expect—and you exit the theater changed.

Williams, writing so very precisely about the human condition, forges a daring list of charged topics: homosexual identity (*Cloudy/Clear, Cat, Suddenly Last Summer*), disability (*The Glass Menagerie*, "One Arm"), race ("Desire and the Black Masseur," "Why Did Desdemona Love the Moor?"), homelessness and definitions of family (*Streetcar, Cat, Camino Real*), domestic abuse and victimization (*Streetcar, Cat, Suddenly*), fertility (*Streetcar, Cat)*, drugs and aging (*Cat, Sweet Bird of Youth, The Roman Spring of Mrs. Stone*), sex tourism (*Suddenly, Roman Spring, Iguana*), health care (*Streetcar, Cat, Summer and Smoke, Suddenly*), immigration (*Cloudy/Clear, Orpheus Descending*), and women's rights (throughout his canon). Without explaining himself or his plays, he leaves the messages to Western Union. Tennessee Williams, influenced by writers Hart Crane, D. H. Lawrence, and Rainer Maria Rilke, is the most poetic of American dramatists and the most dramatic of American poets.

The emerging joy of Tennessee Williams' "unpublished" plays—precisely like this singular version for this New York Art Theater—is the sense of discovery of the person, of the author himself, as times change into new rich readings of his autobiographical work. After we know the big plays of the last midcentury, we want to know the artist, because the artist, in our time, matters as much as the art. Vanessa Redgrave, more than once famously outcast for her humanist mixing of art with politics, in 1997 dug up and starred in Williams'1938 play about fascism, *Not About Nightingales. Variety* reviewed it in 1998 as "angry, propagandistic Williams, a young firebrand with an idealist's fervor."

Williams adored Redgrave. He proclaimed, "Vanessa Redgrave is the greatest actress of our time." The Redgrave dynasty has long championed Williams alongside his beloved Chekov. Vanessa triumphed as Lady Torrance in *Orpheus Descending*, the final version of *Battle of Angels* which Williams was writing while living the action of what became *Cloudy/Clear.* Her brother Corin Redgrave starred in *Not About Nightingales*, directed by

Trevor Nunn. Her sister Lynn Redgrave played Arkadina in *The Notebook of Trigorin*. Her daughter Natasha Richardson played Blanche in *Streetcar* and Catherine Holly in *Suddenly Last Summer*.

Amazingly, *Trigorin* is an almost perfect fusion of two great international playwrights: Chekov and Williams. In the free-wheeling last year of his life, Tennessee re-wrote *The Seagull* as *Trigorin*. He made the text his own in more ways than turning Chekov's plot bisexual—something he could not do to Kip Kiernan. In 1963, during Vanessa's marriage to Tony Richardson, the bisexual Richardson was directing *The Milk Train Doesn't Stop Here Anymore* starring Williams' longtime bisexual friend Tallulah Bankhead. About her who appears fictively in a brief dream in *Cloudy/Clear*, he wrote she is "The strongest of all the hurt people I've ever known."

The Williams-Redgrave solidarity was a long, strong bond. In 1980, Tennessee flew to Boston to support Vanessa in her lawsuit against the Boston Symphony which had canceled her appearance because of pressure opposing her political views. Banned from the Boston Symphony stage, Vanessa booked herself into Boston's Orpheum Theatre where in a protest performance she offered songs and dances from *As You Like It*, *The Seagull*, and *Isadora*.

Tennessee twice joined in and ascended the Orpheum stage with Vanessa, his star of *Orpheus Descending*, to read his essay, "The Misunderstanding and Fears of an Artist's Revolt." That year, before his death in 1983, isolated and suffering the cruelty of the commercial art world, Tennessee, Redgrave wrote, was so out of fashion the newspapers did not bother to report his appearance.

The action in *Cloudy/Clear* happens three years before *The Glass Menagerie*, his second memory play, made Williams famous in 1944. The characters, except for Clare, are real people. Kip was Williams' straight lover, a Canadian dancer who resembled Nijinsky, who had changed his Russian-Jewish name, Bernard Dubowsky, to Kip Kiernan. Kip feared Tennessee was so good a gay lover that he was turning him homosexual. In 1947, after the estranged Kip died in 1944, Frank Merlo became his lover for the next fourteen years.

In the cast of *Cloudy/Clear*, filmstar Miriam Hopkins, who in 1940 starred as Myra Torrance in his ill-fated flop, *Battle of Angels*, became his fictitious "Caroline Wales." Producers Lawrence Langner, his wife Armina Marshall, and the Theatre Guild's Theresa Helburn were merged into the self-serving cannibal agents "Maurice and Celeste Fiddler" to whose tune August does not dance.

So many of Williams' characters on the beach—which is the proscenium stage of planet Earth—endure the gravitational pull of the moon and sea on the geography of the body. Stranded like Sebastian's Encantada turtles on the sands of beaches calling for help, even on the shore of Moon Lake, they, like the Reverend Shannon in *Iguana* want to take the long swim from the beach to China knowing that Christopher Flanders, the angel of death in *Milk Train*, is no catcher in the rye come to save them. He is their escort, their final walker—there to help them die. He is a "lifeguard in reverse" who helps suicidal desperadoes stuck on the shore step into the long swim in the drowning sea.

Penning poetry in his free-style dialogue, Williams observes Aristotle's strict unities of time, place, and action while thrusting forward with a dramatic dialectic. Structurally, in play after play, thesis meets antithesis and creates synthesis. Everyone in Williams' world of determinism is on a collision course. Stanley says to Blanche, "We've had this date from the very beginning." In *Cloudy/Clear*, gay identity arm-wrestles with straight identity. The play itself repeatedly intones that there are Clare's and Kip's "exigencies of desperation" and "negotiation of terms." Williams, the humanist, keeps the humanity of diverse sexual identities alive.

He is not at all like his New Orleans friend, the flamboyant poet, Oliver Evans, whom he first met in Provincetown on the wharf in the summer of 1941 while writing *Cloudy/Clear*. He and Evans became lifelong friends, traveled together, and enjoyed, *à trois*, many a *ménagerie*, Evans told him over drinks in a New Orleans bar on September 14, 1941: "A healthy society does not need [homosexual] artists....We are the rotten apple in the barrel...in fact all artists ought to be exterminated by the age of 25." Williams, never a self-hating homosexual, responded to Evans' problematic take on homosexuality, "I am a deeper and warmer and kinder man for my deviations."

With incredible tenderness, Williams closes *Something Cloudy, Something Clear* when August intones: "Child of God..." August is now almost become Saint Augustine. The Episcopalian Williams, who based the structure of *Streetcar* on the dramatic structure of the Anglican/Catholic Mass, became a Roman Catholic in 1969 because he liked the theatrical pageantry and incense.

August addresses Kip and Clare in the last lines of this version of this script for this production about which director Fourmantchouk, distancing himself from the 1981 version that did not contain this exchange, wrote: "The New York Art Theater is working from a copy of an original uncensored and unpublished version of the play."

Touching Kip's face and throat, August says to Kip: "Child of God—you—don't exist anymore." Clare chimes in, "Neither do you." August, the poet, finally clear about his cloudy existence, asserts in one defining sentence the sustaining magic and power of memory, of storytelling, of theater, of writers voicing theater, of actors performing theater, of audiences watching theater. He retorts with his Proustian reason for being: "At this moment, I do, in order to remember."

Film producer Terry LeGrand on set in a Mistress-owned S&M dungeon shooting *Fit to Be Tied*, Dusseldorf, June 26, 1989. Photo by Jack Fritscher.

TERRY LEGRAND

1939-2018

BORN TO RAISE HELL
Once upon a time, there were no gay movies

Pioneer gay film producer Terry Rodolph Grand was born to raise hell as "Terry LeGrand" in Denver in 1939. He died from AIDS complications at his West Hollywood home April 18, 2018. The Tom of Finland House honored his life with a memorial garden party in Los Angeles on June 3. As the founder of Marathon Films, Terry produced the classic leather film *Born to Raise Hell* (1975) directed by Roger Earl starring their discovery, Val Martin, whom *Drummer* editor Jeanne Barney featured on the cover of issue 3. *Born to Raise Hell* and *Drummer* opened the closet door on leather, kink, and BDSM.

At the violent police raid of the "Drummer Slave Auction" on April 11, 1976, the foursome of friends (Terry, Roger, Jeanne, and Val) were among the 42 arrested—partially because fascist LAPD Police Chief Ed Davis knew *Drummer* was promoting *Born to Raise Hell* which Davis decreed would never be screened in Los Angeles. Davis was a documented fuckup. He knew how to entrap fags and bust fairies. But he couldn't stomach the new breed of homomasculine leathermen who looked more authentic in cop uniforms than did many of his officers. When his late-night storm troopers cuffed the straight Jeanne Barney, they asked if she was a drag queen, and she snapped: "If I were a drag queen, I'd have bigger tits."

Harassed in LA by Davis who called him into his office, Terry told me Davis pounded his desk and threatened him against screening his film at any theater in LA. So Terry moved the world premiere of *Born to Raise Hell* to San Francisco at the Powell Theater, near the Market Street cable car turn-around, where we first met on the Leather Carpet in June 1975.

Terry and Roger, never lovers, were dear friends to each other for forty-four years, and Terry was the sole owner of Marathon Films. They met while Roger was working behind the scenes at NBC Television in Burbank in 1974. Roger was a guest at one of those ever-so patio parties in the Hollywood Hills where the talent stood on one side of the pool and the wallets stood on the other. It was the kind of backstage sex-mixer described by party host Scotty Bowers in his book, *Full Service: My Adventures in Hollywood and the Secret Sex Lives of the Stars.*

At that soiree, Roger's erstwhile leather-bottom George Lawson, who had gotten him his job at NBC, introduced him to Terry who needed a director for his new S&M leather picture. Lawson who was originally slated to direct the film told Terry that Roger would be a better choice because of his stage experience at NBC.

Remembering that night, Roger told me that driving back to his West Hollywood apartment where he has now lived for more than fifty years, "The title *Born to Raise Hell* just came to me. I pictured a motorcycle guy with a tattoo."

Roger wanted to find a Brando, like Marlon in *The Wild One*, while Terry wanted to find a cast as authentic as Kenneth Anger's in *Scorpio Rising.* As a double-bill, those two films can represent a prequel to *Born to Raise Hell.* That lineage makes a trilogy of masculine-identified films that looked virile and made thematic sense screened together.

"I needed a really dynamic guy," Roger said, "to carry this movie. Otherwise it was going to be the same old shit. Terry couldn't have agreed more. I thought of the Colt model Ledermeister, but he was not into the S&M scene. I was lucky to find Val Martin tending bar. He scared me, and I'm a top, so I knew he was perfect for the part of 'Bearded Sadist.'"

Terry's casting of authentic leathermen recruited from LA bars made *Born to Raise Hell* a transgressive play-within-a-play like Jean Genet's *The Maids* and *The Blacks.* Not that Terry or Roger were film students particularly aware of Genet or the coincidence. Just as Genet's poetic, sensual, homomasculine S&M prison film *Un chant d'amour* (1950) was declared obscene by Berkeley, California, police on its American release in 1966, Terry's brutal X-rated S&M cop-and-biker film would be censored and prohibited in 1975 by Los Angeles law enforcement.

The climax of both films, made twenty-five years apart, is a sex chase through the woods. In Genet's film at the climax, a cop forces a gun into his victim's mouth; in Terry's film at the climax, the cop forces a nightstick into the victim's anus. In his meta film, Terry cast non-actors role-playing themselves as characters who are themselves. Years and years before reality TV, that practicality was his genius. In 1975, the LA cops saw *Born to Raise Hell* as a depraved fag movie; but the new leathermen coming out of the S&M closet to be born again in kink saw it as a sex-education film.

This raises the question: are gay porn films fantasy fiction or authentic documentary? This ambiguity alarmed Davis, who feared the film was *real*, and charmed Terry, who knew it was. The 1960s cultural revolution was in the 1970s air. Shot in the styles of *Mondo Cane* and *Scorpio Rising* (both 1963), *Born to Raise Hell* is also a perfect backstory of William Friedkin's controversial S&M film *Cruising* (1980) with which it makes an adventurous cinema quartet.

In the LA gay press, *Drummer* called Davis "Crazy Ed" after he went on local television news demanding a portable gallows to hang captured skyjackers on airport tarmacs. He was riding high on his horse because he had recently arrested the Manson Family for the torture murders of pregnant Hollywood actress Sharon Tate and her friends which confused him about sadomasochism and consent. He reveled in his famous shootouts with the Black Panthers and with the Symbionese Liberation Army, six of whom in 1974 he had burnt up in a house fire he set trying to arrest them for the kidnap and torture of newspaper heiress Patty Hearst who later made a camp of herself in John Waters' films *Cry Baby* and *Serial Mom*.

Terry dared produce his erotic leather documentary in LA despite Crazy Ed raiding leather bars, tapping phones at *Drummer*, and freaking out over the two "cops" in *Born to Raise Hell*, and the high-profile coverage of the film in *Drummer*. Like the politically-correct myopic gays who ran screaming "rape" from the Powell Theater premiere, Davis confused the film's consensual S&M action, including the wild cherry-popping fisting scene, with violence. He feared being played a fool by fags. He inspired gay resistance. Terry along with his friends *Drummer* publisher John Embry and leather author Larry Townsend became his nemeses in gay media. *Drummer* columnist Guy Baldwin, Mr. IML 1989, penned a pertinent commentary about gay fundamentalist opposition to leather culture in *Drummer* 168: "Beware of the Politically Correct Sex Police."

From the 1970s onward, Terry led local gay resistance on several fronts as a political activist, filmmaker, and host of his chat show on LATalk Radio, and as the founding president of the Gay Film Producers Association.

For LATalk in 2010, he created two shows. For the first, *The Alternative*, he hosted personalities like Carol Channing, Armistead Maupin, Johnny Weir, Peter Berlin, and Tyler McCormick, the first transgender Mr. International Leather who was also the first Mr. IML to roll across the stage in a wheelchair.

For the second, *Journey to Recovery*, he called upon his "twenty-five years in the addiction field." Roger claimed that during the AIDS emergency, "Terry felt he would be able to better serve his community by becoming a doctor. He went to school and received his degree." *The*

Alternative called him a "retired physician," but what school, what degree, and what kind of doctor remain to be detected.

Terry was also a stage hypnotist at C Frenz, the longest operating gay and lesbian bar in the West San Fernando Valley which advertised: "Master Hypnotist Terry LeGrand Hosts Charity Show, C Frenz, Reseda, CA. Terry LeGrand brings campy hilarity to his hypnotism show, performed live on stage the first Sunday of every month. Come see one of the gayest and funniest shows around. Guaranteed to entertain you and your friends. Hysterical and real the first Sunday of every month starting at 9:00 PM Reservations are recommended."

It is true that in the 1980s, Terry and his friend Robert Bonin created the AIDS/HIV Health Alternatives, "Forming Opportunities Under New Directions" (FOUND), which opened Menlo House, 1731 S. Menlo Avenue, offering, from his own experience, recovery maintenance to drug-addicted ex-convicts with AIDS. Terry was a recovering alcoholic like his longtime friends Jeanne Barney and Larry Townsend with whom he and Roger lunched for years at the French Market restaurant at 7985 Santa Monica Boulevard in West Hollywood which was their stomping ground.

On his radio show, often hosting in tandem with Will Meyerhofer, JD LCSW-R, "The People's Therapist," he used his experience to encourage his audience to keep conscious of the real impact of alcohol and suicide on gay lives, especially in mixed HIV-status couples when beset with holiday blues. His other topics covered kinky sex, gay therapists for gay persons, gay adoption, ACT UP/LA, Don't Ask Don't Tell, dating and internet dating, being gay and Christian, and misconceptions gay and straight people have about each another.

The money-spinning producer of almost thirty films like *Gayracula*, *Men of the Midway*, and *Pictures from the Black Dance*, was as provocative off screen as he was on. In 1991, he produced what Dave Rhodes at *The Leather Journal* called the best-ever regional Mr. Drummer Contest. Rhodes then added: "LeGrand received heavy criticism for what some said was $40,000 he spent on promoting and producing the event while others were awestruck by the production that rivaled the finals in San Francisco."

What great character has no flaw? Like Genet who was, in Steven Routledge's words, "an odd hybrid: part criminal and part literary celebrity," Terry, who sewed many panels for the AIDS Quilt, often caused people to ask where the money went because Terry like John Embry had a touch of larceny about him, often of the amusing kind found in British film comedies of the 1950s. Terry was famous for writing bad checks which is a misdemeanor crime for amounts under $950 in California.

When some folks, including crew from one of his films, went to the LA County Sheriffs who were empowered to collect funds owed in bounced checks, a deputy reported back, delivering the money owed, saying she had never met a character like Terry LeGrand in her entire career.

Somehow, it was funny that Terry had in him a bit of Max Bialystock from Mel Brooks' *The Producers*, and few grew angry at him who, like Max, slowly made good on his debts. When he contracted me in spring 1989 to shoot three films with a single camera in Europe, I suggested he also hire my husband, film editor Mark Hemry, for a two-camera shoot to get better coverage to make a visually richer movie because Mark and I shot in a matching style, and he would be perfect to handle technical design for lighting and sound.

Money was never an issue between us because we told Terry that in exchange for his footing our travel, food, and lodging expenses, he would not have to pay us to shoot the videos.

With that satisfactory arrangement, instead of editing our two cameras together as action and reaction shots, he and Roger—mindful of Hollywood sequels—felt free to look at our hours of footage, and, instead of the three movies, cut six. That's the inside story of how their trilogy, planned to match their 1988 *Dungeons of Europe* trilogy, became the six titles in Marathon's *Bound for Europe* series.

As happened in the karma and chaos around AIDS, those six films we shot for them were their swan song. They were the last movies Terry produced and Roger edited.

Terry was a business man, a showman, a producer, an impresario. In Europe, he generously lodged us crew in hotels like the grand Victoria Hotel in Amsterdam on the Damrak across the street from the Amsterdam Centraal Station. He wasn't an artist or an auteur filmmaker, but he, who was Co-Chair of ACT UP Southern California, was a dedicated force in film, politics, and AIDS. And he was kind, fun, and fair.

As president of the Gay Film Producers Association, he told *The Los Angeles Times* that erotic filmmakers like Catalina should practice what they preach when they put a caution warning about safe sex on a cassette that contains a film showing unsafe sex. Putting a caution label on a film glamorizing unsafe sex "...is stupid. We have to stop making films with unsafe sex in them. The dollar cannot be important to us. Saving lives has got to be the important thing." In affirmation, *Drummer* publisher Tony DeBlase wrote of Terry's *Pictures from the Black Dance*: "...the 1988 action is much closer to 1975's *Born to Raise Hell* ...and still all safe sex! Like

Born to Raise Hell, this *Dungeons of Europe* trilogy will be one of the major contributions to the erotic media for SM men."

On *The Alternative* broadcast on January 10, 2011, Terry counseled: "For many in our community, there's a second coming out that's less fun, but equally important—coming out as HIV+." In 2012, he and his radio show were cited in the *Journal of Criminal Law and Criminology*, 102, issue 4, in Sharon Dolovich's article: "Two Models of the Prison: Accidental Humanity and Hypermasculinity in the L.A. County Jail."

Hypermasculinity, often caused some say by XYY chromosomes, is a toxic exaggeration of normal primary and secondary male sex characteristics. It is not a synonym for XY homomasculinity which is a natural human expression of male gender that, far from canceling the female principle, offers the valid gender balance of man-to-man male animus that respects what the female anima demands and deserves.

In the 1980s, Terry's annual Producers Awards Show at the Hollywood Century Theater at 5115 Hollywood Boulevard gave "Oscars" to the best erotic films with proceeds going to the support of the Gay and Lesbian Community Center. Terry had a soft spot for the Hollywood Century that had become a gay adult theater a decade before on November 21, 1973, with the premiere of director Richard Abel's big box-office hit *Nights in Black Leather*.

That film starring the already iconic Peter Berlin became a kind of template for Terry who smelled money, and immediately understood its episodic documentary style following Peter cruising through his life in San Francisco. Terry had considered casting the popular Peter Berlin as a lead in *Born to Raise Hell*, but Roger thought Peter, who was best as a solo performer, too young, too blond, and too sweet. In 2008, the magazine *Gay Video News*, sponsor of the GAYVN Awards, inducted Terry into its Hall of Fame, and in 2009 granted Roger the GAYVN Lifetime Achievement Award.

As birthday twins turning fifty in 1989 in Holland, Terry and I laughed with Roger Earl and Mark Hemry on the evening of June 20 when Terry spontaneously jumped up and joke-kissed me to great hilarity while we were chatting on a little supper boat cruising the canals of Amsterdam. Terry was born thirteen days after me in summer 1939, and like an existential punch-line two months later, Hitler invaded Poland. The joke was on us. So was the violence we had to process as children.

Born into a world dangerous to everyone, and always more risky for gays, we war babies who became teenagers in the homophobic 1950s were all too aware there were no gay magazines or movies. Then came

Stonewall. By the 1970s in our thirties while the shameful real violence of the Vietnam War wound down, Terry was the producer of the "violence" in *Born to Raise Hell*, and I was the editor of the "action" in *Drummer*. It was our generation of war babies who alchemized real-life toxic violence and empowered the 1970s culture of liberating resistance with the curative of orgasm.

My own attraction to BDSM was counter-phobic. I eroticized what scared me. People naturally do that. The violence of the Second World War became insanely surreal with the kind of terror that can only be survived by making it erotic. I wanted to turn sex into art because art makes sense of life. *Born to Raise Hell* is the fever dream of war baby counter-phobes ritualizing action that discharges fears by making them erotic.

Talk about performance art! Talk about disruption of the norm! Terry dared put this kind of ritual cleansing up on the screen to address and relieve gay fear. *Born to Raise Hell* is a horror film with "happy endings" on screen and in the audience. At that packed Powell Theatre premiere, leathermen openly masturbated. Safely. Because if gay fantasies of dominance and submission came true, they'd be nightmares. Every pornographer knows that orgasm is the best review.

Marathon's films were "conceived by Roger Earl," but were unscripted. That's what made them such wonderful accidental documentaries of real leather life. "Terry and I preferred to let guys do their own thing on camera to keep it real."

Roger remembers Terry as a mindful producer. "I give a 1000% credit to Terry. He was the one with the guts to dare go out and hire the cast. I'd say 'I want this one' and he'd go convince the guy. Remember: this was back in the day when gay men feared cameras as tools of blackmail, and nobody had yet really seen a gay S&M leather movie. We worked wonderfully together."

That production summer of 1974 was a key turning point in the birth of the commercial gay porn-film industry kick-started in the 1940s by Bob Mizer at his Athletic Model Guild studio in Los Angeles, and in the 1950s by leather kingpin Chuck Renslow at his Kris Studio in Chicago. Terry wanted to earn big bucks at the box office because money and fame empower visibility, and he enjoyed the good life. On location in 1989, I remember him standing in the hallway at the Victoria Hotel showing us his latest high-tech toy, a tiny new camera that he said did not use film and would revolutionize photography. He was an opera buff who dreamed operatic porn dreams after watching *Deep Throat* break through to make millions in 1972.

As a marketing activist, he was keen to fill gay gaps and loud gay silences. He fused trends. He saw an unserved audience of leathermen standing in bars eager to see themselves on screen, but not in the sleazy way San Francisco leather bars were portrayed as special rooms in hell in the 1973 Hollywood film, *The Laughing Policeman*. He understood the red-hot popularity of Kenneth Anger's *Scorpio Rising* and Fred Halsted's *LA Plays Itself*. Why not produce a film to uncloset bondage, fisting, cop worship, and S&M for that audience wanting authentic identity entertainment seeing themselves on page and screen?

For the same reasons at the same moment, Terry's lifelong frenemy, John Embry, founded *Drummer*. That film and that magazine suddenly gave masculine-identified leathermen visions and voices and visibility. For instance, in the *Drummer* personals ads written by grass-root readers profiling themselves and the sex partners they sought, the most repeated words, by count, were *masculine* and *masculinity*. In perfect synergy, the producer needed *Drummer* to publicize *Born to Raise Hell*, and the publisher needed stills from the film to fill *Drummer*.

Drummer published so many photos from Terry's films on covers and on inside copy that it sometimes seemed like a LeGrand fan zine. Covers included *Drummer* 3, October 1975, *Drummer* 114, March 1988; *Drummer* 125, February 1989; *Drummer* 147, March 1991. Interiors included *Drummer* 2, August 1975; *Drummer* 3, October 1975; *Drummer* 78, 1984; *Drummer* 116, May 1988; *Drummer* 126, March 1989; *Drummer* 133, September 1989; *Drummer* 137, March 1990; *Drummer* 141, August 1990. *Drummer* also featured photographs I shot in Europe of his work on the covers and interiors of its Super Publications: *Mach* 20, April 1990, and *Tough Customers* 1, July 1990.

When the Museum of Modern Art in its own fever dream inducted Halsted's S&M-themed *LA Plays Itself* into its permanent collection in 1975, that validation gave Terry a green light more certain than the great Gatsby's to follow his commercial passion. Politically, Terry had no question about his rights as a gay filmmaker. Nor did Roger or Halsted. "We would never have made it," Roger told me, "if it hadn't been for Fred putting out *LA Plays Itself*."

In *Beyond Shame*, Patrick Moore observed in 2004: "What is being explored in both films is a kind of sex that depends not only upon erections and ejaculations, but rather on an emotional stretching that remains shocking today, but must have seemed nothing short of revolutionary in the early 1970s." He is correct. At the Powell Theater premiere, the invited audience gave a standing ovation calling out for more.

LeGrand-Earl helped grow that "emotional stretch" (literally in a fisting film) dramatizing men bonding together in the special trust of leather psychology. In that post-Stonewall decade of emerging liberation, the new gay S&M porn, like sadomasochism itself, was roaring out of the closet and into the art of popular culture. Terry calculated that mainstream producers and directors were educating gay and straight audiences into sadomasochistic literacy with international hit films like *The Night Porter*, *Salo: a 120 Days of Sodom*, *Seven Beauties*, and the camp *Ilsa: She-Wolf of the SS.*

Because Terry and Roger made *Born to Raise Hell* as equals, they deserve co-star billing, but, as often happens in Hollywood, one name can outshine another, and reviewers and queer historians seem to side with French auteur theory which identifies a movie by its director: a Truffaut film, a Hitchcock film. Terry and Roger deserved double-billing like Ismail Merchant and James Ivory, but self-effacing Terry, who produced twenty-two of their films, made Roger the star in their advertising, which buried Terry's name in Marathon publicity.

It was Terry who planned and coordinated the actual film production for *Born to Raise Hell.* He created the safe environment needed in order to work free from harassment by Davis. It was Roger who helped Terry finance this little gay art film with a personal loan of $10,000 dollars from singing star Dean Martin while Roger was Martin's dresser and production coordinator on *The Dean Martin Show* at NBC. (Martin, who liked Roger, did not ask what the loan was for.) Terry protected Roger, and the cast and crew Roger directed, including Tim Christie, one of the incestuous pornstar Christie twins, as sound recordist, and Ray Tomargo and Vince Trainer as the cinematographers.

Terry managed their shoot on location outdoors in Griffith Park, and inside the old Truck Stop bar way out in the San Fernando Valley. With a half-dozen reels in the can, while Terry held his breath, Roger spent four risky weeks in post-production guiding Trainer in cutting the 16mm Eastmancolor footage on a Moviescope set on Roger's kitchen table. "It was dangerous," Roger said of those analog-film times, "Because we could not afford a work print for back up, I was cutting the negative of the original 16mm footage, and didn't want to screw it up."

In 1988, as a grand finale to cap their life's work in LA, Terry decided to use their international success with *Born to Raise Hell* as a calling card to hire European leathermen and locations by traveling to London to shoot Marathon's first three-film series, *Dungeons of Europe*, with British tattoo-and-piercing artist Mr. Sebastian opening his studio for the first of the trilogy, *Pictures from the Black Dance*, after which they flew to Amsterdam to film *Like Moths to a Flame* and *Men with No Name*. At the height of the AIDS emergency, a new generation of film fans got hard on kink offering safer-sex. Everything old at Marathon was hot again.

Trying to remake and upgrade the intensity of *Born to Raise Hell*, Terry banked on finding more of the sex-magic he'd found in Europe in 1988. He could rely on his director and he needed a reliable cameraman to shoot the cast of local men he'd recruit in bars. So in 1989, Terry hired Mark and me because he liked the cinematography we were shooting for our Palm Drive Video studio. We also bonded in that moment because our mutual friend, Fred Halsted, had just committed suicide. Flying to Amsterdam, we four traveled on a wild month-long shoot for our six-film series, *Bound for Europe*, documenting Dutch and German S&M: *The Argos Session*, *Fit to Be Tied*, *Marks of Pleasure*, *Knast*, *The Berlin Connection*, and *Loose Ends of the Rope*.

Our simultaneous two-camera shoot was a first for Marathon Films. Terry credited two cinematographers for *Born to Raise Hell*, but the two took turns shooting with one film camera. Terry and Roger were pleased we shot enough digital footage to keep Roger busy at his editing console cutting the six films over the next two years.

Four months before the Berlin Wall came down, something sexually electric and wonderfully debauched was in the air because the men and the bars and the action seemed very Weimar! Very *Cabaret*! It was romantic being part of a film crew shooting leathermen on location during the last summer West Berlin existed.

In a way, the Second World War was also not over for some German war babies. One afternoon, Terry and Mark and I walked to the city center to shoot exteriors of the bombed-out Kaiser Wilhelm Memorial Church on the famous Kurfürstendamm, the Champs-Élysées of Berlin. The pile was a tall gothic ruin preserved behind a chain-link fence as an anti-war memorial. Suddenly, two young German punks with spiked hair barged into our shoot, pointed at the ruined church, and said, "See what you Americans did?" I looked up from my viewfinder and said, "You started it." That ended that conversation.

That July, we eyewitnessed the efficiency of Roger and Terry working together. Terry assembled an exhibitionist cast eager to do their own thing. Roger put the men—like the East German sex-bomb Christian Dreesen, who needed little direction—on set, and yelled, "Camera. Speed. Action."

Roger was an engaged director when we shot with large casts in the main rooms of bars. Thinking of the fourteen-year-old *Born to Raise Hell*, he set out directing his standard vision of American-movie S&M until he relaxed as much as he could and let the cast do their improvisation from life of authentic German S&M which was the fresh new thing Terry and he said they wanted. Oftentimes, Mark and I, lying on the floor filming only six inches from the action were impressed with the hot German ingenuity and severe intensity.

Once while we filmed in the funky cellar of the Knast bar, Roger retreated to another room where, nursing a beer, he quietly watched the S&M talent on Mark's live feed from our cameras to his video monitor. By that time, he'd learned to leave well enough alone. He gave no direction, and couldn't be heard if he had. The soul of cool, he simply watched what the leather masters and slaves did best until he figured we had shot enough running time for the scene, and he yelled "Cut."

Neither Roger or Terry ever said one word about how we should shoot the movies because they wanted a Palm Drive video inside a Marathon production. We had no intention of repeating the straight-on declarative 1970s shots of *Born to Raise Hell.* So we added some of the italic Palm Drive flair we'd been hired for. We decided to shoot these 1980s films from the tilted point of view of an audience tripping on acid.

In Amsterdam, Terry produced a location whose heritage and realism inspired the actors. At the dark hour of 2AM on a two-night shoot, we began filming *The Argos Session* inside the Argos Bar documenting that midcentury interior gay bar that opened in 1957 and closed in 2015. I remembered that sex pit fondly from 1969 when I had slept in a rented room for a week backstairs at the Argos on Heintje Hoekssteeg, where on one long rainy spring afternoon, I amused myself by letting some dude tattoo my taint as a permanent souvenir.

By 1989, the wooden floor in the Argos bar and the road-asphalt coating the floor in its sex cellar were so filthy, we told Terry we could not get down on our knees or lie on our bellies to shoot exotic-erotic angles. To travel light, we had packed only a few changes of clothing. So Terry bought us Class 6 Hazmat suits that protected against toxic and infectious substances that solved the problem because it is hard to do laundry on a trans-Europe road trip in a time of viral plague.

Terry had expected me to shoot video and stills, but I told him, after shooting both the first night in the Argos, it was impossible to stop for stills without interrupting the flow of the video. We recommended he contact the London photographer and painter David Pearce who had shot the stills the year before for the *Dungeons of Europe* trilogy. From that first night's shoot, I remember a signature photo I lensed specifically to illustrate Marathon's VHS video-box cover glamorizing the two stars of our cast standing on the stairs in the historic gay space of the venerable Argos. Terry liked it enough to publish it on the cover of the *Drummer* sibling magazine, *Mach,* issue 20, April 1990, along with twelve more of my Argos shots inside the issue.

Leaving Holland, Mark was the only one skilled and brave enough to drive our rented Mercedes van, speeding with six passengers (Terry, Roger, David Pearce who was our translator, production assistant Harry Ros of Rotterdam, Mark, and me) through the terrifying traffic on the Autobahn, so we could film in Dusseldorf and Hamburg by way of Cologne where we did not shoot.

Terry left us for two days in Cologne shooting exterior shots for the final edits while he traveled ahead by train to Dusseldorf scouting models and securing our one-film shoot in a dominatrix's straight S&M brothel. When our filming there ran overtime, the leather ladies of Dusseldorf waited patiently off camera watching, smoking, whispering, and, finally, applauding.

In a private gay S&M dungeon Terry rented in Hamburg, we shot one and a half films. Because of international treaties limiting how many Americans could be in West Berlin at one time, we had to leave the van and fly over East Germany to West Berlin where we shot two more features in two gritty *wunder*-bars, the Knast and the Connection, on Fuggerstrasse, Schöneberg.

1. *Argos: The Sessions*, shot in Amsterdam
2. *Fit to Be Tied*, shot in Dusseldorf
3. *Marks of Pleasure*, shot in Hamburg
4. *The Knast*, shot in West Berlin
5. *The Berlin Connection*, shot in West Berlin
6. *Loose Ends of the Rope*, a compilation from extra footage shot in Amsterdam, Dusseldorf, Hamburg, and West Berlin

Terry booked us to shoot after 2 AM in so many abandoned rooms and brick-strewn cellars lacking even toilet facilities that tension broke out with the ever-changing cast who wanted more pay for play. What film shoot does not go over budget? We were well fed and lodged, but no longer staying in hotels like the Victoria in Amsterdam. The actors were paid equitably, but some gimlet-eyed leathermen wanting more American dollars trashed Terry for his tight bankroll just as some trashed Roger for his Hollywood hauteur. Roger won no fans accusing everyone in the West

Berlin cast of stealing a wallet, it turned out, he had lost himself. Mark and David Pearce and I, staying clear and becoming fast forever friends, dubbed the European shoot "Trouble in the Rubble."

At the end of the tour, David, who was a noted London painter living on the dole, flew home with us and stayed a month while he painted our portrait on an easel in our Palm Drive studio.

During the nights after every shoot, Terry was happy that Mark, on his own initiative, woke every two hours to make copies of the day's hours of original footage so there would be two copies in separate luggage in case the tapes got confiscated in German or American customs. At that time to get in or out of West Berlin, which was a post-war political island surrounded by East Germany, every traveler had to go through East German customs run by iron-handed Communist women in uniform. It was the last exciting and romantic summer in a nervous West Berlin just a hundred days before the fall of the Berlin Wall.

As a publicity stunt for advertising, Terry wanted to shoot in East Berlin, but at Checkpoint Charlie we turned around because no one on the crew, except Terry, felt it was safe for a Mercedes full of gay pornographers to cross over to East Germany to solicit East German men to beat each other up for a decadent American film studio. The East German secret police, the Stasi, were not disbanded until the next June in 1990.

Instead, on our last night in West Berlin, something fun happened during our farewell supper that the generous Terry hosted in the Michelin-starred Restaurant Bieberbau on Durlacher Strasse 15. Its awesome interior that survived the war was famous for its dramatic dark beams and dazzling white plaster walls sculpted with high- and low-relief flora and fauna showcasing the figurative stucco work created in 1894 by German master-plaster sculptor Richard Bieber.

Over dessert, a hot young Berliner on our crew asked if we would like to go scream under the arch of the elevated railroad bridge at Bahnhof/ Station on Bleibtreustrasse at Savignyplatz, ten minutes by taxi, where, in the almost-perfect movie *Cabaret*, Liza Minnelli taught Michael York how to scream their bloody howl against the coming fascism.

After a month of very long nights on set, it relieved our stress and anxiety. After all, during that month, with AIDS rampant, we were living a pure zipless fuck. We had no sex with any of the tempting locals or with any of the cast whose sex we sucked up untouched into the camera to give all the sex to the viewers which was our job.

Roger and Terry didn't care a fig about *Cabaret*. From his days with Dean Martin in Las Vegas, Roger announced at the candle-lit Bieberbau table he wouldn't go scream because he hated Dean's co-star Liza. But Mark and David Pearce and I, HIV-negative in an age of incurable viral plague, had reason to scream. We waited breathless, stoned on grass, leaning against the brick wall under the viaduct bridge for a train to roar past over our heads and we screamed till our screams turned to laughter. For Christmas 1989, Terry sent each of us a small souvenir chunk of cement that he said was from the Berlin Wall.

In 1991, Terry founded Parkwood Productions with Louis Jansky, and became the founding publisher of *Leatherman Magazine* whose title he wrote in *International Leatherman*, issue 2, 1994, he took from my novel *Some Dance to Remember.* Capitalizing on *Leatherman* in 1994, he sold the title to Brush Creek Media in San Francisco who were the publishers of *Bear* magazine. He closed Marathon when he broke his hip in 2007. He was pleased in 2017 when Marco Siedelmann's Editions Moustache in Germany published my photos of him and Roger making the last films of their careers on location in Holland and West Germany in the book *California Dreamin': West Coast Directors and the Golden Age of Forbidden Gay Movies.*

In France in 2017, *Neons Fanzine* #3 invited a new next-generation to tune in to view the enduring *Born to Raise Hell* and a similar rough S&M documentary, Jean-Étienne Siry's *Poing de Force* [aka *The Warehouse* aka the glorious 1976 fisting film *Erotic Hands*] which "...are each a tasty experience to enjoy at least once in your lifetime. These grimy and nihilistic pieces of sleaze are a great opportunity to let you, through their mondo-style filming and dirty, gritty picture, dive into the leather underground subculture where Hell is Heaven and pain is the key..."

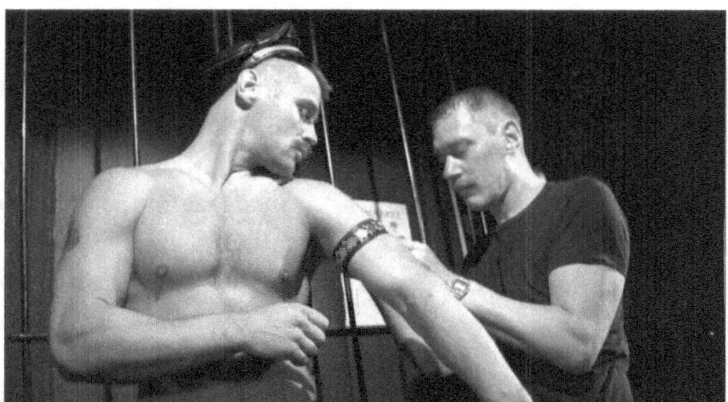

London photographer/painter David Pearce styles Christian Dreesen who on his third attempt had escaped East Germany through the Berlin Wall, Knast Bar, Fuggerstrasse 34, West Berlin, July 4, 1989. Photo by Jack Fritscher.

After filming in Europe, Roger Earl and Terry LeGrand flew to fans in San Francisco and sold VHS-cassette tapes in front of their poster of Christian Dreesen, star of their two series *Dungeons of Europe* and *Bound for Europe*. They were headlined by Karen Mendelsohn at her "QSM (Queer S&M) Art Faire" while screening their film *Like Moths to a Flame* in tandem with erotic book readings by authors Pat Califia and Jack Fritscher, Leather Pride Week, the Firehouse, Fort Mason Center, San Francisco, September 23, 1989. Photo by Mark Hemry.

Roger Earl Warnix directing *The Knast* at the Knast leather bar, Fuggerstrasse 34, West Berlin, July 4, 1989. Photo by Mark Hemry.

Terry LeGrand kisses Jack Fritscher on board an evening Amsterdam Canal Cruise, Amsterdam, June 21, 1989. Photo by Mark Hemry.

Roger Earl and Terry LeGrand on set shooting *Fit to Be Tied*, Dusseldorf, June 26, 1989. Photo by Jack Fritscher.

ROGER EARL

1939-

Born to Raise Hell: Two Filmmakers in Conversation
April 22, 1997

Curating the BDSM Film History of Roger Earl and Terry LeGrand Popularized in *Drummer* Magazine

Roger Earl: [Answering phone] Hello from Los Angeles.

Jack Fritscher: Hello from San Francisco.

Roger Earl: Hi, Jack. Right on time. I love that.

Jack Fritscher: Are you ready for your closeup?

Roger Earl: Absolutely.

Jack Fritscher: How are you doing?

Roger Earl: I'm doing fine.

Jack Fritscher: Good. Is it alright with you if I record this?

Roger Earl: Fine.

Jack Fritscher: OK, we're recording. Let's start in the middle of things the way Greek dramas start. Let's go back to that romantic night in June 1989, when Terry [LeGrand] kissed me on the boat in Amsterdam, on the canal. Remember that? We all had a laugh.

Roger Earl: Terry probably did it. Do I remember it? No.

Jack Fritscher: We have a photo Mark [Hemry] shot. He and I had just flown in from California hauling your huge trunk full of lights and cameras that at a couple hundred pounds was not so much carry-on luggage as it was freight. We had just landed at Schiphol [Airport] to shoot on location for you.

Roger Earl: Probably that's why Terry kissed you. We were both so happy to see you.

Jack Fritscher: [Laughs] That first night, you and Terry took us on a dinner-boat tour on the canals of Amsterdam. Two couples. You: a pair of friends. We: lovers. Very romantic with all the lights on the bridges and buildings. It was sweet. Mark and I always remember your gesture very fondly.

Roger Earl: Terry and I had been there in 1988 shooting films.

Jack Fritscher: Just to be clear: that was for your *Dungeons of Europe* trilogy which came out [in 1988] just before your *Bound for Europe* series of six videos we shot for you [in 1989].

Roger Earl: Exactly. *Dungeons* was filmed in England, Holland, and West Germany.

Jack Fritscher: And we shot *Bound* in Holland, Germany, and, more specifically, West Berlin, which was, as it turned out historically, the last summer that West Berlin existed. Did you know that the Christmas after the Berlin Wall fell in November Terry sent us a small chunk of souvenir cement from the wall?

Roger Earl: Terry is a good and thoughtful producer.

Jack Fritscher: And an industrious entrepreneur! Remember how he provided the crew with new leather vests identifying our names embroidered in red on the front and "Marathon Films" on the back. Mark and I were happy he admired the fetish and S&M reality features we shot for our Palm Drive Video studio enough to trust us to shoot in our style for your Marathon Studio. Even though I was with you on location, I'm curious. I remember you told me that *Born to Raise Hell* was your calling card because it was so famous in Europe that it opened doors and dungeons. Men were eager to work with you. How did you feel as an American director shooting twice in Europe with European leathermen personally and authentically dedicated to S&M?

Roger Earl: Actually, I consider the 1989 *Bound* shoot with you as a continuation of our first experience of shooting in Europe.

Jack Fritscher: Your first three European features in *Dungeons* were *Pictures from the Black Dance*, *Moths to a Flame*, and *Men with No Name.*

Roger Earl: Yes. Three films. So the six-video series you shot for me was sort of a continuation of that…

Jack Fritscher: There's definitely a narrative thread connecting your last nine films [*Dungeons* and *Bound*]. I can see that in the fact that Terry contracted Mark and me to shoot three features on two cameras out of which footage you actually cut six interconnected features for *Bound*.

> [*Bound for Europe*: The Six-Feature Video Series, Directed by Roger Earl and Produced by Terry LeGrand of Marathon Films, Cinematography by Jack Fritscher and Mark Hemry of Palm Drive Video; Production Date: June-July 1989, Released Serially: 1990-1994
>
> 1. *Argos: The Sessions*, shot in Amsterdam
> 2. *Fit to Be Tied*, shot in Dusseldorf
> 3. *Marks of Pleasure,* shot in Hamburg
> 4. *The Knast*, shot in West Berlin
> 5. *The Berlin Connection*, shot in West Berlin
> 6. *Loose Ends of the Rope,* shot variously in Amsterdam, Hamburg, Dusseldorf, and West Berlin]

Roger Earl: …And [in that connective narrative] we were using Christian Dreesen again, and shooting in locations we had not gone to earlier.

Jack Fritscher: Ah. Making a connection of shooting Christian in the Connection Club bar in West Berlin for *The Berlin Connection*. Christian was sex-bomb star. When Terry brought him into the hotel lounge to introduce him to us crew, the entire room fell silent. [Dreesen later became both Mr. Germany *Drummer* and Mr. Europe *Drummer*: *Drummer* 147 cover, March 1991]. How much of *Dungeons* was shot in England?

Roger Earl: A lot in England. Most of the rest in Amsterdam.

> [As the founding San Francisco editor-in-chief of *Drummer,* may I recommend journalist Kevin Wolff's interview, "Roger Earl: S&M Auteur," in *Drummer* 126 (March 1989) in which Earl explained that he decided to shoot *Dungeons* in Europe because no American director "had done this, and I'd read so much about Europe in *Drummer,* and in some of the magazines I'd gotten through Larry Townsend from Europe. It looked like a pretty good scene over there…. It all developed from starting to talk to

> Bryan Derbyshire, of *HIM* Magazine. Larry Townsend had put us in touch with most of these people...credited at the end....We didn't know what we were getting into, what kind of locations we'd have, or if we'd even get people. We went over there really on speculation."]

Jack Fritscher: So our *Bound* crew then went to five cities in Germany and met all those wonderful German leathermen.

Roger Earl: The *Bound* series got us to Hamburg and...

Jack Fritscher: Dusseldorf and Cologne and Frankfurt...

Roger Earl: And West Berlin. But I'm thinking about that wonderful club [Terry scouted] in Hamburg, the famous German S&M club, where nobody had ever been allowed to shoot before, and it turned out wonderfully.

Jack Fritscher: That was the dominatrix's place?

Roger Earl: No, no. There was an upstairs and a downstairs, and they had the cages and everything. It was like a clubhouse. The one you're thinking of is in Dusseldorf.

Jack Fritscher: As a cameraman, my recall of the locations is limited because I mainly saw them through my black-and-white viewfinder. In my memory, what was in the camera is more real and lasting than the reality that was real and evaporated. As the director, you processed the entire *mise en scene*. But, yeah. I do remember the Hamburg club you're talking about because that's where that hot "Beast of Hamburg" appeared in the door. That breed of German leathermen was fierce and wonderful.

Roger Earl: What a turn-on they were. They were very serious people who knew what they were doing. It was like watching a ballet to see them play.

Jack Fritscher: When I look at our footage that you've edited together, and it's a good job of editing, by the way, I really like what you've done. That shoot that Mark and I did was your first two-camera shoot, wasn't it?

Roger Earl: Yes, it was.

Jack Fritscher: And that requires a whole new set of conceptual editing skills. A novice can sit down and edit the footage from one camera, start to finish; but to interpret and cut footage from two cameras is really…

Roger Earl: It becomes a little more difficult, but I like it mainly because [with footage from two rolling cameras giving twice the dailies] I feel that I don't really miss any on-set action while one or the other camera is moving to another angle. When you're shooting an S&M sort of [reality] thing, it's not like you can say, hey, *cut*, *wait*, let's go back and start at the beginning.

Jack Fritscher: Going back to the beginning, to your debut film *Born to Raise Hell.* I remember going with a group of leathermen to its San Francisco premiere at the Powell Street Theater, just by the cable car turnaround at Market Street. Standing room only. The struggling Powell was just then turning into a porn theater. Terry must have four-walled it, because the premiere of *Born* started at 10 AM so the manager could start screening his scheduled triple-X double feature at noon. Was it 1975?

Roger Earl Marathon Filmography in *Drummer*

- *Drummer* 3 (August 1975) Cover and photo feature, *Born to Raise Hell*
- *Drummer* 78 (September 1984) Back cover and photo feature, pages 10-17, *Chain Reactions*
- *Drummer* 114 (March 1988) Back cover and photo feature, pages 8-15, *Pictures from the Black Dance*
- *Drummer* 125 (February 1989) Cover: Christian Dreesen, *Like Moths to a Flame*
- *Drummer* 126 (March 1989) "Roger Earl: S&M Auteur," an interview of Roger Earl by Kevin Wolff with photo spread, pages 42-45
- *Drummer* 133 (September 1989) Photo feature, *Men with No Name*
- *Drummer* 144 (November 1990) Cover, Christian Dreesen as "Mr. Europe Drummer"
- *Drummer* 147 (March 1991) Cover, Christian Dreesen as both "Mr. Europe Drummer" and Mr. Germany Drummer," with *Dungeons of Europe* guided-tour feature
- *Drummer* (Special Publication as separate magazine) *Born to Raise Hell* (still photography), 64 pages, 1975

- *Drummer* (Special Publication as separate magazine) *Chain Reactions* (still photography), 64 pages, 1985
- *Mach* 14 (February 1988) Interior photo spread, *Pictures from the Black Dance*, pages 34-41
- *Mach* 15 (May 1988) Interior photo feature, *Like Moths to a Flame*, pages 30-35 (misnamed on the cover as *Pictures from the Black Dance*)
- *Mach* 17 (March 1989) *Like Moths to a Flame*, pages 30-35
- *Mach* 19 (January 1990) *Men with No Name*, pages 46-51
- *Mach* 20 (April 1990) Cover and interior photo spread, *The Argos Session* (cover and stills shot by Jack Fritscher)

More details: www.DrummerArchives.com

Roger Earl: Close to it.

Jack Fritscher: I often see the *Born* release date misquoted as "late 1970s" when it was actually shot in mid-1974, and released in 1975.

Roger Earl: I believe it was.

Jack Fritscher: In a timeline, I remember that *Born* was immediately showcased on the cover and inside the third issue of *Drummer* magazine in August 1975, as well as in the special *Drummer* spin-off publication of your stills titled *Born to Raise Hell.* You were good for *Drummer* business and *Drummer* was good for yours. I counted nearly a dozen *Drummer* covers and interior spreads dedicated to your work. Plus covers and coverage in five issues of the *Drummer* sibling magazine, *Mach*, including the cover of *Mach* 20 which, you remember, I shot the first night in the Argos bar, for *The Argos Sessions*, when I was shooting the stills before you hired David Pearce to do that because, as you may recall, I told you it was impossible for me to shoot both the Hi-8 video and the 35mm stills of scenes that were one-take chances. Your relationship to *Drummer* was symbiosis. Perfect marketing. Your photos were a hit with readers who turned into viewers of your films.

> [During twenty-four years, the 214 issues of *Drummer*, with a 42,000 press run per issue in the 1970s, were read, quite literally, by millions worldwide.]

Roger Earl: You know *Drummer* better than I do.

Jack Fritscher: Just as *Drummer* depended on you to fill our hungry monthly pages, the gay films of the 1970s depended on gay magazines to get publicity and esthetic respect. When I see your name in magazine ads for your very successful Marathon film company, and people writing reviews, they always call you a filmmaker. And you are a filmmaker, but like all us directors, you evolved into a video maker in the early 1980s. Do you remember coming out into the hallway of our hotel in Amsterdam? That wonderful hotel, the Victoria, directly facing Centraal Railway Station? Terry had a little device in his hand, and you and he told us it was the latest high-tech thing: a camera that did not use film.

Roger Earl: Absolutely. I'm a filmmaker who graduated to video. And to digital. Way back when, I edited *Born to Raise Hell* on my dining room table, cut from original 16mm film.

Jack Fritscher: On a Movieola?

Roger Earl: No, not on a Movieola. On one of those little Moviescopes.

Jack Fritscher: How long did it take you to edit *Born*?

Roger Earl: Oh God, three to four weeks. Mainly because I had hired someone to do the actual cutting while I was making all the decisions. We were cutting the original color footage because I couldn't afford to make a work print. Believe me: I didn't want to screw up the original. His name was... He was a lover of one of the Christy twins. He did a couple of films as a director/photographer.

Jack Fritscher: Yes, the twins. Did you know the Christy twins?

Roger Earl: One of them used to come over and sit in the patio while we did our editing. [On *Born*, Tim Christy was assistant sound editor and sound recordist.]

Jack Fritscher: Tim and Chris Christy and their gay porn films! Twincest as taboo in that first decade after Stonewall. [I shot my Palm Drive feature *Twincest* with the Blake Twins in 1992.] Were they from the South?

Roger Earl: I think so, from the San Diego area originally. *Vince*. That's it. *Vince* was the first name of the editor on *Born to Raise Hell*. I'll think of his last name before this is over. *Vince Trainer*. That was his name. He did the physical cut.

Jack Fritscher: How many prints did you make for theatrical showing?

Roger Earl: I don't really know. Terry did that and I think he had three or four made.

Jack Fritscher: How did you meet Terry?

Roger Earl: I was working at NBC, had gotten a job there, in Burbank. I had gone to a party in the Hollywood Hills and met this older gentleman named George who was very hunky and I ended up in the basement with him, whipping his ass on the staircase. He had got me my job at NBC. Later on, he came to me and said, "I've got some friends who want to make a very heavy S&M film, and I told them that I would only do it if you would do it with me." And I said, "Well, OK." There was a meeting to go to. He never showed up at the meeting, and he never wanted anything to do with the project afterwards. He said, "I don't know anything about directing. You just go ahead and do it." So that's how I met Terry and got involved with *Born to Raise Hell.*

Jack Fritscher: How did Terry know this guy?

Roger Earl: He was a friend of George. He had known George for years and years.

Jack Fritscher: Can we use his last name?

Roger Earl: George has passed away, so I guess it's OK. It was Lawson, George Lawson.

Jack Fritscher: So you had those theatrical prints made, and that went on to great sales in Super-8 film, right, in the 1970s when gay mail order was beginning? I remember watching Wakefield Poole in his home office, busy stuffing Super-8 copies of *Boys in the Sand* into envelopes for his Irving mail-order.

Roger Earl: I guess we sold it on Super-8. You know, Terry handled all of that business. All I was interested in was the creative part. Of course, that's why I didn't get what I was supposed to, because I didn't get involved.

> [In West Berlin in 1989, Roger Earl told Mark Hemry and me how during pre-production in West Hollywood in 1974 he had taken out a personal loan of ten-thousand dollars from his boss, singer Dean Martin, to finance *Born to Raise Hell.*]

Jack Fritscher: Well, you helped launch the gay-lib 1970s as the "Golden Age of Gay Film," because, soon after Stonewall, gay movie houses popped up in big cities and did big box office until video came out in 1981 and audiences stayed home jerking off to VHS cassettes. The majority of gay movie theaters where you could watch porn and get blown lasted little more than ten years before they were killed by the VCR and HIV.

Roger Earl: [About that decade of 1970s gay film] I want to say one thing, too, about making *Born to Raise Hell* and that is that I would never have made it, never had a part in it, if it hadn't been for Fred Halsted putting out *L. A. Plays Itself.*

> [Actor/director Fred Halsted's 1972 American experimental film, which he began shooting in 1968, a year before Stonewall, was almost immediately accepted in the permanent collection of the New York Museum of Modern Art which for a time had the only complete original copy because censorship and marketing caused Halsted to re-cut the film several times, deleting the fisting, to please nervous distributors. *L. A. Plays Itself* was something new, a gay *film noir* of violent urban sex between Halsted and a "Texan" that ends with a montage of newspaper headlines about an S&M murder. In that way, *L. A. Plays Itself* is a precursor to William Friedkin's controversial leather film, *Cruising.* Mistaken in his thinking that Halsted's film was a documentary, Police Chief Ed Davis of the LAPD increased his harassment of leather bars, gay movie theaters, and, particularly, *Drummer* whose staff he arrested, causing *Drummer* to flee from LA to San Francisco.]

Jack Fritscher: In July 1975, Jeanne Barney [September 13, 1938-November 3, 2018]. published Halsted's newest film *Sextool* on the cover of *Drummer*, issue two, and your *Born to Raise Hell* on the cover of issue three.

> [Before the "Leather Bloomsbury Group" circling *Drummer* in Los Angeles was busted by the LAPD in 1976, the *prima inter pares* editor-in-chief of *Drummer*, Jeanne Barney, was a kind of straight dowager matrix to the group. She was the lifelong friend of *Drummer* columnist Fred Halsted and the trusted keeper of his secrets. She was the longtime friend of Roger Earl and *Drummer* artist Chuck Arnett who drew her. She was frenemies forever with *Drummer* publisher John Embry. She imagined *Drummer* to be a

leather version of *The Evergreen Review*. She understood how gay films and *Drummer* could be symbiotic in creating the revolutionary art and eros that ignited the Golden Age of Gay Cinema in the 1970s on page and screen years before gay film/video review magazines first appeared in the 1980s. In the San Francisco *Drummer* Salon that followed the LA Bloomsbury Group, various filmmakers such as Wakefield Poole, the Gage Brothers, and Mikal Bales of Zeus Studio, benefitted from such hand-in-glove covers at least once. Terry LeGrand had noticed that of the many covers I shot for *Drummer*, including my *Drummer* 30 cover of his star Val Martin, four covers featured my Palm Drive Video films. In the same synergy that LeGrand and Earl had with *Drummer*, my Palm Drive videos were regularly featured in centerfolds and photo spreads. I liked that *Drummer* aggressively promoted the popularity of gay cinema in most issues, as well as in periodic Special Publications each designed as a separate movie magazine, each featuring stills from the film title: *Sextool*, 48 pages, 1975; *Born to Raise Hell*, 64 pages, 1975; and *Chain Reactions,* 64 pages, 1985.]

Roger Earl: Having seen *L. A. Plays Itself*, and having admired it, and saying, OK, it's safe to show gay sex on screen, I no longer thought of it as something that you can't go and do. I think Fred was truly the one who started it all, and without him I would never have done it. I really had a lot of respect for Fred.

Jack Fritscher: He liberated you.

Roger Earl: He was a friend, and I admired him very much.

Jack Fritscher: I did too. He was a pioneer [who owed much to the master underground filmmaker, Kenneth Anger, director of the quintessential S&M piss-and-blasphemy leather-biker film, *Scorpio Rising* (1964)].

Roger Earl: Absolutely.

Jack Fritscher: Even before I succeeded Jeanne Barney as editor of *Drummer*, when Barney first started, Fred was a regular columnist. He was a writer as well as a filmmaker and a great creative spirit who went on to publish his own *Drummer*-style magazine, *Package*.

Roger Earl: Exactly. I had wonderful times with him, too.

Jack Fritscher: Everyone so regretted Fred's suicide [1941-1989] after Joey Yale [his lover and muse] died of AIDS [1949-1986]. Tell me about your wonderful times with Fred.

Roger Earl: Fred always came and bottomed for me. He was a wonderful bottom, and we just had wild, wild sexual times together.

Jack Fritscher: Halsted was a bottom? How different from his dominant image on screen. Can you describe a typical scene?

Roger Earl: We made love, that's literally what we did.

Jack Fritscher: Lucky you, with Fred Halsted.

Roger Earl: We did that on many occasions.

Jack Fritscher: Everybody always thinks of him as the ideal top.

Roger Earl: Exactly. I'm not out to destroy this. He was a wonderful man, and a creative, terrific person. He was wonderful to play with.

Jack Fritscher: Did he like to get whipped or spanked or tit-play?

Roger Earl: Absolutely. He was game for everything.

Jack Fritscher: What about fisting? Which you so scandalously depicted in *Born to Raise Hell*?

> [The first films to include fisting were Fred Halsted's *Sex Garage* and *L. A. Plays Itself*, both 1972, and his *Sextool*, 1975. Under threats from the LAPD, Halsted was forced to cut the fisting scenes from all three films so he could screen them in Los Angeles. Because of this, LeGrand premiered *Born* intact in San Francisco where a politically correct someone ran from the theater making a rape accusation that its vivid handballing scene was not consensual. The "scandal" was either an urban legend that failed to credit Earl for his ability to direct actors in characterized ways that seem real, or it was a great self-generated publicity stunt by master showman Terry LeGrand who was not above hiring a stooge to create exciting or contentious "word of mouth" which is a marketing dynamic that sells tickets at the box office. In 1976, French filmmaker Jean-Étienne Siry released his gorgeous 20-minute classic *Erotic Hands* starring "Bill [blond-bearded],

B. Dick, and Don." "B. Dick" was Richard Trask, owner of the Wizard's Emerald City gift shop at 1645 Market Street in San Francisco for whom I wrote and designed an advertising brochure. Trask and "Don" both played at the Slot Hotel on Folsom Street where they individually went bottoms up for me who found it an exciting challenge to surprise their insatiably experienced holiness. *Erotic Hands* consists of two scenes sourced from two other Siry shorts: "Entrepôt 026" aka "The Warehouse Part 1" and "Poing de Force" aka "The Warehouse Part 2." Siry's soundtrack to the "Poing de Force" ("Fists of Force") section of *Erotic Hands* can be heard on YouTube.]

Roger Earl: Fisting. Fred and I didn't get into all that.

Jack Fritscher: That gives me some idea of the range of you two LA filmmakers at play.

Roger Earl: But it's wonderful memories. Very beautiful memories.

Jack Fritscher: Yes, Halsted is a saint in the S&M pantheon; but he is often ignored or distorted by politically-correct gay film historians who too often look at homomasculine cinema through a feminist lens that confuses male-sex action on screen with the non-consensual action of violence. You give a vision of male history; they give their female revision. Perhaps they do this because S&M films are not really about sex itself as much as they are about the intense male bonding and human psychology of the participants. Jeanne Barney always discerned the difference.

Roger Earl: You know, I agree with you, Jack. And that's why [I was pleased] when they asked me to guest-edit an issue of *International Leatherman* [founded by Terry LeGrand who, from his twenty years of exposure in *Drummer*, understood fully the power of gay magazines in promoting films]. As editor, I did a whole thing on Fred, two pages, because I thought it was very important for me to testify. Like I said: *Born to Raise Hell* would not have happened without Fred.

[The cover of LeGrand's *International Leatherman*, issue 3, January 1990, published by his Parkwood Publications, listed Roger Earl as editor, and featured Christian Dreesen on the cover shot by David Pearce on location at the Knast Bar, Berlin, June 1989; including twenty centerfold photographs from the Knast. In issue two, LeGrand wrote that he had titled his new magazine, a doppelganger for *Drummer*, after a fictitious magazine titled *Leatherman*, which was also a doppelganger for *Drummer*, in my *Some Dance to Remember: A Memoir-Novel of San Francisco 1970-1982*.]

Jack Fritscher: While Vince Trainer did your editing, did you show Fred any of the rushes?

Roger Earl: Oh yeah. Fred liked the film, admired it, and was my greatest fan. He was wonderful.

Jack Fritscher: Did you ever meet the Gage brothers whose homomasculinist films we also featured in *Drummer*?

Roger Earl: No.

Jack Fritscher: Few have. That's why I wondered if you did. At *Drummer*, we published dozens of stills of Gage films without personally meeting Joe Gage [aka Tim Kincaid, a charming man I met at my home in 2011 when he arrived to interview me on camera for a documentary he was trying to make on David Hurles].

Roger Earl: Then I don't feel so bad.

[As editor of *Drummer* seeking a hot film to follow *Born to Raise Hell*, I introduced into the pages of *Drummer* 19 (December 1977) the work of the Gage Brothers who proved a perfect fit for *Drummer* covers and photo spreads with their homomasculine trilogy: *Kansas City Trucking Co.* (1976), *El Paso Wrecking Corp.* (1978), and *L. A. Tool and Die* (1979). Like their contemporary, Roger Earl, the Gages were storytellers of episodic sex featuring the picaresque escapades of reality actors like Fred Halsted, Jack Wrangler, and the mature Richard Locke who was *Drummer* 's first "Daddy"—at age 37! In content and style, the Gage *mise en scene* embraced technique, material, eros, and casting that were embraced in 1976 by fans of the new genre of homomasculine action movies kick-started by Halsted (1972) and Earl (1974).]

Jack Fritscher: You had the good luck to meet Val Martin.

Roger Earl: God, yes, did I ever.

Jack Fritscher: So tell me. In a sense, you and Terry are the director and producer who discovered Vallotte Martinelli [1939-1985] who was an immigrant from Brazil, a porn model, and a star in the leather bars in Los Angeles. As soon as you finished shooting *Born*, Fred Halsted cast him in *Sextool* (1975).

> [Val Martin was one of the forty-two leatherfolk arrested with *Drummer* publisher John Embry and founding LA editor-in-chief Jeanne Barney and Roger Earl and Terry LeGrand during the raid by the LAPD on the *Drummer* Slave Auction, April 1976, that drove *Drummer* to freedom in San Francisco. Because Val became the "Face of *Drummer*," I photographed him with his partner, the model Leo Stone (Bob Hyslop), for the cover of our Fourth Anniversary Issue, *Drummer* 30, June 1979, and for the centerfold of *Drummer* 31.]

Jack Fritscher: When you introduced Val to *Drummer*, it was a perfect fit. We put him on more covers than any other person, including the cover of the second issue publicizing *Sextool*, and the cover of the third issue trumpeting *Born to Raise Hell*. He was so popular that in 1979, John Embry, Al Shapiro, and I appointed him the first "Mr. Drummer" without even bothering to pretend he won in competition.

Roger Earl: I will tell you the truth. Leaving that first meeting with George Lawson, and driving from there, the name *Born to Raise Hell* came to me. I pictured the motorcycle guy with the tattoo "Born to Raise Hell." The name came straight from that meeting. I knew that I had to have a real dynamic guy to carry this thing. Otherwise it was going to be the same old shit. So I went on my search. There was a guy who I thought would be wonderful, a Colt model, name of Ledermeister. I knew that Paul [Gerrior aka Ledermeister, April 19, 1933-January 18, 2021] hung out at some of the baths. I talked to him briefly. He really was not into the scene, although I liked his look.

Jack Fritscher: I did too. He's iconic as a pioneer super-model in gay media.

Roger Earl: I went out to the bars, thinking, how was I going to shoot this thing? I don't have anybody—when in walks Val! I knew he was right from the minute I saw him. I said, "You've got to ask him." But I was afraid to ask him. He might smash me right through the fucking wall. Finally,

I screwed up my nerve and went over to him. He was very nice to me. He said, "Why don't you give me your card and I'll call you tomorrow. This is not the proper place to talk about anything like this." I gave him my card and at 10:00 the next morning he called me. He was a man of his word, a real gentleman.

Jack Fritscher: Yes, he was also supporting, so he said, his eighteen siblings back in South America, and his two children from a former marriage. We hung out in the *Drummer* Salon of leathermen after he moved from LA to San Francisco. Forty of my photographs of Val were published in the centerfold of *Drummer* [issue 31, September 1979].

Roger Earl: He was a terrific guy, nice, kind. I made a panel for Val [who died April 13, 1985] for the AIDS Memorial Quilt. I put all kinds of studding in it, the whole thing, the name. At the bottom of the panel, I put the words: "A Leatherman and a Gentleman." That's the way I felt about him, a true gentleman.

Jack Fritscher: He was. And he was terribly, wonderfully hot, too. It's interesting that you considered Ledermeister because he is such a great gay porn icon from the 1960s and 1970s. He was, in fact, a lineman for a utility company [Pacific Telephone and AT&T], one of those guys you see all geared up opening manholes and climbing poles.

Roger Earl: He was just the first guy that came to mind. I needed someone for this film that was going to be a dynamic personality.

Jack Fritscher: I know his dynamism. I shot some twenty-minutes of Super-8 footage of Ledermeister in 1973 when he was out on 15th Street near the Castro doing his lineman work, wearing a tank top and sitting with his legs down inside a manhole while he stripped wire between his knees. But as you say, he wasn't really into the scene although I often saw him at the Folsom leather bars, one time coming out of the No Name on crutches because he'd wrecked his motorcycle and broken his leg. I thought, hmmm, he's limping. I can finally catch him. And I did. In my home. In my bed. I've never washed those sheets. He's had an interesting career as a legit stage actor in San Francisco. I think you and Ledermeister would have been great together.

Roger Earl: Well, *Born* wouldn't have worked [validly or realistically] without someone who was into the scene. Val was into it. He was very talented and easy to look at [playing the part of "Bearded Sadist"].

Jack Fritscher: We put Val on four *Drummer* covers. You are right: he was so easy to look at. Right after *Born*, he went on to attempt a fisting scene with Casey Donovan in Wakefield Poole's *Moving*. Poole was another director featured in *Drummer* [issue 27, February 1979]. Who else in the cast of *Born* did you enjoy?

Roger Earl: I have never really had a problem with cast members. I've enjoyed everyone I've ever worked with, and the ones that I didn't, I got rid of.

Jack Fritscher: I mean their performances on screen. Whose do you think was successful?

Roger Earl: Well, I liked that little kid, John Detour [who plays "Barroom Victim #1"] in the beginning scene in the bar. He's the one that starts out in the bathroom and then moves onto the pool table. When he finished that and I told him thanks and that he was going to be dynamite, he said, "Is that all they're going to do to me? I was hoping for so much more." I said, "Just give me a couple of minutes and we'll arrange something." So we went on with the alligator clips and everything.

Jack Fritscher: I think that's one of the wonderful things about S&M movies: your personal casting of guys personally committed to the scene. The actors, role-playing themselves, seem to be eager and able to go farther, faster, deeper into their real kinks than you might even hope for. In vanilla movies, the actors often seem like hired dicks, disinterested and ready to break for lunch.

Roger Earl: Well, I've done vanilla movies, of course. One I was on, there was this cute little "boy," looked like he was from Arkansas, with this little wiry muscular body, and being fucked by this big bear-type guy, and all of a sudden I hear snoring. The kid is sound asleep.

Jack Fritscher: Tired? Drugged? Jaded?

> [Adding to the concept of "scandal" above: It's a problem during a shoot if questions of consent arise. It must be addressed that through no fault of Earl's, a few in those early 1970 audiences, because they had never seen an S&M film before, were not esthetically prepared for the consensual role-playing intensity on screen which their limited experience mistook as nonconsensual violence. Few had ever witnessed fisting, which was a rather new sex

practice in the 1970s. So they had no way to judge the negotiated consensuality of the on-screen fisting scene that was meant to be a thrill even as the bottom acted out his "resistance." True players know that in a sling, with or without a camera present, the dialogue is a constant stream of yesyesnoyesnonoyeeeeesss! *Born to Raise Hell* is meta-cinema, like a play within a play by Jean Genet where actors play actresses playing the role of maids playing the role of their mistress who in turn plays the role of the maids playing actresses playing actors. Earl cast non-actors to play themselves as role-playing characters who are themselves. Falling through the looking glass of the screen, *Born* dramatizes a normal leather night's sex play by authentic men within a fantasy film about S&M reality directed by Roger Earl. As sadomasochism came out of the closet in the 1970s with fictitious international films like *The Night Porter* and *Salo*, audiences grew into sexual literacy, and stopped freaking out like fundamentalists that a documentary director as skilled as Earl could overpower them with *film verite* dialogue and images that would shake their willing suspension of disbelief—which is the goal of a storyteller.]

Roger Earl: The big guy is just fucking him like crazy and he's snoring.

Jack Fritscher: Very different from the sex excitement on your *Bound* sets. I remember Terry would have an authentic twosome or threesome of kinksters standing by to film their sequences, and all of them were ready and hot to trot, and were so intense that you decided not to yell "cut" when their scene ran longer than you had planned. That's one of the reasons *Bound* which was pitched as three features ended up being six.

Roger Earl: You just go with it [the actors on a shoot] and get what you can and tear it apart [in post-production] when you get it home.

Jack Fritscher: Sure, if the players want to beat each other up for another hour, it's cheaper to roll tape than it was to shoot film. Sometimes all the excitement was not on screen. Remember when we were shooting in the Knast? The long line-up of steel plates that were the floor-covering of the bar somehow got electrified from all our power cords, and the cameras and lights kept shorting and blinking. Mark and I spent much of that shoot lying on the floor aiming angles up to heroize the action, and our bodies started tingling, head to toe. Cheap thrills on Fuggerstrasse! We were all being electrocuted. And you immediately saw to everyone's on-set safety.

Roger Earl: For me, the key to it all, the thing that I think I have the most talent at is editing. I take a lot of pride in that. I see so many films, I say to myself, why didn't they cut that? They went right to this. Tighten this up. I see so many films where there is no rhythm. You've got to have a rhythm. Some of the people who do pornography don't understand that.

Jack Fritscher: I call those people "tripod queens." They put the actors on one side of the room and the camera on a tripod on the other side. They never move the camera, never zoom in, and basically release CCTV footage. They haven't made a film. They made footage. They've just turned on the camera. Yet it sells because most people will watch shit as long as it's *new.* From my thirty years in the business, I figure that consumers rarely even care that gay video could be better than it is. In fact, I think it's ironic that gay people are supposed to be so much smarter and have such better taste than straight people, except when it comes to gay video, and we often make worse videos than they do, except for you. You have a rhythm.

Roger Earl: That's important to me.

Jack Fritscher: You do have a good editing rhythm. Mikal Bales [1939-2012] of Zeus Studio, whose first bondage films I introduced in *Drummer* [issue 30, June 1979], has a rhythm, but it's a camera rhythm, not an editing rhythm. He moves the camera around the action very nicely. He cuts differently from the way you cut because of your two completely different artistic styles, both of which suit your work.

Roger Earl: Right.

Jack Fritscher: *Born to Raise Hell* was your first movie. How many have you made over all?

Roger Earl: Hmmm. Probably 45. Which includes all the vanilla stuff.

> [Roger Earl told Kevin Wolff in *Drummer* 126: "I'm doing another non-S&M film shortly. I've got quite a background doing porno films. Non S&M films are always scripted. S&M porno films are unscripted for me. You can do a light script, but I prefer to do segment things and just let guys do their own thing without me telling them, 'You're playing a part.' …Once I give them a character, and have them play a part…, it takes away from their real self. I think that's more important in an S&M type thing….

Maybe I should try scripting an S&M film sometime. I feel I get more out of people by not doing it."]

Jack Fritscher: I think highly of your *Gayracula*, *Men of the Midway*, and *Chain Reactions* which was also published as a special *Drummer* photo book. You were at your production peak by the close of the 1980s. So I was delighted that Terry, because he had liked how Mark and I, two cameramen shooting with matching style, invited us to film with you at the height of your career in 1989. I know that when we all met on the boat in Amsterdam that Terry and I were celebrating our June birthdays. How about you?

Roger Earl: I was born in January 1939. Aquarius.

Jack Fritscher: I'm June. Gemini. 1939. Where were you born?

Roger Earl: A town called Barstow, California. In the Mojave Desert.

Jack Fritscher: What was it like growing up in Barstow?

Roger Earl: I grew up in Ludlow, a town of thirty-five people, fifty miles from Barstow [East, on I-40], but I went to school in Barstow. It was wonderful growing up where I did. I was the only child in a town of thirty-five people, spoiled rotten not only by my parents but by the entire town. I could do no wrong and they couldn't do enough for me. My dad had a truck stop, garage, motel, café, all of that. I started in on [sex with] truck drivers when I was seven years old.

[For twenty years, beginning in the 1940s, Roger's parents, Earl and Lillian Warnix, ran the popular Art Deco Streamline-Moderne Ludlow Cafe and Union 76 gas station in the Mojave Desert on the legendary Route 66 in Ludlow, California. When the incoming Interstate 40, known as the "Needles Highway," bypassed the town in 1964, they sold their historic building which lasted several more years as a business before it burned down into ruins that remain in the ghost town where Roger once greeted incoming traffic.]

Jack Fritscher: You grew up living Halsted's *Sex Garage*.

Roger Earl: I was well known up and down the line. They would come in and want to know if there was a kid here named Roger. And I would take on the truck drivers. If I didn't like the looks of them, I'd say, "I don't know what you're talking about."

Jack Fritscher: How did it dawn on you at the age of seven to do this?

Roger Earl: I was a horny little bastard, I was very sexual at the age of seven. I had an uncle who was an incredible looking man. He was just beautiful, big muscles, hairy chest, and all that. Of course, it is very hot in the desert around Barstow and he ran around with his shirt off all the time. When I was a kid, I ran around in my underwear, just a pair of jockey shorts. He used to pick me up and hold me in his arms and, wow! the electricity would just fly.

Jack Fritscher: Was he aware you were turned on?

Roger Earl: I don't think so.

Jack Fritscher: The point I'm getting to is, most people instinctively know that if someone has sex with a seven-year-old boy, the boy is being abused.

Roger Earl: I know. That's the dumbest thing in the world. I was a real aggressor like you wouldn't believe.

Jack Fritscher: Mark was the same at about the same age. He knew what he wanted and went out and got it. Both of you seem to have understood *consent* at an early age. If that's even possible.

Roger Earl: You couldn't blame anybody but me. I guarantee you.

Jack Fritscher: Did anybody else in the town find out about this?

Roger Earl: No, and let me tell you honestly, Jack, I could have sucked dick right in the middle of Highway 66 and nobody would have believed it because I was the perfect person. I could do no wrong. I was the best little boy in the whole wide world. It was one of those situations where I had the best of everything.

Jack Fritscher: So you went down on these guys and sucked them?

Roger Earl: Sure.

Jack Fritscher: What about anal sex, anything like that until you were a teenager?

Roger Earl: I did, yes. They fucked me. When I got to be seventeen or eighteen, I suddenly decided that I didn't like that at all anymore and basically haven't done it since.

Jack Fritscher: How old were these guys? All different ages?

Roger Earl: Anywhere from their twenties to late forties or fifties. There were some fifty-year-old guys that were incredible.

Jack Fritscher: Most people, Roger, will have difficulty understanding this fact of your own psychology.

Roger Earl: It was a wonderful experience. And, of course, the movies! Once in a while I would get to go to Barstow to the movies, and I would get all worked up, especially if it was a Tyrone Power movie where he was tied up in a dungeon and put on the rack. It drove me right up the fucking wall, and I'm talking seven-eight years old.

Jack Fritscher: Was your family religious?

Roger Earl: No. There was no church in Ludlow. I mean they were religious, but not [practicing] when they came to Ludlow.

Jack Fritscher: I was wondering if your sadomasochistic interests were fueled by religious tales, like heroic Christian martyrs tortured by gladiators in the Roman Coliseum. Or something like that.

Roger Earl: I never went to church. Religion has never been part of my life.

Jack Fritscher: That probably accounts for the guilt-free purity of your movies. What is your second favorite film after *Born to Raise Hell*?

Roger Earl: There are a few. I definitely like *Like Moths to a Flame* because that was the first one I did with Christian Dreesen. Christian is very special to me just like Val was.

Jack Fritscher: Tell me how you met him. He was a refugee who had somehow escaped from East Germany.

Roger Earl: Strangely enough, I saw him in one of those little European S&M books. I think it was called *Mr. S&M* or something like that [actually *TOY*], in one of the ads. Terry and I had already met one guy in England, the guy that owns Fetters [custom leather shop] in London...

Jack Fritscher: Maurice Stewart known also as "Jim Stewart"? [British stage-and-screen actor and director, James Maurice Stewart-Addison, 1932-2012; not American leather author and photographer Jim Stewart, 1942-2018, who wrote the memoir *Folsom Street Blues*.] He founded Fetters. He owns it. I've known him since we met in swinging London in 1969 when we were having sex at his home and he was so proud of the leather toys he was just then inventing before he went into business. He introduced me to his circle of leather bikers who hung out at the Coleherne bar, out on Old Brompton Road.

Roger Earl: Yes. That Jim: Maurice. He designed and built the S&M equipment used in the film. He was friends with these other [leather] people. Anyway, we were going to see Stewart, and we talked to these two other guys, David and John, about doing a film. David [Pearce] was John's, mmm, I don't know what. He lived with John [my friend John Howe], but I never could figure out if they were lovers or not.

Jack Fritscher: David lived on the dole and depended on the kindness of strangers. When you introduced us to him in Amsterdam, he held out his arms to Mark and me and said, "Are you the gentlemen I've been expecting?" We three became friends until David disappeared during the AIDS crisis in the early 1990s. David was as great a painter as he was a photographer, and he knew everyone who was anyone in London.

Roger Earl: Yes, and in pursuit of Christian, I was going on and on about this gorgeous guy in this book, and I showed his picture to David who Terry hired to be our still photographer for *Dungeons*, and David said, "Well, I took the picture. That's Christian." I said, "Well, call him, damn it! I want him in my movie." And that's how we met Christian.

Jack Fritscher: So you flew him in from West Germany to London.

Roger Earl: Exactly. He worked with John [Howe] in the first film, *Like Moths to a Flame*. Down in John's little basement area.

Jack Fritscher: John's done some interesting work as an extra in a number of films shot in England, Hollywood-type movies. When the Operation Spanner scandal happened in England in 1987, what did you think of that witch-hunt that started with seizure of a gay S&M video the Manchester cops thought was real torture leading to a gay snuff film? [The fundamentalist British court ruled that an adult person does not have the legal right to consent to receiving what they considered bodily harm in BDSM play.] One of your actors, Mr. Sebastian [Alan Oversby, 1933-1996, British pioneer body piercing and tattoo artist], was one of the sixteen men arrested. Refusing to consider the issue of consent, the judge sentenced him to a fifteen months suspended sentence for performing genital piercings on willing clients.

Roger Earl: I kept thinking, I hope to God the criminalizing of S&M has nothing to do with us. I was afraid it did, and then later on I found out it [Spanner] didn't have anything to do with us.

Jack Fritscher: Still, that fundamentalist wave of new British and American censorship as the 1980s became the 1990s was very threatening to us all. If you recall, because Mark had a lifelong career within the U.S. Government, and because I was so affected by the censorship against the photographs of my dear friend Robert Mapplethorpe, we asked Terry to remove our credit as cameramen for caution against legal reprisals because of the very heavy S&M sex in *Bound.* The hot footage we shot in Europe seemed dangerous in the States. So the credits for the videos in the *Bound* six-pack sometimes list us and sometimes do not. That ambiguity is not unusual in the history of gay cinema where legal anxieties often impact the credits of producers, cast, and crew.

Roger Earl: Yes. As you know, movies are copied and bootlegged all over, but we never set up any European distribution of any of these films. So we were safe. We distributed our Marathon films only in the United States, although I am sure our titles were copied and sold by pirates all over the world.

Jack Fritscher: These London leathermen were convicted of performing consensual S&M acts on themselves and you were shooting consensual stuff. I think that society in Europe, England in particular, as well as in the U.S. has grown more uptight with the rise of fundamentalist religion of the kind that caused [the right-wing Republican] Jesse Helms to attack Robert Mapplethorpe for his leather photographs on the floor of the United States Senate in 1989, the same summer you and I were together shooting *Bound for Europe.* There was a wonderful window still open in the culture war when you shot *Dungeons* in 1988, but that window was closing when we shot *Bound.* That last summer of that decade when we went to West Berlin with you was an ironic pivot in gay culture because both Spanner and Helms were shutting down freedom of personal and artistic expression at the same moment the Berlin Wall came down, opening up freedom. Remember how repugnant those hard female East German customs guards were who tore through our suitcases and cameras when our group of gay men stood nervously in line to board our flight over Communist East Germany into West Berlin, which had a limit on its population? One American had to exit West Berlin before another could enter. Five months later the wall came down. Shooting porn in that city that summer, surrounded by Communists, was like something defiant Christopher ("I am a Camera") Isherwood might have done in the Weimar Republic before World War II. It was a magical time and a wonderful time. And a dangerous time.

Roger Earl: Yes it was, and I am just so thankful that we were there then.

Jack Fritscher: Now, eight years later with Reunification, the mood of Berlin has changed. A German shoot now would be less of a political act.

Roger Earl: And so many of our friends are gone now that were there then. The guys that owned the Connection bar.

Jack Fritscher: So many gone.... After everyone's cult favorite, *Born to Raise Hell*, what is your next personal favorite film? In 1980, six years after you shot *Born*, you shot your film, *Rear Admiral*, with Fred Halsted's lover Joey Yale, followed by *Gayracula* (1983). It's seriously hot porn, but has comic elements, and camp in character names like the "Marquis de Suede." I think that *Gayracula*'s fixation on blood at the start of the AIDS epidemic makes it a timely psychological study amidst the terrific sex.

Roger Earl: I'll tell you, *Gayracula* was a fun film. I was crazy about Tim Kramer. Such a sweet, lovely man.

Jack Fritscher: A luscious All-American blond. When he's bitten on the neck, it ain't a normal hickey.

Roger Earl: Another film that I really enjoyed doing was *Chain Reactions.*

Jack Fritscher: A terrific film. *Drummer* published a great review of *Chain Reactions* with eleven photos in issue 78, with cover copy asking the inevitable question: "Sneak Preview: Is the New *Chain Reactions* a Sequel to *Born to Raise Hell*?" *Drummer* followed that feature with the *Drummer* special *Chain Reactions* photo book of sixty-four pages. There's that synergy again between *Drummer* and film. The review, which I have at hand, mentions you and Terry hosting *Drummer* with Ken Bergquist (Mr.

Drummer 1984, first-runner-up) at your home "where Roger whipped out over a thousand photographs of their new film, *Chain Reactions*, which was almost finished." You struck a deal to cast Bergquist in the final motorcycle orgy scene which was shot at the bar "'Chains," which was made over from the [bar] the "Pits" in Los Angeles, much as *Born to Raise Hell* was shot at the old "Truck Stop" [bar] out in the San Fernando Valley. And what a compliment *Drummer* pays you! Your name becomes a brand name in the line: "The action is uniquely 'Roger Earl,' very leather with a flair that few filmmakers can approach."

Roger Earl: I understand that today *Chain Reactions* has unfortunately been chopped up by distributors.

Jack Fritscher: That film had orgy sex, spankings, slings, and enemas. Was that Daniel Holt that you tied up in the spider-web? For *Bound*, I remember how you had the "Dutch Master" Harry Ros spend hours before our shoot tying a slave into a rope spider web.

Roger Earl: That was Dwan tied up in the *Chain Reactions* web. I designed the whole smoky thing with the candle wax and all that. Those were fun scenes that I thought turned out sort of artsy-fartsy and were still erotic. That one kid here in LA who made artsy videos and just died…

Jack Fritscher: Bad Brad. Nice kid. [Brad Braverman, 1961-1996, porn star and director, invoked Roger Earl's *Gayracula* in his feature video *Disconnected* (1992) with its vampire sequences.]

Roger Earl: Yes, him. His videos are artsy, but I don't find them erotic.

Jack Fritscher: I agree. I interviewed him last year right before he died and I thought he was way more of a film editor than he was a filmmaker. He was a stylist with little content. It was unfortunate that he died so young because he might have eventually learned how to use both content and style to compose a film. I doubt if anyone could cum to his work, which was like a soap or car commercial, very MTV.

Roger Earl: That's the key to me. If I can't get off on it, it's a waste of my time.

Jack Fritscher: I told Bad Brad nobody ever shot their load to a special effect on screen.

Roger Earl: Never will.

Jack Fritscher: CGI special effects. Salad-shooter editing. Not hot. The best art conceals itself to help the audience suspend their disbelief. Overt technology calls attention to itself and distracts sexual heat. It's often the ruination of eros when people get too "high tech." My friend, the San Francisco filmmaker Michael Goodwin [1937-2006, founder of "Goodjac Productions"] who does the *Goodjac Chronicles* also gets too artsy. He yearns to be an artist, but he should make art films on one side and erotic films on the other, and not mix the two. Art school is one thing. In the real world, art and sex rarely seem to mix because horndog viewers are voyeurs who don't want to start thinking while they are masturbating to forget the workday they spent thinking about real life. Robert Mapplethorpe, in many people's minds, mixed style and content together for perfect moments that are maybe intellectual and esthetic, but not hot moments. He was more of a stylist. I doubt anybody has ever jerked off to a Mapplethorpe photograph.

Roger Earl: He never did film or video, did he?

Jack Fritscher: Yes. And he screened his rushes for me. Shortly after he and I met, he directed Patti Smith in *Still Moving* [10 minutes, 1978] while Lisa Rinzler ran the 16mm camera for him as we did for you. He also directed bodybuilder Lisa Lyon in *Lady* [1984]. He was a static artist in search of the perfect moment, the perfect film "still," not the perfect "motion picture." He was a master of "still life" art whether it was a flower, a fetish, or a face. Roger, there is nothing "still life" about your athletic films. Your guys look like sex-action heroes: sweaty hot dudes with some tread on their nipples like Christian Dreesen escaping from the East German Stasi, and Mr. Sebastian [1933-1996] working with filmmaker Fakir Musafar [1930-2018], the founder of the modern primitive movement, in creating the body modification scene.

Roger Earl: What a wonderful person Sebastian was. Another reason that I'm crazy about *Like Moths to a Flame.*

Jack Fritscher: Do you know that when Sebastian died eleven months ago, his obituary made international news in the *New York Times* and the UK *Independent*?

Roger Earl: Really? I was not aware of it. How wonderful.

Jack Fritscher: Mark and I were on a plane to Paris and found it. I thought, well, here's a nice little connection. It was like "Six Degrees of Roger Earl," and there's Mr. Sebastian in the *New York Times.*

Roger Earl: I thought you were going to tell me that he and his tattoos had been made into a lampshade.

Jack Fritscher: He was one of the most pierced, tattooed persons in the world. What was he like personally?

Roger Earl: Charming, sweet, adorable, loving. I was just crazy about him. You couldn't help it. He was a very vulnerable man too.

Jack Fritscher: But a heavy duty S&M player?

Roger Earl: Not so much, just really into all this clinical piercing and tattoos.

Jack Fritscher: More of a real practitioner of body modification than an erotic exhibitionist?

Roger Earl: Yes. But for me his scene worked in the film.

> [Roger Earl told Kevin Wolff in *Drummer* 126: "Mr. Sebastian in *Like Moths to a Flame*...We shot the whole thing [the Mr. Sebastian sequence] in his [tattoo] studio, because he insisted. See, I wanted to shoot it somewhere else, in kind of a scene thing, but he said, 'In my studio I know there can never be an infection, and for sanitary reasons I will not do this outside the studio.' The minute he told me that, I said, 'There's no more discussion. You're absolutely right.'" Earl told former *Drummer* publisher John Embry, who had cloned his new magazine, *Manifest Reader*, out of *Drummer*, that other scenes in *Moths* were shot in the cellar of "Expatiations of London" and "in Germany." *Men with No Name* was shot in the cellar of RoB of Amsterdam. "Time was running out...We knew we had to go back home. That was how series two, *Bound for Europe*, came about." *Manifest Reader*, 33, 1997]

Jack Fritscher: I see gay history listing you as a filmmaker and a videographer, but I've never seen you called what I would like to call you: a documentarian. You search out and cast people who are the real thing and then give them permission to do the real thing in front of your camera. You told *Drummer*: "I work with men who are into the scene one-hundred percent." Plus, I know from experience that the "Roger Earl camera" is a power tool. The presence of the camera encourages real players to dig deep to represent their scene with an intensity greater than it might be without the motivation of the camera which they are very aware documents them and their trip forever.

Roger Earl: At this point, Jack, I have to tell you I give a thousand percent credit to my partner and friend, Terry LeGrand, because without him—he's the one who has the guts to go out and really get these people. I say I want this one and he gets him. We work wonderfully together.

Jack Fritscher: Indeed you do. I've seen Terry in action interviewing new talent to populate your set. In Europe, while you were directing one scene and thinking about the next scene, Terry was out convincing very hot, but camera-shy, tops and bottoms to come let it all hang out on your set. How many films have you worked on together?

Roger Earl: Everything I've done.

Jack Fritscher: So you and Terry are business partners, not lovers. Not ever?

Roger Earl: We are not lovers.

Jack Fritscher: Do you have a lover?

Roger Earl: Not now.

Jack Fritscher: Have you had lovers?

Roger Earl: I have had.

Jack Fritscher: How many? Were they domestic partners or just lovers?

Roger Earl: One was somebody that I lived with for five or six years, until he got so jealous of me that he had to leave.

Jack Fritscher: Turning again to hired talent. What is your opinion of that British David Pearce as a photographer? He shot the stills for all three titles of *Dungeons of Europe* and five of the six titles of *Bound for Europe*, except *The Argos Session* which I shot.

Roger Earl: Quite a lot of his work was good, and some of it I was disappointed in; but everything is not going to be a masterpiece.

Jack Fritscher: *Drummer* certainly relished his photos which have become famous.

Roger Earl: For what I needed, he did some wonderful stuff. He was fine. Didn't he come and stay with you and Mark for awhile?

Jack Fritscher: The first time he came to our home, he stayed for three weeks and painted quite a wonderful oil painting of Mark and me. That was 1990.

Roger Earl: He was a very talented artist.

Jack Fritscher: In 1993, he asked to come visit us again, and we looked forward to seeing him. I'm sad to tell you that he, like so many others, had been driven to deep depression by the AIDS epidemic because he thought he might be positive. He was living on the dole and complaining he'd been kicked in the teeth by Margaret Thatcher. He was a mess. He had missed his flight from Heathrow because he and his leather traveling companion were too stoned to board. So he showed up loaded a day late, actually at 4 AM, with his drugged-out friend he had not told us existed. Obviously unwashed for weeks, the two of them were circling the drain. It was a sad and long way from the starry night you introduced us in Amsterdam, because David Pearce had become a beloved friend and was an extraordinary artist with brush and camera. He was so demanding, tweaked, unwashed, and far gone that within a day, we asked them to leave. They were not the gentlemen we were expecting.

Roger Earl: So sad, indeed. AIDS has robbed us all of so much.

Jack Fritscher: Swept away. All the more reason to look at the documentary qualities in your films. In a sense, most of the people whom you've shot would have disappeared into history if you hadn't shot them because many of them have died in this unfortunate plague and the only thing they left behind, the only creative thing that people will even pay attention to, are the images that you've captured of them on film. Fred and Val—your entire casts—still live on screen. I think that's a very significant thing you've done. You couldn't have known that you were doing that on such a scale, making films for the ages, when you shot *Born to Raise Hell*, but it turned out that way. When did you sense that *Born* was a true phenomenon? When you hired Val Martin? While you were shooting it?

Roger Earl: Not while I was shooting it. It was after it had been screened. The way it was received. This being my first movie. I was happy with it. To me it wasn't erotic because I had looked at it two thousand times before the damn thing was edited and in the can. So at that point it wasn't erotic for me, which worried me very much. I thought, Jesus, nobody will find it erotic because I can't find it erotic. It's full of the kind of things I love, but why can't I find it erotic?

Jack Fritscher: I can't find the films I shoot erotic either.

Roger Earl: You look at it over and over so many times.

Jack Fritscher: A filmmaker has so many camera and editing decisions to make, the footage becomes a mathematical thing that you have viewed so often that, while you work professionally to edit it to increase its heat for viewers, it loses its personal heat for you.

Roger Earl: Exactly, and *Born* was definitely not erotic to me.

Jack Fritscher: If you could find the actual date of the premiere at that Powell Street theater, I'd appreciate it because that was the day you and I first met.

Roger Earl: You know, I don't have the foggiest idea how even to research that, Jack. I don't even know when *Born to Raise Hell* was first shown in LA. I have no concept.

Jack Fritscher: Maybe Terry would know.

Roger Earl: I'll ask Terry if he can figure it out. If he has any records.

Jack Fritscher: It was in June, I think, of 1975. At that time, I was already writing about gay history and I thought, God, gay liberation is wonderful because we're going to a real movie theater, not a porn theater, to see an S&M movie. So [my then partner, *Drummer* photographer] David Sparrow and I went to the premiere. The crowd loved it.

Roger Earl: We got a very good response, and I certainly was thrilled by that.

Jack Fritscher: Did that get reviewed, do you remember, in the San Francisco *Chronicle* or *Examiner*?

Roger Earl: It got reviewed in *Variety*.

Jack Fritscher: *Variety* is the show biz bible. It should have it listed. *Variety* reviewed Wakefield Poole's *Boys in the Sand* [1971] and Fred Halsted's *L. A. Plays Itself* [1972]. Do you have the *Variety* review?

Roger Earl: I think I do somewhere. I'll have to look for it. I have a scrapbook somewhere.

Jack Fritscher: If you could make a copy of that for me, I'd love it.

Roger Earl: *Variety* liked it.

Jack Fritscher: Great. What are your plans right now for the future of your film career?

Roger Earl: I don't really know. When I was in San Francisco, I spoke to Beardog Hoffman and Joseph Bean, and I might make some films for them [Brush Creek Studio who bought *International Leatherman* from LeGrand]. I don't know if that will come to pass. I'm one of those people who doesn't want somebody else controlling their creativity or anything like that. If they can live with that or not, I don't know.

Jack Fritscher: Then also, you have to sort who owns the rights to what you shoot.

Roger Earl: It's the kind of thing where I have to draw up a proposal which I haven't had time to do. If they like it, fine. If they don't, then I'm not interested. That's just the way I am. My way or no way. Not everybody is going to accept that, let's face it. Good old Terry would always accept it.

Jack Fritscher: Because you two are a famous couple like Rogers and Hammerstein, Kander and Ebb, Mickey and Judy. You work together to put on a show.

Roger Earl: Terry and I each did our own thing and did it well.

Jack Fritscher: And the two of you produced magazines as well?

Roger Earl: No. Terry did the magazines. I was allowed to edit that one issue of *International Leatherman*. He begged me to, and I finally said OK. It was the best issue they ever did.

Jack Fritscher: I'm on the cover of the current issue [April/May 1997]. I mean, it's not actually me, but a photograph I took of Chris Duffy during one of my Palm Drive Video shoots.

Roger Earl: I thought you were on the cover.

Jack Fritscher: No, Turning sixty, I'm a bit past being on the covers of gay magazines. It's my shot of Chris Duffy, Mr. America, on the cover.

Roger Earl: I keep running across this photo of you naked, with rubber boots on?

Jack Fritscher: Hmmm. Yes. Photos like that exist in the *Drummer* archives, but have they escaped?

Roger Earl: I'll have to look it up. I think I have it on my computer. I think I pulled it off the Internet.

Jack Fritscher: Really. Oh. I've been turned into a screen saver.

Roger Earl: Indeed.

Jack Fritscher: Is there anything you would like to say about your career or your life? This is an opportunity to do that.

Roger Earl: I must say I'm always a happy person, and I've had a happy life, and have experienced some of the most wonderful things through my film career and through my other career. So am I a happy person? Damn right, I am. I don't know what else to say. I'm not good at expressing myself, in talking. I express myself in film.

Jack Fritscher: You're doing fine. Let's wind this up with your birth date again and some heritage.

Roger Earl: January 27, 1939.

Jack Fritscher: You're six months older than I am. You're my elder.

Roger Earl: I'm usually everybody's elder.

Jack Fritscher: Are you Scottish?

Roger Earl: No, maybe a little bit, but I'm German and everything else. A mongrel.

Jack Fritscher: From Barstow. The cocksucking boy from Barstow. I always think of you rather as the royal "Roger, Earl of Warnix." Where did "Earl" come from?

Roger Earl: It was my father's name. His first name.

Jack Fritscher: And "Roger"?

Roger Earl: Old family name. Part of my family had a last name of Rogers.

Jack Fritscher: OK. Outside of your dick size, I don't need anything else right now.

Roger Earl: Well, we ain't going to give that.

Jack Fritscher: Good answer. I would like to thank you very much.

Roger Earl: My pleasure.

Jack Fritscher: As a journalist, may I say you give good interview.

Roger Earl: Well, you just have to go with the flow of my words because I don't express myself well, Jack.

Jack Fritscher: Roger, you express yourself just fine. Thank you very much for this, and for the opportunity you gave Mark and me to be cameramen on your films.

Roger Earl: Say hello to Mark. You guys take care.

The Ludlow Café, Route 66, in Ludlow near Barstow, with garage, service station, and motel owned and run for 20 years by Earl and Lillian Warnix who raised their young son Roger Earl on the premises from the 1940s to the 1960s.

Other Books by Jack Fritscher

Novels

Some Dance to Remember:
A Memoir-Novel of San Francisco 1970-1982
The Geography of Women
What They Did to the Kid
Leather Blues

Short Fiction

Rainbow County
Corporal in Charge of Taking Care of Captain O'Malley
Stand by Your Man
TITANIC: Forbidden Stories Hollywood Forgot
Stonewall: Stories of Gay Liberation
Sweet Embraceable You: Coffee House Stories

Non-Fiction

The Life and Times of the Legendary Larry Townsend
Gay Pioneers: How "Drummer" Shaped Gay Pop Culture 1965-1999
Gay San Francisco: Eyewitness Drummer
Mapplethorpe: Assault with a Deadly Camera
Popular Witchcraft: Straight from the Witches Mouth
Anton LaVey Speaks: The Canonical Interview
Love and Death in Tennessee Williams
When Malory Met Arthur: Camelot
Television Today

www.JackFritscher.com

www.ingramcontent.com/pod-product-compliance
Lightning Source LLC
Chambersburg PA
CBHW030747190726
48285CB00003B/737